THE BEST COAST

A ROAD TRIP atlas

ILLUSTRATED ADVENTURES
along
the WEST coast's
HISTORIC HIGHWAYS

CHANDLER O'LEARY

SASQUATCH BOOKS
SEATTLE

Printed in China

Published by Sasquatch Books

26 25 24 23 22   10 9 8 7 6 5 4 3

Editor: Hannah Elnan | Production editor: Bridget Sweet
Copyeditor: Kirsten Colton | Design: Anna Goldstein

Credits: On page xi, California State Park logo used with permission from the State of California Department of Parks and Recreation, Oregon State Parks logo used with permission from the Oregon Parks and Recreation Department, and Washington State Parks logo used with permission from the Washington State Parks and Recreation Commission. On page 179, dragon art piece created by Meng Huang, Heather Presler, and Kevin Lorentzen; owned by Chinatown-International District Business Improvement Area; and used with permission.
The Portland Oregon sign on page 160 is a registered trademark of the City of Portland, Oregon, and is used with permission.

Library of Congress Cataloging-in-Publication Data
Names: O'Leary, Chandler, author.
Title: The best coast : a road trip atlas : illustrated adventures along the
   West Coast's historic highways / Chandler O'Leary.
Description: Seattle, WA : Sasquatch Books, [2019] | Includes index.
Identifiers: LCCN 2018014338 | ISBN 9781632171740 (pbk.)
Subjects: LCSH: Automobile travel--Pacific Coast (U.S.)--Guidebooks. |
   Pacific Coast (U.S.)--Guidebooks. | Pacific Coast (U.S.)--Description and
   travel. | LCGFT: Guidebooks.
Classification: LCC F852.3 .O44 2019 | DDC 917.904--dc23
LC record available at https://lccn.loc.gov/2018014338

ISBN: 978-1-63217-174-0

Sasquatch Books
1904 Third Avenue, Suite 710 | Seattle, WA 98101
SasquatchBooks.com

For my three favorite road trip companions:
Dad, Donald, and Mary-Alice

CONTENTS

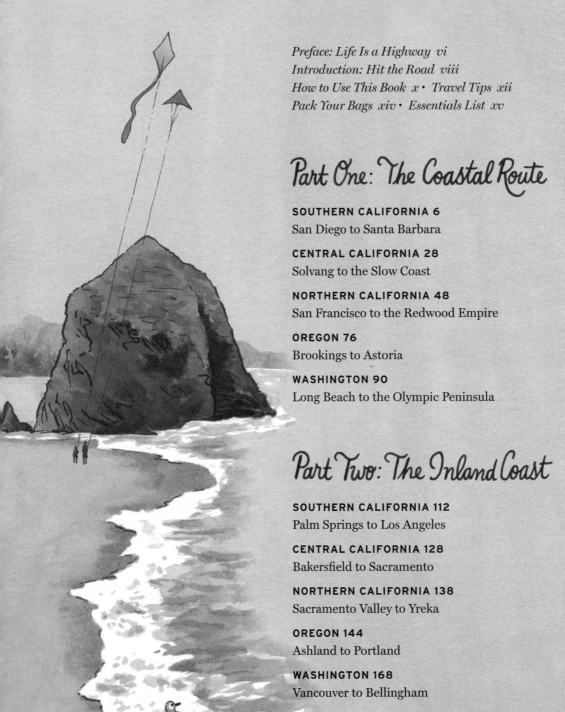

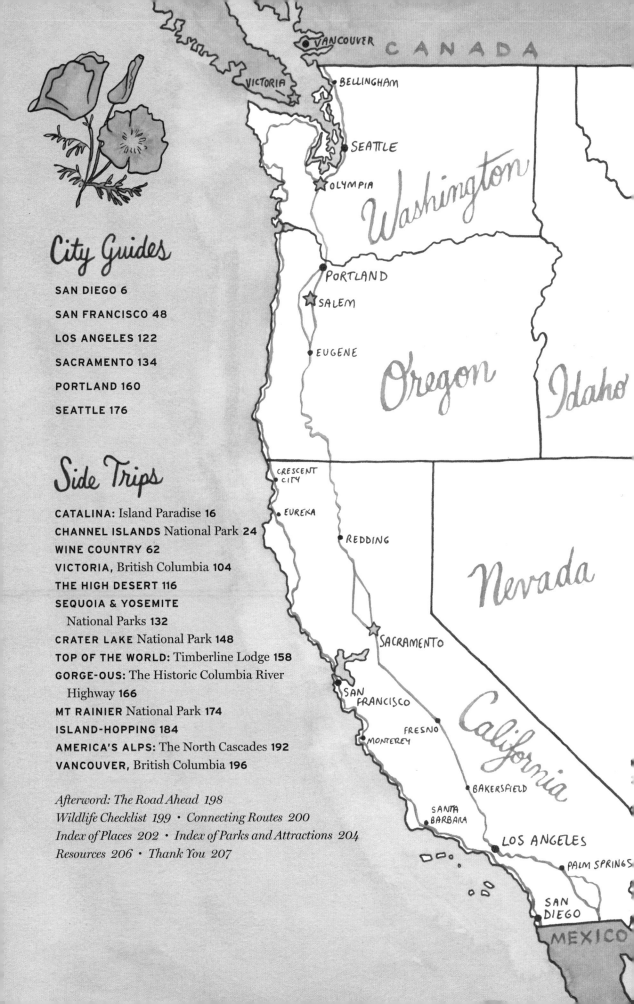

City Guides

Side Trips

Life Is a HIGHWAY

I am an illustrator, a lettering artist, and (these days) a writer. Telling stories through a combination of words and images is what I do, and I am never more eager to tell a story than when it involves a sense of place. For as long as I can remember, I have organized my life around the idea of *where*. I was born fifty miles west of Wall Drug, that legendary tourist trap in western South Dakota (I think this explains a lot about me). I grew up in a military family, moving from place to place every few years. While starting over was never easy, I looked forward to the moves themselves because they meant traveling somewhere new—and more specifically, driving cross-country to get there. My dad shared my love of road trips, and together we'd spend hours planning potential routes or reminiscing about favorite back roads.

▼ On road trips my car becomes a mobile art studio; everywhere I go I carry a sketchbook, a watercolor paint box, and a set of brushes and drawing tools.

AN EVER-SPINNING ODOMETER

As an adult I've spent every moment (and dollar) I could crisscrossing the continent on back roads. Whether I travel alone or with others, my priorities are the same: to see as much as possible and to try to get to know a place on its own terms. I will always choose the slowest road, the squiggliest line on the map—for me, the joy is the journey and the landscape itself. I've logged well over one hundred thousand road trip miles to date and visited all the Lower Forty-Eight states, but I still feel as if I've barely scratched the surface.

HAVE SKETCHBOOK, WILL TRAVEL

For many years I've documented my travels through my sketchbook drawings, which now number in the thousands. I'm both blessed and cursed with being interested in absolutely everything—which means I never run out of things to draw, and I *always* run out of time. Some of my favorite subjects are the hokey roadside attractions and vintage neon signs of the historic highways. Even more than their humor and somewhat random nature, what I love most is the sincerity with which they were made. An interesting side effect of all this travel sketching is that my sketchbooks mostly satisfy my urge to collect travel souvenirs. And that's a good thing: after a lifetime of traveling, I'd otherwise be drowning

in Bigfoot mugs and bumper stickers by now. (Though I'm far from immune: ask me sometime about my Mount Saint Helens "before and after" salt and pepper shakers.)

FINDING THE THREAD

These days the lines between business and pleasure have blurred, and road trips have become an increasing part of my work as an artist. In 2013, at the urging of a friend, I started an illustrated travel blog to share my sketchbook drawings. The blog, called *Drawn the Road Again*, is arranged thematically rather than chronologically. My images and stories jump around in time and space, linking disparate places together into narrative arcs. Time and again I'm drawn (no pun intended) to fading, vulnerable, forgotten places. Sometimes I think my main "job" is to capture the things I see and to tell their stories before they succumb to progress and disappear.

I have found, to my delight, that I am far from alone in my love of place. Many fellow travelers have found my blog over the years; my readers are equally passionate about the road less traveled and just as eager to tell me their own anecdotes. This gives me hope that our collective stories of place will be remembered—and reminds me that *where* is as important as *who* and *how* and *why*.

SHARING THE BEST COAST

In 2008 my husband and I relocated to Washington State. As much of the region was new to me at the time, I have spent the past decade exploring the history and geography of my adopted home—always along scenic back roads and the old highways. I love seeing the landscape, climate, and culture shift as the road moves up and down the West Coast—it is this that inspired me to write this book. I hope that by the time you reach the last page, you'll be dreaming of your own road trip adventure and eager to discover the beauty and quirks that make the West Coast the *best* coast.

▼ The reward for taking the time to draw on my travels is the discovery of surprises hidden in plain sight—like this walrus frieze in Seattle.

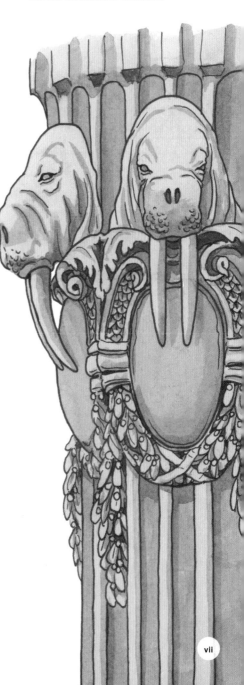

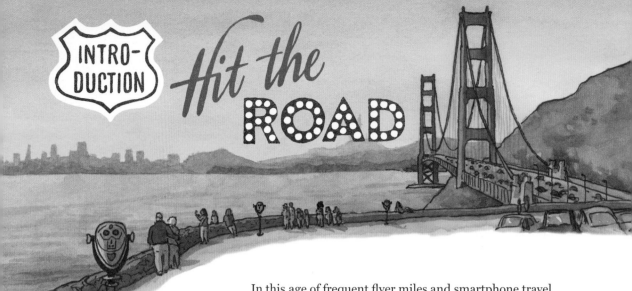

Hit the ROAD

▲ Early highway builders recognized the tourist appeal of their utilitarian constructions, adding scenic pullouts and pedestrian overlooks to many bridges and roadways.

▼ From the 1880s until about 1960, West Coast growers advertised their produce as exotic delicacies to eastern and midwestern travelers, offering pricey shipments of pears and fresh citrus back home.

In this age of frequent flyer miles and smartphone travel apps, an old-school road trip seems hopelessly nostalgic. Yet the immense size and distinct regions of the West Coast make car travel the ideal mode for exploring in depth. This has been true for more than a century, since America's love affair with the open road began.

FROM MUD TO CONCRETE

The West Coast's highways follow the logic of the landscape, retracing ancient Indigenous trade routes, following river systems, picking their way over and between mountains. After white settlers arrived, communities were connected by a disjointed network of dirt tracks, gravel paths, and even wooden-plank roads. Eventually the Pacific Highway evolved as the first continuous border-to-border route from Mexico to Canada. The federal government took over its management in 1926, paved it from end to end, and renamed it US Highway 99. As a new national highway system developed and grew, engineers designed marvels like the Golden Gate Bridge to carry the ever-growing flow of traffic. Depression-era alphabet soup agencies like the CCC (Civilian Conservation Corps) and the WPA (Works Progress Administration) took charge of infrastructure and beautification.

THE GOLDEN AGE OF ROAD TRIPS

In the 1920s, and again in the post–World War II era, personal automobile ownership soared. Families used their paid vacation time—another twentieth-century innovation—to drive cross-country for fun and family togetherness. Early highway promoters foresaw this and developed intentionally scenic roads (like the Historic Columbia River Highway, page 166) designed to highlight the natural beauty of the landscape—and enhance the experience of motorists traveling through it.

Savvy entrepreneurs cashed in on all this wanderlust. Cars need fuel, so gas stations popped up first. Then came lodging, in the form of newfangled motor courts, later renamed motels (a contraction of "motor hotel"). Guests needed to eat, so restaurants and drive-throughs appeared, offering meals on the go in service of making good time. And of course, *having* a good time was the basis for every roadside attraction and tourist trap along the way. Farmers supplemented their income with roadside fruit stands and souvenir citrus. Small towns put themselves on the map with "world's largest" statues and homemade amusement parks. Businesses raked in the dough, and families racked up the memories.

SHADOW AND DECLINE

These golden years, however, existed only for white travelers. Many establishments refused to serve travelers of color or non-Christians. For Black motorists, whole communities—called sundown towns—were forbidden to them after dark. In response *The Negro Motorist Green Book*, published from 1936 to 1966, compiled safe lodging and other options for Black travelers, and warned them of dangers to avoid. The book was inspired by similar guides for Jewish vacationers who had developed their own resort industry in upstate New York in response to anti-Semitism on the road.

For good or ill, the era of roadside America was short-lived. Built between 1956 and 1992, the federal Interstate Highway System slowly replaced the old US highways, shaving off precious travel minutes by bypassing towns and cities with high-speed roadways. After Interstate 5 was completed in 1969, Highway 99 was decommissioned as a national route. It didn't take long, then, for the pleasure-trip economy to dry up.

RETRACING OUR STEPS

Today's travelers are rediscovering and reclaiming the road trip. The remaining vestiges of roadside Americana have aged into eerie, absurd non sequiturs—attracting writers, preservationists, and international tourists. The old highways, now the "back roads," appeal to anyone who views the journey itself as the true destination. A voyage on these historic routes is a link to the past, to our most unique landscapes—and to each other.

▲ Neon signs made their American debut in Los Angeles in the 1920s. They quickly became a dominant roadside fixture for their eye-catching designs and bold typography.

▲ A type of novelty architecture, a "duck" is a building shaped like what it houses. West Coast examples include the Cabazon Dinosaurs (page 118) and a shoe-repair shop in Bakersfield, California.

▼ Maps in this book highlight main or recommended routes in red, with optional side trips in purple. Other nearby roads (including, at times, the interstate) are drawn in gray.

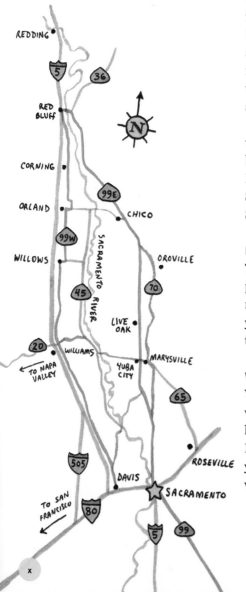

This is not your typical guidebook, nor is it an exhaustive list of features and attractions. Instead, think of it as a curated starter kit for your own West Coast adventure.

ORIENT YOURSELF

This book is arranged geographically, moving from south to north. The main reason for this is that the American highway system (for both federal and state roads) is organized from south to north (and west to east). Mile markers count up from the southern (or western) borders of each state, or from the southern (or western) terminus of each highway. In similar fashion, this book begins in Southern California and ends in Washington. For easy reference, each region is marked with a color-coded tab on the right-hand side of the spread, placed from bottom to top as the book moves south to north.

Furthermore, in keeping with the American system—as well as the signs you'll see on the road—measurements in this book are imperial (miles and feet), not metric (kilometers). If you're looking for city guides, you'll find San Diego and San Francisco in Part One (page xvi), and Los Angeles, Sacramento, Portland, and Seattle in Part Two (page 106).

DETOURS AND TANGENTS

This book also details a number of side trips, which highlight points of interest accessible from, though not directly *on*, the main routes in each part. These side trips are marked with a yellow tab placed in the same spot on the page as the tabs for the region that contains the detour.

WHAT THEME PARKS?

While many road trippers might feel that no West Coast vacation is complete without a stop at Disneyland or Legoland, you won't find these mega theme parks in this book. Instead, since the trips here focus on historic highways, you'll find a number of historic amusement parks and vintage roadside attractions.

A JUMBLE OF TERMS

In America we use the terms "freeway" and "highway" and "interstate" interchangeably, but there are distinct differences. In this book, "freeway" refers to limited-access (by way of exits and on-ramps) high-speed roadways. Only freeways have exit numbers. "Highway," on the other hand, is a generic term. Highways may be historic or modern, two or many lane, local, state, or federal. "Interstate" refers to the Interstate Highway System, the numbered federal freeways that connect major cities across America. What's more, interstate exit numbers match the mile-marker numbers, but some state freeway and US highway exit numbers do not!

A ROAD BY ANY OTHER NAME

Everyone knows Interstate 5; when you hear someone mention "I-5" or "the 5," you'll know what they mean. The historic highways, though, are another story. Before American highways were numbered, they were named routes. On the West Coast, many old highway names survive today in some form. (Some places use the old name only!) This can get confusing, so for quick reference, here is a list of the most common regional names used for each historic highway referenced in this book:

US HIGHWAY 101

- El Camino Real
- Coast Highway
- Redwood Highway
- Oregon Coast Highway

HIGHWAY 1

- Pacific Coast Highway
- The PCH
- Cabrillo Highway
- Shoreline Highway
- Coast Highway

HIGHWAY 99

- Pacific Highway
- Old 99
- Jackson Highway

OTHER HISTORIC ROUTES MENTIONED IN THIS BOOK:

- Palms to Pines Scenic Byway (CA): page 117
- Route 66 (CA): pages 21, 85, 108, 118, 120, 121, 122, 126
- Angeles Crest Highway (CA): page 126
- 17-Mile Drive (CA): page 38
- 49-Mile Scenic Drive (CA): page 47
- The Silverado Trail (CA): page 64
- Historic Columbia River Highway (OR): page 166
- North Cascades Highway (WA): page 193
- Sea to Sky Highway (BC, Canada): page 197

SHOW ME A SIGN

Below are some common signs and symbols you'll see along the way:

guide signs
(exits, towns, etc.)

recreation
(parks, historic sites, etc.)

services
(gas, food, hospital, etc.)

warnings
(curves, crossings, etc.)

temporary
(construction, detour, etc.)

Interstate   US
Highway   Highway

CA   OR
Route   Route

CA   WA
Landmark   Route

CA Parks   OR Parks

WA Parks

TRAVEL TIPS

Safety First

PACE YOURSELF. Road trips involve long distances and many hours of driving each day. Give yourself enough time to get to your destinations safely, without arriving exhausted. A good rule of thumb is to time each day so that you're done driving by mid or late afternoon.

KEEP YOUR GAS TANK FULL. It's easy to fill up in urban or suburban areas, but in many places gas is scarce and cell coverage is spotty. Get in the habit of topping off the tank whenever you're about to enter a remote region.

BE SMART ABOUT YOUR STUFF. An out-of-state, packed car can be a target for thieves, especially in large cities. Empty your vehicle (or at least the cab) each night, and keep whatever you don't need at hand out of sight in the trunk. Never leave valuables behind when you park.

RESPECT THE WILD. If you venture into remote or wilderness areas, take your surroundings seriously, pack accordingly, and let others know of your travel plans.

NEVER TURN YOUR BACK ON THE OCEAN. On the beach, note posted warnings about tsunamis and sneaker waves. Stay off jetties and breakwaters; evacuate if you hear a siren. Carry tide tables to help plan your activities.

Rules of the Road

BE A SAFE DRIVER. Obey all posted speed limits, traffic laws, and warnings, and respect construction zones. Always carry your license and proof of insurance.

MIND THE ONE-WAYS. In many towns, the historic highway ran along the main thoroughfare. Later, as traffic levels grew, the flow of traffic was often split between two one-way streets running in opposite directions. Depending on your direction of travel, you may find yourself on the "off" route and may need to do a loop to see any historic landmarks from the old highway.

DITCH THE CAR FOR A DAY. In cities where parking is tricky, consider leaving your car in an all-day garage (or at your hotel) and exploring by public transit or on foot.

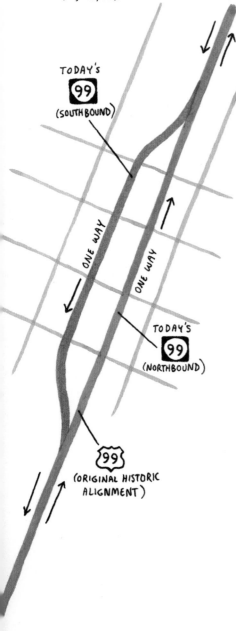

▼ This diagram shows the parallel one-way pattern you'll find in many towns, like Port Angeles, Washington (Highway 101), and Salem, Oregon (Highway 99).

TODAY'S
99
(SOUTHBOUND)

ONE WAY

ONE WAY

TODAY'S
99
(NORTHBOUND)

99
(ORIGINAL HISTORIC ALIGNMENT)

CHAIN UP. On many mountain roads, travelers are legally required to carry or use tire chains in the winter. Fines for disregarding these laws can be hundreds of dollars.

PICK THE RIGHT LANE. On freeways around major cities, keep an eye out for carpool or HOV (high-occupancy vehicle) lanes. There are rules for when and how you may use them—when in doubt, stick to the regular lanes.

PULL OVER. Use traffic pullouts to allow faster cars behind you to pass. This allows you to travel safely, without stressing out or feeling pressured to speed up.

Lost and Found

PAPER MAPS ARE YOUR FRIENDS. GPS isn't accurate (or even functional) everywhere. Carry paper maps and learn to read them properly. State and local atlases are wonderfully detailed and especially great for back roads.

CALLING FOR HELP? If you need roadside assistance, note the nearest mile marker and memorize your license plate number so help can find you as quickly as possible.

Wise Planning

TO BOOK OR NOT TO BOOK? Though it's not spontaneous, researching and booking your lodging in advance is best for your budget and your peace of mind.

CHANGE YOUR OIL BEFORE YOU GO. Car repairs on the road can be expensive, so get a tune-up before you leave. Carry an emergency repair kit and extra oil with you.

BUY ANNUAL PARK PASSES. Park entry fees can add up quickly (see the long list of state parks in this book on page 205), so get a state parks pass for every state you visit, as well as one for national parks (page 204). Your investment will pay for itself after just a handful of parks.

BE BEACH SAVVY. Except in Oregon (where all beaches are open to the public), be aware of public-private beach boundaries to avoid trespassing. In California, public state beaches have entry fees.

ARE YOU SURE ABOUT THAT CLAMBAKE? Fishing and shellfish harvesting require a license for each state, and there are seasonal and location-based restrictions. Hotels often have rules about storing or cleaning fish on-site.

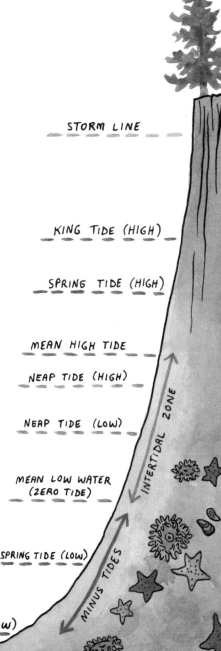

▼ Minus tides offer the best chance to explore tide pools. The highest (spring) tides happen at the full moon; super moons (when the full moon is closest to Earth) cause king tides.

STORM LINE

KING TIDE (HIGH)

SPRING TIDE (HIGH)

MEAN HIGH TIDE

NEAP TIDE (HIGH)

NEAP TIDE (LOW)

MEAN LOW WATER (ZERO TIDE)

INTERTIDAL ZONE

SPRING TIDE (LOW)

MINUS TIDES

KING TIDE (LOW)

Pack Your BAGS

For your West Coast trip, you'll need to prepare for every possible climate, from blazing-hot sun to mountain snow, from soggy rain forests to parched deserts.

Clothing

- Layered clothing
- Warm outerwear
- Rain jacket
- Hats (winter and sun)
- Gloves and scarf
- Swimwear

West Coast weather can vary wildly, even on the same day. Dress in layers, and prepare for both wet and dry conditions.

Footwear

- Walking shoes
- Flip-flops
- Galoshes/rain boots
- Hiking boots
- Dress shoes

Whether for lounging in hot weather, splashing in tide pools, hiking a mountain trail, or stepping out for a fancy meal, bring a variety of shoes with you.

Personal Items

- Sunglasses
- Sunscreen
- Umbrella
- Backpack or day bag
- Toiletries
- Medications

Take sun protection seriously—and bring sufficient quantities of any prescription medications you use.

Identification

- Valid driver's license
- Proof of car insurance
- Emergency contact info
- Passport (for Canada or Mexico)

Sadly, border officials are known to subject travelers to racial profiling, even at interior immigration checkpoints. Carrying your passport, even if you don't plan to visit Canada or Mexico, can save you a huge headache.

Other Paperwork

- Printed reservations
- Park and transit passes
- Tickets and other important papers
- Tide tables

While many travelers now keep their reservations and tickets on their smartphone, having a paper version is useful for areas with spotty cell coverage. Also, some older hotels haven't gone digital. Paper isn't dead yet!

Essentials LIST

The beauty of a road trip is not having to distill your belongings down to an airplane carry-on. Pack sensibly, but prepare for both fun and not-so-fun adventures.

Navigation Tools

- Atlases (national and state)
- Folded paper maps
- Guidebooks (like this one!)
- Travel club membership

Stock up on those old-fashioned maps. While membership with a travel club (AAA, AARP, Better World Club, etc.) is optional, many provide useful things like free maps and roadside assistance.

Car Essentials

- Motor oil, windshield washer fluid
- Tire chains for snow
- Spare tire, basic repair kit
- Roll of toilet paper

Use common sense when it comes to car gear. (You're laughing at the TP, but you won't be when you need it!) For safety reasons, it's generally better not to carry extra gasoline with you.* Instead, stop to refuel frequently.

Safety

- Cell phone
- Extra battery chargers
- Flashlight and batteries
- Emergency blankets
- Flare/reflectors
- First aid kit

Again, use common sense here. Carry the basics that will allow you to take care of yourself and call for help, should you need it.

Food and Drink

- Water bottles
- Large water jug
- Healthy snacks
- Tea or instant coffee
- Travel mugs
- Small electric kettle
- Resealable bags
- Insulated cooler

Pack extra water in the car for desert treks (hence the big jug). The kettle can be a lifesaver if you want hot tea in your hotel room.

Just for Fun

- Camera
- Binoculars
- Music for the road
- Notebook or journal
- Postcard stamps
- Pens and pencils

Bring extra camera batteries and memory cards (or film, if you're old-school). And people *love* receiving travel postcards!

*Unless you'll be in a truly remote area for an extended period of time.

PART ONE

The COASTAL ROUTE

Get ready for an unforgettable adventure: this coastal route, a combination of US Highway 101 and State Route 1, commonly called Highway 1, gets you up close and personal with nearly every twist and turn of the Pacific shore. These historic highways will show you sunny SoCal beaches, the cliffs of Big Sur, the hills of San Francisco, towering redwoods, rugged Northwest sea stacks—and mile upon mile of breathtaking ocean views.

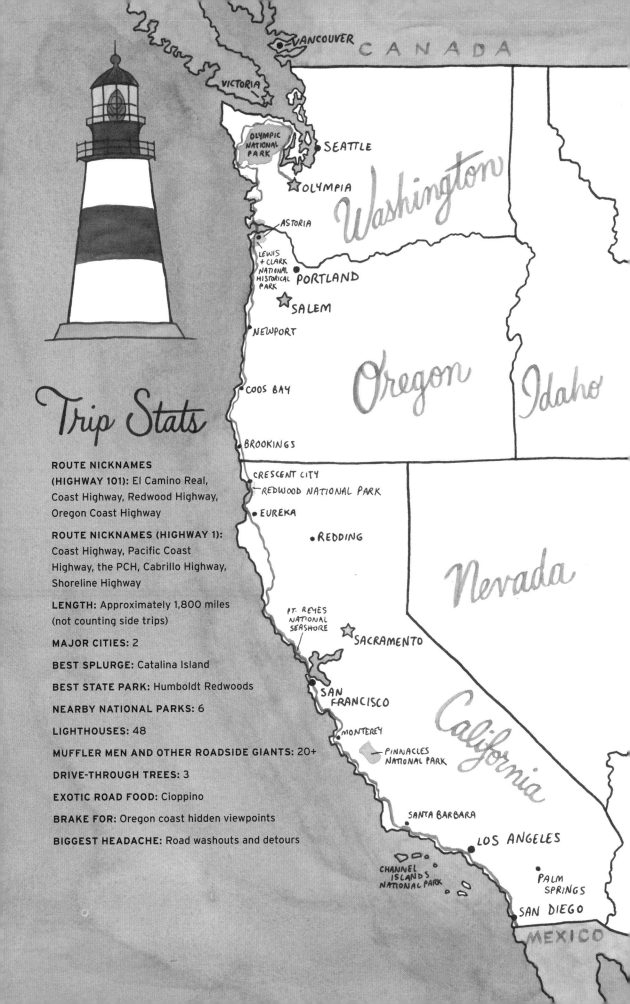

Trip Stats

**ROUTE NICKNAMES
(HIGHWAY 101):** El Camino Real,
Coast Highway, Redwood Highway,
Oregon Coast Highway

ROUTE NICKNAMES (HIGHWAY 1):
Coast Highway, Pacific Coast
Highway, the PCH, Cabrillo Highway,
Shoreline Highway

LENGTH: Approximately 1,800 miles
(not counting side trips)

MAJOR CITIES: 2

BEST SPLURGE: Catalina Island

BEST STATE PARK: Humboldt Redwoods

NEARBY NATIONAL PARKS: 6

LIGHTHOUSES: 48

MUFFLER MEN AND OTHER ROADSIDE GIANTS: 20+

DRIVE-THROUGH TREES: 3

EXOTIC ROAD FOOD: Cioppino

BRAKE FOR: Oregon coast hidden viewpoints

BIGGEST HEADACHE: Road washouts and detours

CANADA

VANCOUVER

VICTORIA

OLYMPIC
NATIONAL
PARK

SEATTLE

OLYMPIA

Washington

ASTORIA

LEWIS
+ CLARK
NATIONAL
HISTORICAL
PARK

PORTLAND

SALEM

NEWPORT

Oregon

COOS BAY

Idaho

BROOKINGS

CRESCENT CITY

REDWOOD NATIONAL PARK

EUREKA

REDDING

Nevada

PT. REYES
NATIONAL
SEASHORE

SACRAMENTO

SAN
FRANCISCO

California

MONTEREY

PINNACLES
NATIONAL PARK

SANTA BARBARA

LOS ANGELES

CHANNEL
ISLANDS
NATIONAL PARK

PALM
SPRINGS

SAN DIEGO

MEXICO

▲ While the driving might be a challenge, the road itself can become a scenic addition to the view—as in this spot near Jenner, California.

▼ The highest mountains on the West Coast can be found on Washington's Olympic Peninsula. Thanks to these snowcapped peaks, there isn't a single road across the interior of the 1,400-square-mile peninsula.

Drive the Pacific Shore

A West Coast road trip is like no other in America—and that's because the "best coast" is something altogether unique. Here, the seaboard lies beyond a series of coastal mountain ranges that run almost continuously from Mexico to Canada. To reach the Pacific Ocean, travelers must first cross these natural barriers—yet while the terrain might make for a daunting passage, it is also the source of the West Coast's unparalleled beauty. The network of historic coastal highways, which traverses more than 1,800 miles of coastline, puts this rocky shore within reach.

Not only are the Pacific coast highways some of the most scenic routes in America, but they also, in many cases, provide the *only* means to reach many coastal sights. With the exception of southernmost California, the modern freeway of Interstate 5 runs inland—in places by more than a hundred driving miles. So rather than visiting the left coast via a series of spur trips from the interstate, it's far more rewarding to hug the coast in one grand back-roads adventure. Although you won't find any major cities along the coastal highways north of San Francisco (page 48), what lies beyond is not the middle of nowhere, but the gateway to a different world.

HIGHWAY 1: FORTUNE FAVORS THE BRAVE

When most travelers picture a West Coast road trip, California's Highway 1 springs to mind. This is the most famous (and infamous) West Coast route, a thin ribbon of blacktop clinging to every curve of the California coastline. Driving this route is not for the faint of heart. Sharp curves, impossibly steep drop-offs, unpredictable weather, patches of heavy traffic, and even landslides are hallmarks of this drive. (Pro tip: another reason this book moves from south

to north is that it allows the driver to stick to the *inside* of all those hair-raising curves.) Yet the rewards far outweigh the risks here. The jaw-dropping vistas alone are worth the trip. And the drive itself feels like graduating from a stunt course—a feather in one's cap for anyone who loves a challenge.

Highway 1 came together in piecemeal fashion, starting with the most challenging section, Big Sur (page 32), in 1919. Surplus explosives from World War I blasted tunnels and carved roadbeds out of cliff sides, while New Deal funding during the Great Depression provided thousands of jobs and expanded the route's range. During World War II the road hosted a line of watchtowers to search for invaders from across the Pacific. Finally, in 1964 the various sections of coastal highway were connected and united under Highway 1. Today the route is still preserved, in its original form, from end to end. Drivers travel this road for both business and pleasure, zigzagging between major cities, small coastal communities, and a variety of state and federal parks and natural reserves.

Highway 1 covers much of the California coast, stretching 655.8 miles between San Clemente (page 14) and Leggett (page 70). Yet this is only a taste of the West Coast as a whole, and for travelers hungry for more, Highway 101 delivers the rest of the Pacific Coast, from Leggett to Washington's Olympic Peninsula (page 90).

▶ Spectacular sights like Oregon's Yaquina Head Lighthouse mean a long detour for interstate travelers, but Highway 101 brings coastal road trippers within shouting distance.

▲ The grizzly bear is California's state animal and the emblem on its state flag. American settlers unveiled the design near Mission San Francisco Solano in Sonoma as part of the 1846 Bear Flag Revolt against Mexican rule.

▼ Look for the roadside mission bell markers that mark Highway 101 between San Diego and Sonoma, California.

HIGHWAY 101: THE COASTAL BACKBONE

An inland route that parallels much of Highway 1's route, Highway 101 hugs the shore once Highway 1 ends. In Southern California, historic 101 is relegated to two-lane highways and urban surface streets, as modern interstates have taken over the shore. Yet in Northern California and all of the Pacific Northwest, 101 is still the main (and often only) coastal thoroughfare.

While Highway 1 was a product of the twentieth century, 101 has a lineage tracing back to one of the earliest roads in North America. Before California was annexed by the United States in 1848, its southern two-thirds were part of the Alta California (meaning upper California) territory of the colony of New Spain (hence all those Spanish-language place names). Beginning in the 1680s, Catholic priests established missionary outposts for the subjugation and forced conversion of Indigenous peoples like the Chumash, Miwok, and many others. The coastal missions stretched all the way from the tip of the Baja California peninsula (now Mexico) to what is now Sonoma, California. The twenty-one Alta California missions are a distinct group begun by Father Junípero Serra in 1769, with each outpost placed a long day's horseback ride (roughly thirty miles) apart. The path connecting these points was El Camino Real (the Royal Highway). Modern Highway 101 is remarkably faithful to this original road and still links most of the missions.

In Northern California, Highway 101 runs inland until it reaches the remote Redwood Coast (page 70), carrying tourists, locals, and logging trucks to increasingly rainy shores. The Oregon coast (page 76) is spectacular and accessible, with every inch of its coastline preserved as public land. In its northern reaches, 101 runs almost all the way to the northwestern tip of Washington State, before hooking back around in a three-hundred-mile near loop of the Olympic Peninsula (page 90). The state capital of Olympia is the end of the road, where the old northern terminus of 101 intersects historic Highway 99 (see page 170) downtown.

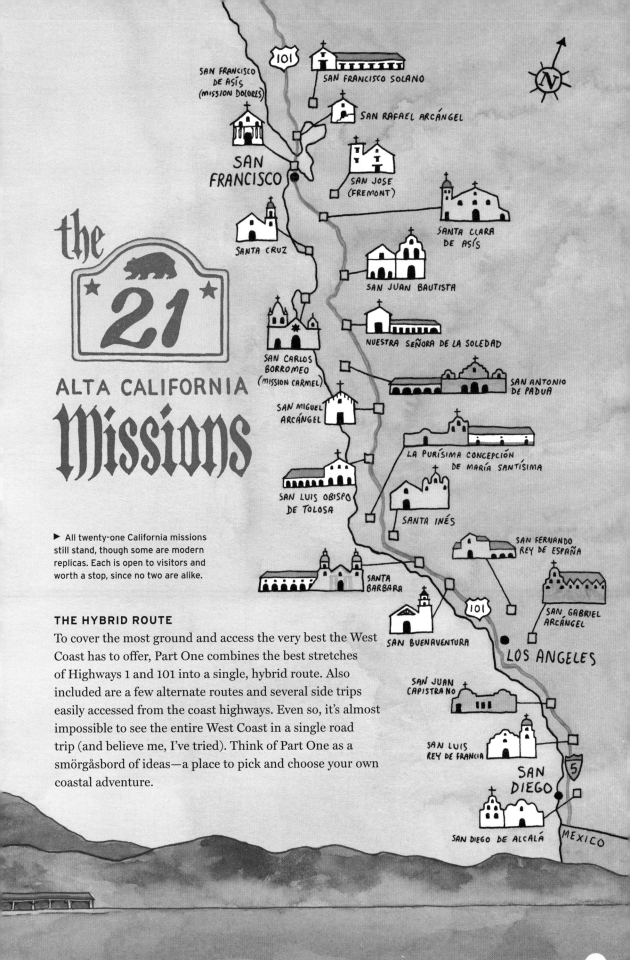

SAN FRANCISCO DE ASÍS (MISSION DOLORES)

SAN FRANCISCO SOLANO

SAN RAFAEL ARCÁNGEL

SAN FRANCISCO

SAN JOSE (FREMONT)

SANTA CRUZ

SANTA CLARA DE ASÍS

SAN JUAN BAUTISTA

NUESTRA SEÑORA DE LA SOLEDAD

SAN CARLOS BORROMEO (MISSION CARMEL)

SAN ANTONIO DE PADUA

SAN MIGUEL ARCÁNGEL

LA PURÍSIMA CONCEPCIÓN DE MARÍA SANTÍSIMA

SAN LUIS OBISPO DE TOLOSA

SANTA INÉS

SAN FERNANDO REY DE ESPAÑA

the
21
ALTA CALIFORNIA
missions

▶ All twenty-one California missions still stand, though some are modern replicas. Each is open to visitors and worth a stop, since no two are alike.

SANTA BARBARA

SAN BUENAVENTURA

SAN GABRIEL ARCÁNGEL

LOS ANGELES

SAN JUAN CAPISTRANO

SAN LUIS REY DE FRANCIA

SAN DIEGO

SAN DIEGO DE ALCALÁ

MEXICO

THE HYBRID ROUTE

To cover the most ground and access the very best the West Coast has to offer, Part One combines the best stretches of Highways 1 and 101 into a single, hybrid route. Also included are a few alternate routes and several side trips easily accessed from the coast highways. Even so, it's almost impossible to see the entire West Coast in a single road trip (and believe me, I've tried). Think of Part One as a smörgåsbord of ideas—a place to pick and choose your own coastal adventure.

San Diego

▲ The famous Gaslamp Quarter contains ninety-four historic buildings, constructed between 1850 and 1923.

San Diego's glittering harbor and near-perfect climate seem like living symbols of Southern California. Here, odds are that your West Coast road trip will get off to a sunny start. With a population of three million people, a melting-pot culture, and a plethora of events and activities, San Diego has all the ingredients of a major metropolis. Yet its natural beauty, patchwork geography, and distinct neighborhoods lend the place a small-town atmosphere that keeps visitors from feeling overwhelmed. Plan to spend a good chunk of time here: with plenty to see in this gorgeous setting, you'll find it hard to leave.

LISTEN TO THE MISSION BELLS

Located on the northeastern edge of town, Mission Basilica San Diego de Alcalá feels a bit separate from the city that grew out of its foundations. Beyond being an oasis of quiet gardens and gleaming painted tile, it's also a splash of Europe: check out the fourteenth-century choir stall imported from Spain. Festooned with wooden gargoyles and hand-painted lions, the stall is built with interlocking pieces, without using a single nail.

ON THE WATERFRONT

Thanks to two world wars, the San Diego waterfront has been a military hub for more than a century. Get a taste for the city's naval history with a tour of the USS *Midway*, expand your newfound nautical knowledge at the Maritime Museum of San Diego, and buy salty souvenir tchotchkes at Seaport Village.

◀ Mission Basilica San Diego de Alcalá, founded in 1769, is the oldest of the California missions—as well as the first stop for mission hunters headed north.

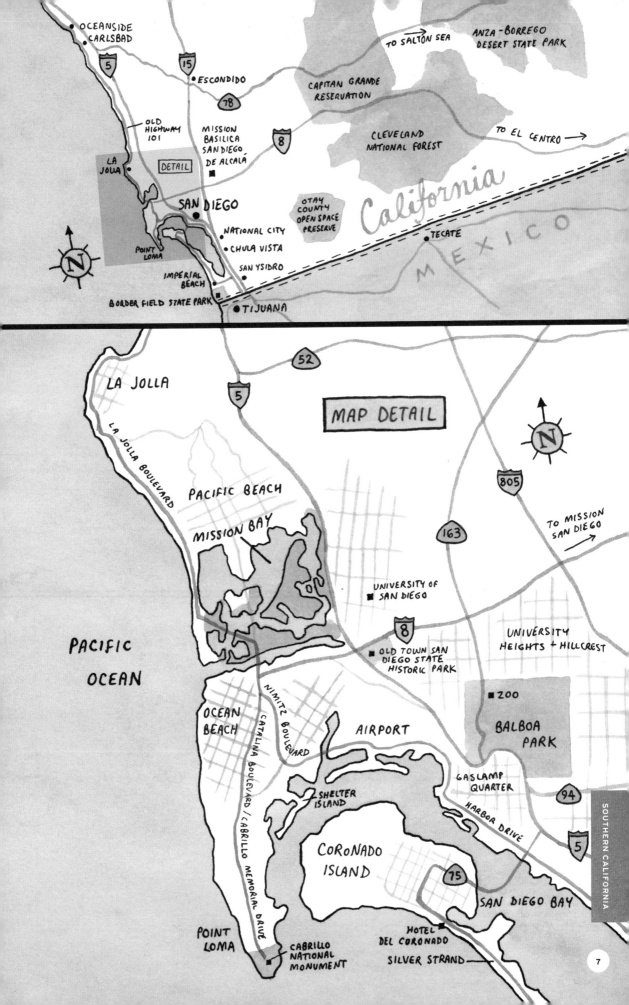

▲ The Point Loma peninsula affords picture-postcard views of downtown, the harbor, and Coronado Island.

▼ Old Town is home to a number of open-air markets and alfresco dining areas.

A BLAST FROM THE PAST

Downtown comprises seven distinct districts, but its beating heart is the sixteen-block Gaslamp Quarter, home to restored Victorian buildings and a vibrant nightlife. Don't miss the showstopping Louis Bank of Commerce Building on Fifth Avenue. Nearby is the still-operating Santa Fe train depot on Kettner Boulevard. End your urban sojourn with a Padres baseball game, where even the ballpark comes with a scenic view.

URBAN ANCESTOR

The original Mexican pueblo (chartered town) founded in 1834 is now Old Town San Diego State Historic Park, the most-visited state park in California. The surrounding neighborhood is a mix of old houses, Mexican restaurants, and multicultural souvenirs. Accessible either by trolley or by a short drive from downtown.

FIRST CONTACT

Cabrillo National Monument commemorates the 1542 landing of Spanish explorer Juan Rodríguez Cabrillo, the first European to step foot on the West Coast, at Point Loma. The park also boasts two lighthouses, a series of tide pools, and breathtaking sea and city vistas.

A JUMBLE OF LAND AND SEA

A huge swath of the city is occupied by Mission Bay Park, an enormous man-made lagoon built out of a natural tide marsh. Forget navigating the mousetrap of thoroughfares and bridges that skirt the park; ditch the car and explore on foot, by bike, or in a kayak.

THE GREEN HEART OF THE CITY

San Diego's signature Balboa Park is one of America's all-time greats—as well as one of its oldest. In 1915–16 and again in 1935–36, the park played host to an international exposition (similar to a world's fair); both events added permanent architectural pieces to the park. Most recognizable is the California Building, the ornate spire and mosaic-tile dome that now house the Museum of Man. A seemingly endless list of other park highlights includes the Casa del Prado, the Spreckels Organ Pavilion, the International Cottages, the Air & Space Museum, the Spanish Village Art Center, and of course, the hundred-acre, world-class San Diego Zoo. It is impossible to see the whole park in one visit; a smart option is to dedicate a separate day trip to the zoo alone.

UP THE HILL

University Avenue is the central thoroughfare for a number of uptown neighborhoods. Visit University Heights for its cafés, bars, and shops; North Park is a haven for hipsters and foodies; Hillcrest is the hub of a thriving LGBTQ community with roots dating back to the 1950s. Also on this side of town are several specimens of Egyptian-revival architecture—the remnants of an early-twentieth-century design craze.

▶ The California Building employs a pastiche of architectural styles, with baroque, rococo, Gothic, and Spanish-colonial elements.

SOUTHERN CALIFORNIA

9

BAY, BRIDGE, AND BEACH

Across from downtown San Diego is Coronado Island, accessible by the two-mile-long Coronado Bridge. The island's centerpiece is the Hotel Del Coronado, one of the very last of the Victorian era's spectacular beachfront resorts ("the Del" is also the second-largest wooden structure in the United States). A night's stay here comes with a hefty price tag, but you don't have to be a guest to visit the grounds or take a guided tour of the interior. Coronado Island connects back to the mainland via a narrow isthmus called the Silver Strand—the southernmost of sixty-four California state beaches.

▲ Border Field State Park, dedicated in 1971 by then first lady Pat Nixon, is now unrecognizable from its original design as an open, cross-border shared space.

▼ The Hotel Del Coronado is prominently featured in the 1959 Billy Wilder classic, *Some Like It Hot*, starring Marilyn Monroe, Tony Curtis, and Jack Lemmon.

SOUTH OF THE CITY

Greater San Diego extends all the way to the Mexican border, as does the original Highway 101, although the old route is nearly lost amid a jumble of freeways and the international checkpoint on Interstate 5. Yet if you really want to say you drove the entire length of 101, it's still possible to pick up the southernmost thread of the old road. Old Highway 101 runs along Beyer Boulevard in San Ysidro, which becomes Broadway in Chula Vista and continues, under various names (National City Boulevard, Main Street, Harbor Drive, etc.), all the way to downtown San Diego.

THE UNWELCOME MAT

The southwestern corner of the United States is a local curiosity and a well-kept secret. Once accessible by car, Border Field State Park in Imperial Beach is now open only to pedestrians and equestrians. Hiking trails offer views of Tijuana and the ocean—including a high steel fence extending several yards into the sea. On certain days of the year, a restricted area called Friendship Park is open for visitors to approach (though not cross or even touch) the border fence to speak with loved ones on the other side. Border police are continually present; if you go, make sure you carry your driver's license, passport (page xiv), or other identification with you.

SAN DIEGO ICONS

▶ The *Star of India,* an iron-hulled British windjammer built in 1863, is the star attraction of the Maritime Museum of San Diego.

▲ What made the San Diego Zoo famous was its innovative cageless enclosures, which were among the first zoo exhibits to mimic an animal's natural habitat.

▶ San Diego cuisine combines flavors from both sides of the nearby international border. Fish tacos are a specialty of both street vendors and high-end restaurants.

◀ Old Point Loma Lighthouse, built in 1851 at what is now Cabrillo National Monument, is one of the oldest in California.

▶ The Egyptian Garage on University Avenue is encrusted with quirky Egyptian-revival details, like pharaohs' busts, cobras, and turquoise vulture wings.

◀ The Gaslamp Quarter gets its name from the early gas-powered streetlamps that lit the district during the Victorian era.

▼ The Geisel Library at UC San Diego is named for the city's most famous son, Theodor Seuss Geisel (Dr. Seuss).

Splashes of COLOR
NORTHERN SAN DIEGO COUNTY

San Diego proper extends far beyond the harbor and Balboa Park, yet the city's outer neighborhoods are cut off from downtown by a variety of geographical features. For this reason, it often makes sense to tour the northern outskirts on your way out of the city. With the military base Camp Pendleton blocking much of the coastal access and famous Orange County nearby, the northern half of San Diego County is easily overlooked. Still, the region boasts a wide variety of natural and cultural attractions.

▲ While the famous ranunculus blossoms steal the show, the Flower Fields also include unforgettable displays of orchids, poinsettias, roses, sweet peas, and more.

LA JOLLA: THE JEWEL OF SAN DIEGO COUNTY
A derivation of the Spanish word for "jewel," this wealthy seaside enclave is aptly named. Still an incorporated neighborhood of San Diego, it has high cliffs and a protected cove that give the place the feel of a separate world. A variety of upscale shops and restaurants, as well as easy walkability, makes La Jolla the ideal spot for a day trip or fancy outing.

LIFE-SIZE TERRARIUM
At first glance, Torrey Pines State Natural Reserve resembles any other haven for hikers and beachcombers, but its real purpose is the conservation of one of the rarest pines on earth. Only about one hundred Torrey pines remain, because the tree grows only in two places: Santa Rosa Island (page 25) and the narrow strip of cliff land defined by the state reserve.

▼ The Victorian cottage made famous by the 1986 film *Top Gun* still stands on Pacific Street in Oceanside, currently in restoration amid a swath of new development.

▶ Though the skull and crossbones in Oceanside is fake, it references a real Spanish cemetery motif. You can find the real thing in Old Mission Santa Barbara's boneyard (page 26).

BOUNTIFUL BLOOMS

Visit the Flower Fields in Carlsbad in the spring for a chance to see the landscape transform into a living rainbow. Carlsbad Ranch is home to these fifty sprawling acres of blossoms adjacent to old Highway 101. The main attraction is the fields of Giant Tecolote ranunculus; local horticulturist Edwin Frazee spent decades selecting and breeding these sun-loving bulbs, resulting in thirteen color varieties that attract tourists and gardeners alike. The farm and attached garden shop host about one hundred thousand visitors each spring; visit on a weekday morning for the best chance of avoiding the crowds.

ZORRO WAS HERE

The white stucco facade and sky-blue dome make Oceanside's Mission San Luis Rey de Francia one of the most recognizable of California's missions. On site is the first pepper tree, also a California icon, ever planted in the state. Look closely above the cemetery gate to find a skull and crossbones sculpted into the adobe wall. This detail is a modern anachronism added by the Walt Disney Studios in 1957 while filming several episodes of the television series *Zorro* on the mission grounds.

PIER-ING OUT TO SEA

At approximately 1,950 feet in length, the historic wooden Oceanside Pier is one of the largest on the West Coast. It is also Oceanside's centerpiece, perfect for a leisurely stroll, a spot of fishing, or a bit of evening entertainment. A souvenir shop and restaurant are built on the pier itself, and on the beach end is an amphitheater that hosts concerts and other outdoor events.

▼ Bring your binoculars to the Oceanside Pier, an excellent location for spotting both humans and dolphins surfing the waves.

▶ Once critically endangered, the brown pelican has made a remarkable comeback. These birds are once again a common sight along the Southern California coast.

THE OC & THE PCH
SAN CLEMENTE TO LAGUNA BEACH

▲ Visitors looking for cliff swallows can find them nesting in nearby Chino Hills.

◄ La Tour is a sixty-foot tower built in 1926 as a Laguna residence. While the tower itself is private property, it can easily be viewed by visiting the public Victoria Beach.

After mountains and military bases force you onto Interstate 5 at the north end of Oceanside, you can pick up the thread of the old coastal highway once again in San Clemente. This is where Highway 1 begins—dubbed the PCH (Pacific Coast Highway) along the southern half of the route. The towns of Orange County tend to bleed together a bit, but there are memorable highlights.

DARLING DANA
Oddly named streets like Ruby Lantern, Amber Lantern, and others mark Dana Point's historic Lantern District. The names reference the town's early days, when ships docked here would use color-coded lanterns to advertise which products they carried aboard. Today ships are moored in a modern marina built in the 1960s and slated for complete revitalization in the coming years.

LIVELY LAGUNA
Long a haven for artists and environmentalists, Laguna Beach is chockablock with galleries, green spaces, and eccentric locals. In July and August, check out the splendidly kooky Pageant of the Masters, where living models recreate famous paintings in *tableaux vivants*.

THE PAST RESURRECTED
Perched above the PCH, San Juan Capistrano is a treasure trove of history. The Los Rios Historic District dates to the eighteenth century, and Richard Nixon's favorite haunt, the famous El Adobe de Capistrano restaurant, might actually be haunted. Built as a private home in 1797, it was later divided in half to house the local courthouse. The basement served for a time as the town's only jail, then became a wine cellar when the restaurant opened in 1948. Visitors and staff have reported ghost sightings of a young jail inmate in the basement, as well as a headless friar wandering around outside.

LAGUNA BEACH

MISSION SAN JUAN CAPISTRANO

DANA POINT

CATALINA FERRY

SAN CLEMENTE

N

A SLICE OF THE OLD WORLD

The centerpiece of San Juan Capistrano is the town's name-sake mission, founded in 1776. The landmark is unique among California's missions in that it is at once a living church and a preserved ruin. The sprawling mission complex is open to tourists, displaying both the religious history and the secular industry of the compound. Don't miss the stunning gardens, the iconic mission bells, or the Greco-Roman-style ruins of the Great Stone Church, which collapsed in an 1812 earthquake that struck in the middle of Sunday service.

▲ Visit Dana Point in March for the Festival of Whales, which since 1972 has celebrated the return to the SoCal coast of migrating cetaceans like gray whales.

WHEN THE SWALLOWS COME BACK TO CAPISTRANO

What most tourists visit the mission for is not the architecture, however. Instead, the tiny American cliff swallow steals the show. The birds have historically nested at Mission San Juan Capistrano by the tens of thousands on their return from their winter habitat in Argentina. Tradition has it that the swallows depart every year on Saint John's Day (October 23) and return once more on Saint Joseph's Day (March 19). The phenomenon has been the subject of songs and films, plus the town's annual Fiesta de las Golondrinas (Festival of the Swallows).

In recent years the mission's returning swallows have sadly dwindled to just a trickle. This reduction is largely due to the region's increased development, which gives the birds a wider, less concentrated choice of habitat.

SIDE TRIP

Catalina
ISLAND PARADISE

▲ In 1919, William Wrigley Jr., of chewing gum fame, bought most of the island. Along with his money, his personal taste influenced Avalon's unique aesthetic.

▼ In the 1920s, Catalina was home to an artisan tile factory. Avalon is still festooned with tile remnants, including mosaic murals of animals and exotic birds.

Located about twenty miles off the coast of Southern California, Santa Catalina Island (or simply Catalina for short) transports the visitor to an idyllic world. With jewel-bright waters, crystal-clear air, and postcard-perfect views at every turn—as well as steep price tags for lodging and many activities—Catalina feels like a reimagined slice of a Mediterranean principality.

Various private high-speed passenger ferries depart from the mainland, though Dana Point, Newport Beach, and Long Beach offer the most options. Private cars are not allowed on the island, so leave your wheels on the shore and plan to spend your island adventure on foot.

A REAL-LIFE AVALON

The island's only incorporated city is named for the land of Arthurian legend—yet has the feel of the Italian Riviera. Colorful shops line the half-moon harbor, while residential streets snake up the steep hillsides that form the crescent-shaped valley. The pace of life here is easy; the only traffic consists of pedestrians and the island's iconic golf carts. Stop for fish-and-chips at the Green Pleasure Pier, browse the waterfront shops, or hike (or take a rented bike or cart) up Avalon Canyon to the Wrigley Memorial & Botanic Garden.

NOT THAT KIND OF CASINO

At the height of a twelve-story building, the Catalina Casino is the island's most recognizable landmark. You'll find no gambling here, however: built in 1929, the casino is modeled after the Italian word meaning "gathering place." Upstairs is a massive ballroom, the largest circular dance floor on earth. In the 1930s and '40s, famous big-band musicians broadcast

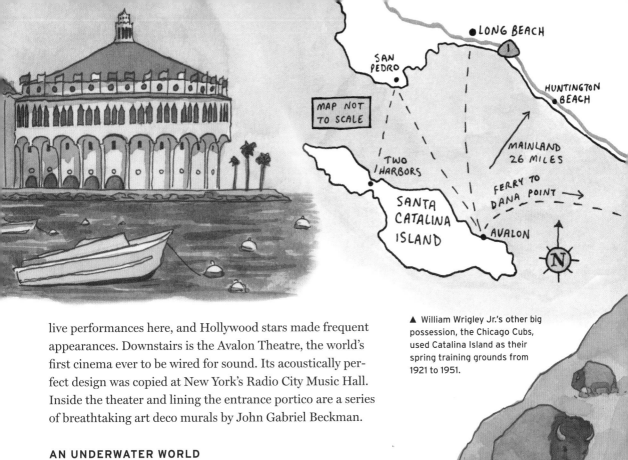

live performances here, and Hollywood stars made frequent appearances. Downstairs is the Avalon Theatre, the world's first cinema ever to be wired for sound. Its acoustically perfect design was copied at New York's Radio City Music Hall. Inside the theater and lining the entrance portico are a series of breathtaking art deco murals by John Gabriel Beckman.

▲ William Wrigley Jr.'s other big possession, the Chicago Cubs, used Catalina Island as their spring training grounds from 1921 to 1951.

AN UNDERWATER WORLD

The waters surrounding the island are their own tourist attraction. Underwater visibility frequently spans a hundred feet, making it the perfect marine photography spot. Kelp forests dominate here, providing ideal habitat for bright-orange garibaldi, California's state fish. If diving isn't your thing, there are glass-bottomed and semisubmersible boat tours to choose from.

THE HEART OF THE INTERIOR

The Catalina Island Conservancy, a private land trust formed in 1972 by the Wrigley family, controls the few roads and trails within the island's interior. To protect the fragile ecosystem, permits are needed for all visits, including hikes. Various tours are available, either by jeep or vintage 1950s tour bus. The rough, primitive road makes for a bumpy ride, but the views at the summit above Avalon are well worth it. Sharp-eyed travelers might see the island's bison herd, brought here in the 1920s for the filming of a western. The very luckiest might spot the endemic, endangered island fox.

SURF'S UP

NEWPORT BEACH TO LONG BEACH

Back on the mainland, Highway 1 flattens out north of Laguna Beach, following a wide and densely populated coastal plain that stretches all the way to Los Angeles (map on page 21).

THERE'S ALWAYS MONEY IN THE BANANA STAND

Located within the sprawling city of Newport Beach are the island and peninsula of Balboa. The peninsula is home to the Balboa Fun Zone, an old-time beachfront carnival and boardwalk. Balboa Island is a residential community consisting of vaguely Venetian-style houses and a small shopping district. Grab a bite at the iconic Sugar 'n Spice—a snack stand that has served up frozen bananas since 1945 and was more recently immortalized by the television comedy *Arrested Development*.

SURF CITY USA

Huntington Beach is home to near-perfect surfing conditions year-round. In 2015, sixty-six people rode the world's largest surfboard all at once, smashing several world records; the board itself is now on display at the International Surfing Museum on Olive Avenue.

URBAN SEASHORE

Long Beach, the third-largest city in Southern California, sprang to life in the 1920s and '30s after oil was discovered offshore. It is a haven for architecture buffs, who will love spotting art deco details on nearly every downtown building. For a bit of seaside fun, walk along the waterfront promenade, stop at the Aquarium of the Pacific, and grab a meal with a view at Parkers' Lighthouse.

▲ For less than the cost of a latte, you can ride the tiny car ferry that runs continuously between Balboa Island and Balboa Peninsula.

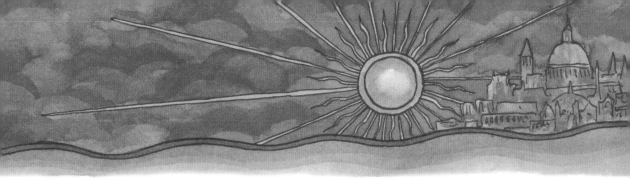

FIT FOR A QUEEN

Long Beach's main attraction is something of an oddity: the RMS *Queen Mary*, a retired British ocean liner. The flagship of the Cunard Line, she made her maiden voyage in 1936 and was the luxury liner of choice for both the English monarchy and Hollywood royalty. During World War II, she was requisitioned by the British navy as a troop transport ship. Her stealth paint job and swift speed earned her the nickname the *Grey Ghost*. After the war she was restored back to her art deco glory and refitted for passenger service, capable of making the transatlantic journey between London and New York in just under four days. However, the rise of air travel in the 1960s made ocean cruises fall out of favor, and in 1967 the city of Long Beach purchased the retired ship to be moored permanently as a hotel and tourist attraction.

WINSTON CHURCHILL SLEPT HERE

Today the *Queen Mary* offers high-class restaurants, excellent guided tours, and one-of-a-kind overnight accommodations. While it's far from a budget hotel, it's well worth spending a night or two here, not least because hotel guests are largely free to explore the ship. Try booking one of the former first-class staterooms, which are perfectly preserved from the days when they hosted movie stars and heads of state. Other ship highlights include the spectacular Observation Bar and the Grand Salon, which hosts an opulent Sunday brunch.

▲ Don't miss the art deco murals, friezes, sculptures, and inlaid wood panels that grace the ship's ballrooms and other gathering spaces.

▼ There's just one drawback to this hotel: the walls are a bit thin, as the engine noise that once soundproofed the ship has fallen silent.

▼ At more than one thousand feet in length, the RMS *Queen Mary* could fit one and a half RMS *Titanic*s inside her massive hull.

BEACH BUMS

REDONDO BEACH TO MALIBU

After Long Beach, Highway 1 turns inland for a time, skipping some of the coastal communities along the way. A side jaunt along the coastal Palos Verdes Drive might be worth the trip, but as traffic lights and the convoluted thoroughfares can be time consuming to navigate, it's easier just to power through on the PCH.

▼ If you manage to find a parking space in either Santa Monica or Malibu, be careful crossing Highway 1 to reach the beach!

THE BEACHES: REDONDO, HERMOSA, AND MANHATTAN
The PCH does cross through this trio of beach communities, which are surprisingly laid back and sleepy despite their proximity to Los Angeles. All three towns boast a municipal pier and are connected to one another by the twenty-mile-long pedestrian and bike path known as the Strand.

RE-LAX
Highway 1 runs along Sepulveda Boulevard to Los Angeles International Airport (LAX). Even if you don't have a flight to catch, it's worth stopping here to see the Theme Building. This midcentury masterpiece is a prime example of Googie architecture, the retro-futuristic style of the 1950s and '60s that celebrated space exploration and the atomic age. Afterward, take a short detour east on Manchester Boulevard for a drive-through stop at Randy's Donuts; look for the giant rooftop doughnut that has been featured in many films and television shows.

WELCOME TO

BEAUTIFUL PARADISE COVE

SEA THE VIEW

BRING THE KIDS

HAVE A SEAT

ENJOY MALIBU

THE OTHER VENICE
Just before the PCH heads back to the shore, it skirts the Los Angeles beachfront neighborhood of Venice, named for its canals, which mimic the famous ones in Italy. The Venice Canal Historic District is nearly invisible from the thoroughfares, tucked away in a residential neighborhood and accessible only from a handful of pedestrian entrances. The district makes for a splendid stroll, with a series of arched bridges for viewing the reflections of colorful houses and pleasure boats.

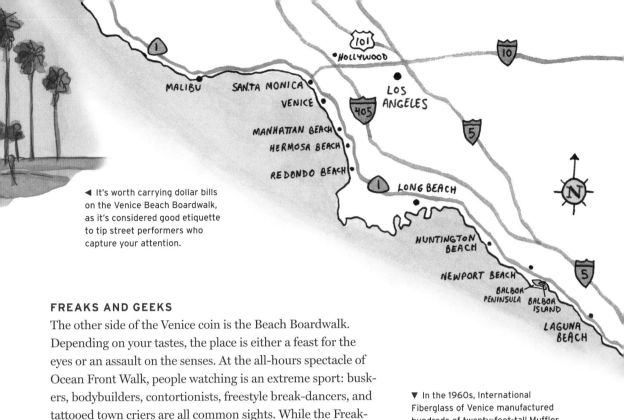

◀ It's worth carrying dollar bills on the Venice Beach Boardwalk, as it's considered good etiquette to tip street performers who capture your attention.

FREAKS AND GEEKS

The other side of the Venice coin is the Beach Boardwalk. Depending on your tastes, the place is either a feast for the eyes or an assault on the senses. At the all-hours spectacle of Ocean Front Walk, people watching is an extreme sport: buskers, bodybuilders, contortionists, freestyle break-dancers, and tattooed town criers are all common sights. While the Freakshow attraction closed in 2017 (bummer!), Muscle Beach is still a highlight, as are the plethora of street performers.

WHERE THE MOTHER ROAD MEETS THE COAST HIGHWAY

Next up is Santa Monica, where Route 66 meets its symbolic end at the PCH and the iconic Santa Monica Pier. Highway 1 widens into a six-lane speedway here—but before you zoom away, check out the candy-colored stucco apartment houses, hotels, and storefronts high above you, along the cliff-top Ocean Avenue.

WAIT—DID I JUST SEE BEYONCÉ?

Long known as the playground of the rich and famous, Malibu isn't quite as exclusive as its celebrity homes and private beaches make it out to be. There are many public access points along the city's twenty-seven-mile coastline, including Zuma Beach County Park, state beaches like El Matador and Leo Carrillo, and Malibu Lagoon State Beach, which encompasses Surfrider Beach and the Malibu Pier. For a dash of roadside kitsch amid the glitz and glamour, keep an eye out for a sombrero-wearing Muffler Man (see caption, right) holding a giant taco.

▼ In the 1960s, International Fiberglass of Venice manufactured hundreds of twenty-feet-tall Muffler Men to advertise gas stations nationwide. Many of these roadside giants still guard the West Coast.

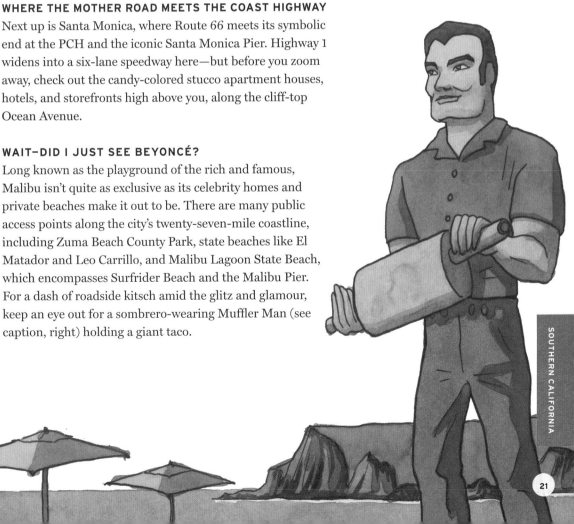

SOUTHERN CALIFORNIA

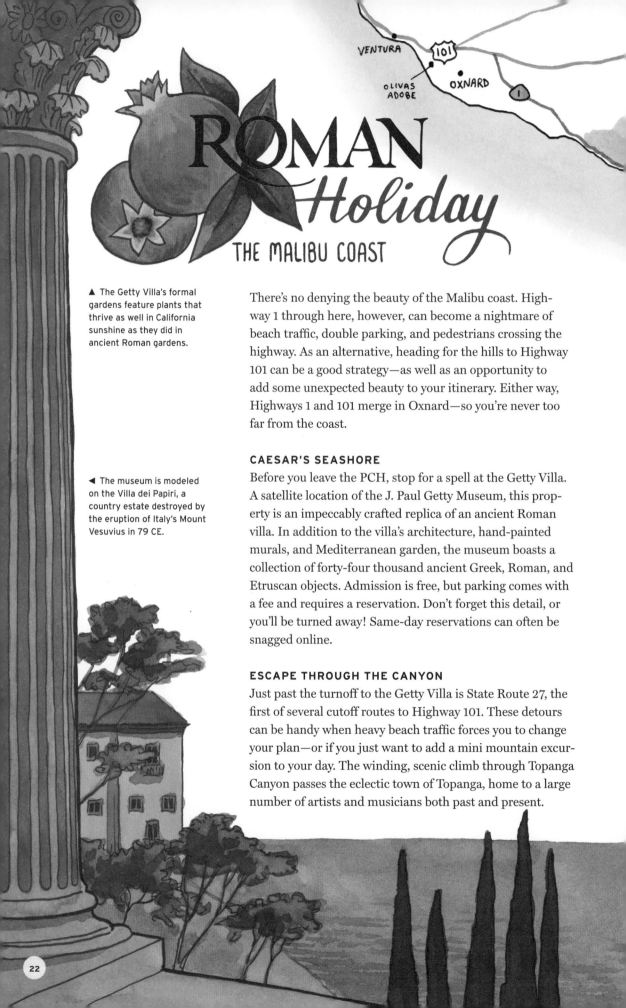

ROMAN *Holiday*

THE MALIBU COAST

▲ The Getty Villa's formal gardens feature plants that thrive as well in California sunshine as they did in ancient Roman gardens.

There's no denying the beauty of the Malibu coast. Highway 1 through here, however, can become a nightmare of beach traffic, double parking, and pedestrians crossing the highway. As an alternative, heading for the hills to Highway 101 can be a good strategy—as well as an opportunity to add some unexpected beauty to your itinerary. Either way, Highways 1 and 101 merge in Oxnard—so you're never too far from the coast.

CAESAR'S SEASHORE

◄ The museum is modeled on the Villa dei Papiri, a country estate destroyed by the eruption of Italy's Mount Vesuvius in 79 CE.

Before you leave the PCH, stop for a spell at the Getty Villa. A satellite location of the J. Paul Getty Museum, this property is an impeccably crafted replica of an ancient Roman villa. In addition to the villa's architecture, hand-painted murals, and Mediterranean garden, the museum boasts a collection of forty-four thousand ancient Greek, Roman, and Etruscan objects. Admission is free, but parking comes with a fee and requires a reservation. Don't forget this detail, or you'll be turned away! Same-day reservations can often be snagged online.

ESCAPE THROUGH THE CANYON

Just past the turnoff to the Getty Villa is State Route 27, the first of several cutoff routes to Highway 101. These detours can be handy when heavy beach traffic forces you to change your plan—or if you just want to add a mini mountain excursion to your day. The winding, scenic climb through Topanga Canyon passes the eclectic town of Topanga, home to a large number of artists and musicians both past and present.

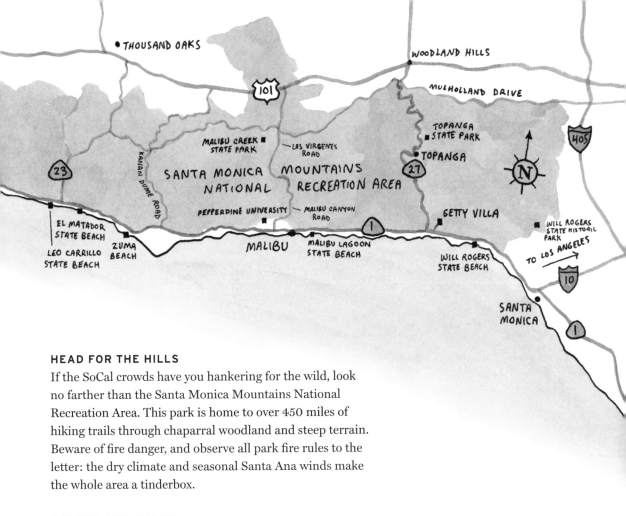

HEAD FOR THE HILLS

If the SoCal crowds have you hankering for the wild, look
no farther than the Santa Monica Mountains National
Recreation Area. This park is home to over 450 miles of
hiking trails through chaparral woodland and steep terrain.
Beware of fire danger, and observe all park fire rules to the
letter: the dry climate and seasonal Santa Ana winds make
the whole area a tinderbox.

BACK TO THE COAST

Eventually the mountains give way to the Oxnard Plain,
which is blanketed with strawberry fields and vegetable
farms. The topography allows Oxnard to sprawl out over a
large area; adjacent Ventura is more compact. About halfway
between is the living-history museum of the Olivas Adobe,
one of the original ranchos (land grants) dating to the Alta
California territory of New Spain. Mission San Buenaventura is the centerpiece of Ventura's historic downtown. Each
city encompasses its own working harbor, and both serve as
gateway ports to the Channel Islands (page 24).

▼ The wild landscape of Topanga
Canyon makes it easy to forget one's
close proximity to urban Los Angeles.

SOUTHERN CALIFORNIA

Channel Islands
NATIONAL PARK

SIDE TRIP →

Often called America's Galápagos, the Channel Islands are a glimpse of what the West Coast looked like before white settlers arrived: pristine landscapes home to isolated species of plants, animals, and birds. Unlike the virgin ecosystem of the Galápagos, however, the natural world of the Channel Islands is a restored one, brought back from the brink of destruction after decades of military and agricultural use. The national park encompasses five of the eight islands off the coast of Southern California; the remaining three are tourist haven Santa Catalina (page 16), US Navy–owned San Clemente, and remote San Nicolas, the setting of the famous children's novel *Island of the Blue Dolphins*. The islands are both unforgettable and extremely sensitive to human visitors; see them with the eyes of a steward as well as a tourist. The standard rules of thumb apply: take only pictures, pack out all trash, leave no trace.

Boat trips to each island are handled by the private charter company Island Packers and depart from both Oxnard and Ventura. The park's official visitor center in Ventura provides up-to-date information, with park rangers on hand to answer questions. Other than a handful of campgrounds and sparsely staffed ranger stations, there are no services, supplies, or cell reception on any of the islands. Be prepared to be self-sufficient during your time there. Carry your own food and ample drinking water, as well as layered clothing, sun protection, and first aid supplies. And don't miss your return boat!

▲ The Santa Barbara Island liveforever is a rare succulent that, aptly, has managed to survive the introduced rabbits that devoured it to the brink of extinction.

▼ An easy hike leads to this spot on Anacapa's western edge—they don't call it Inspiration Point for nothing.

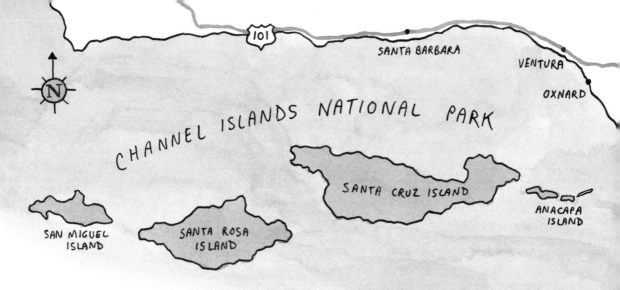

ANACAPA: THE GATEWAY ISLAND

Actually consisting of three tiny islets, Anacapa is perfect for a day trip or an introduction to the archipelago. The treeless terrain makes its lighthouse, the last built on the West Coast, visible from all over the island. Glimpse the natural bridge at Arch Rock from the boat as you arrive.

SANTA CRUZ: THE HISTORY ISLAND

California's largest island, a perennial favorite of hikers and wildlife watchers, is a living scale model of the state itself. Here, you'll find two mountain ranges, a vast central valley, and shell middens (ancient trash heaps) left behind by the Indigenous Chumash people.

SANTA ROSA: THE BIOLOGY ISLAND

Known for its rolling hills, deep canyons, and pristine beaches, Santa Rosa was once home to several prehistoric species, now extinct—including giant mice, flightless geese, and pygmy mammoths.

SAN MIGUEL: THE WILD ISLAND

The westernmost island, San Miguel gets pummeled by the waves and weather. Point Bennett is one of the largest seal and sea lion haul-outs on earth; thirty thousand congregate here in one impossibly raucous hootenanny.

SANTA BARBARA: ISLAND IN TRANSITION

Smallest, remotest, and least visited, this isle nonetheless bears the scars of overpopulation. The ecosystem is healing from past farming and invasive species, however, and spring once again brings an explosion of wildflowers.

▼ Thanks to its isolation, Santa Cruz Island is home to several organisms found only here, including eight plant species and the island scrub jay.

◄ Anacapa is a nesting habitat for fifteen thousand gulls. Visit in April for the ultimate Easter egg hunt, or celebrate the births of peeping chicks in May.

SIDE TRIP

CALIFORNIA'S *Riviera*
SANTA BARBARA

At this point on the coastal highway, that indefinable Southern California feeling begins to shift. The climate changes ever so slightly, and the air of endless summer vacation dissipates. Santa Barbara is widely considered to be the unofficial boundary point between north and south. It's hard to think of a better place to stop and celebrate the transition and wave a fond farewell to SoCal.

Despite an ever-swelling population, Santa Barbara miraculously retains a small-town ambience. Much of this is due to its strict laws on zoning and architectural consistency. After a devastating earthquake in 1925, the city sought to rebuild itself in its own historical image. Spanish-revival architecture was popular in that era anyway, so the city embraced its transformation into a unified, living tribute to its forebears.

A SEA OF RED ROOFTOPS
The most striking of Santa Barbara's Spanish-revival attributes are its terra-cotta rooftops and bone-white or adobe-buff stucco walls. Ceramic tile mosaics in brilliant colors provide accents and adorn the many domes that rise above the skyline. Arched doorways complete the look, along with the odd ornamental bell. Spanish-style courtyards add a layer of surprise and mystery to a neighborhood stroll.

PRETTY IN PINK
Old Mission Santa Barbara, the city's namesake, is perched like a castle up the hill from downtown. Locals call it "Queen of the Missions" for good reason, with its long colonnade of archways, colorful stucco, and twin pink domes. The interior rooms and cloister gardens are well worth the admission fee.

▼ The Flamenco Arts Festival, held each autumn, celebrates the traditional music and dance of southern Spain.

▲ The clocktower of the Santa Barbara County Courthouse offers unparalleled views of city and shore.

DON'T FORGET DOWNTOWN

State Street, with its broadleaf evergreen trees and adobe storefronts, is the centerpiece of all that picturesque city planning. Even if upscale shopping isn't your thing, the walk is its own reward. Downtown extends to the waterfront, home of the historic 1872 Stearns Wharf.

GARDENS GALORE

No Spanish villa is complete without a courtyard garden, and Santa Barbara is overflowing with lush florals and greenery. Many gardens are open to the public; some favorites are Alice Keck Park and the themed gardens at Ganna Walska Lotusland. Home horticulturists can browse and shop at the Santa Barbara Orchid Estate.

▲ Santa Barbara's mild Mediterranean climate completes the illusion of having suddenly stepped into a hillside village on the Riviera.

UNA FIESTA EXCELENTE

Visit in early August for Old Spanish Days, an annual celebration of Santa Barbara's ranchero history. Events include a Mexican market, music and dance performances, and an equestrian parade.

Danes & Dunes

SOLVANG TO PISMO BEACH

With Santa Barbara behind you, the central coast begins, and the coast highway splits in two again. Highway 1 also gains the new nickname the Cabrillo Highway, which it retains until the Golden Gate Bridge.

CHEESE DANISH

In the 1940s, the town of Solvang began boosting its Danish heritage to attract tourists. Business owners added half-timbered facades to their buildings; windmills and even a scale replica of Copenhagen's Rundetaarn popped up around town. Today Solvang feels a bit like a cheesy theme park, but it's still a fun place to stop and stretch your legs.

SOUP'S ON

Nearby Buellton's hokey roadside answer to Solvang's faux Denmark is Pea Soup Andersen's Inn. Its over-the-top theme restaurant has served bottomless bowls of split-pea soup since 1947.

▲ Be sure to try aebleskiver, a doughnut-like Danish sweet treat. Solvang Restaurant, which makes a cameo in the movie *Sideways*, has served them since 1966.

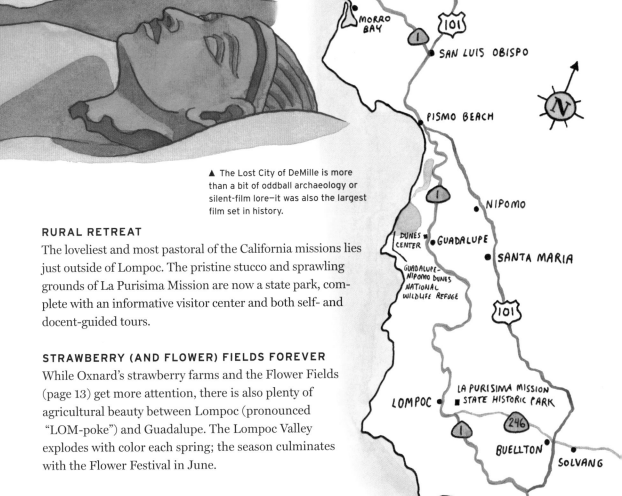

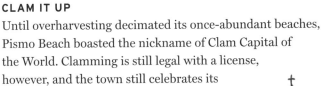

▲ The Lost City of DeMille is more than a bit of oddball archaeology or silent-film lore—it was also the largest film set in history.

RURAL RETREAT

The loveliest and most pastoral of the California missions lies just outside of Lompoc. The pristine stucco and sprawling grounds of La Purisima Mission are now a state park, complete with an informative visitor center and both self- and docent-guided tours.

STRAWBERRY (AND FLOWER) FIELDS FOREVER

While Oxnard's strawberry farms and the Flower Fields (page 13) get more attention, there is also plenty of agricultural beauty between Lompoc (pronounced "LOM-poke") and Guadalupe. The Lompoc Valley explodes with color each spring; the season culminates with the Flower Festival in June.

SECRET SANDS

The Guadalupe-Nipomo Dunes are eighteen miles of coastline set aside for conservation and recreation. In 1923, Cecil B. DeMille filmed *The Ten Commandments* there—and afterward buried the set in the sand. It lay undisturbed and forgotten for sixty years, until archaeologists began digging up several set pieces. The remains of two sphinxes are on display at the Dunes Center.

CLAM IT UP

Until overharvesting decimated its once-abundant beaches, Pismo Beach boasted the nickname of Clam Capital of the World. Clamming is still legal with a license, however, and the town still celebrates its Clam Festival every October.

▼ La Purisima Mission was hand restored in the 1930s, using eighteenth-century methods employed as part of a Depression-era New Deal program.

CENTRAL CALIFORNIA

SLO
Down & Enjoy

SAN LUIS OBISPO TO MORRO BAY

At Pismo Beach the two highways merge yet again, but only as far as San Luis Obispo. This city, nicknamed SLO (pronounced "slow") by some locals, is the perfect place to rest and recharge before the next leg of your coastal journey.

A LOW-KEY GEM

Home to the tech university Cal Poly, SLO shows its affluence in its lovely buildings, nearby wineries, and immaculate streets lined with towering ficus trees. There's a perfect balance between sleepy leisure and bustling vibrance here. A top-notch farmers' market lines a five-block stretch of Higuera Street every Thursday night with produce, food trucks, and live entertainment.

▲ Mission San Luis Obispo de Tolosa, located right downtown, features hand-painted floral murals added during a 1930s-era restoration.

MUCH MO' THAN A MOTEL

Roadside historians should note the Motel Inn, the world's first motor hotel (now part of the Apple Farm hotel). But for a real treat, consider a stay across town at the Madonna Inn. An insane mishmash of baroque and western decor that defies the posh and understated SLO aesthetic, the hotel features one hundred individually themed rooms. There's also a hot-pink dining room, a wagon-wheel-shaped café that serves champagne cake and house-made wine, a staircase from Hearst Castle, and a waterfall-grotto urinal in the men's restroom (don't fret, ladies—you can peek in there, too). The whole thing is over the top, overpriced, and *completely* worth it.

▼ The Madonna Inn is a mix of stately and silly, the perfect destination for anyone who loves roadside Americana.

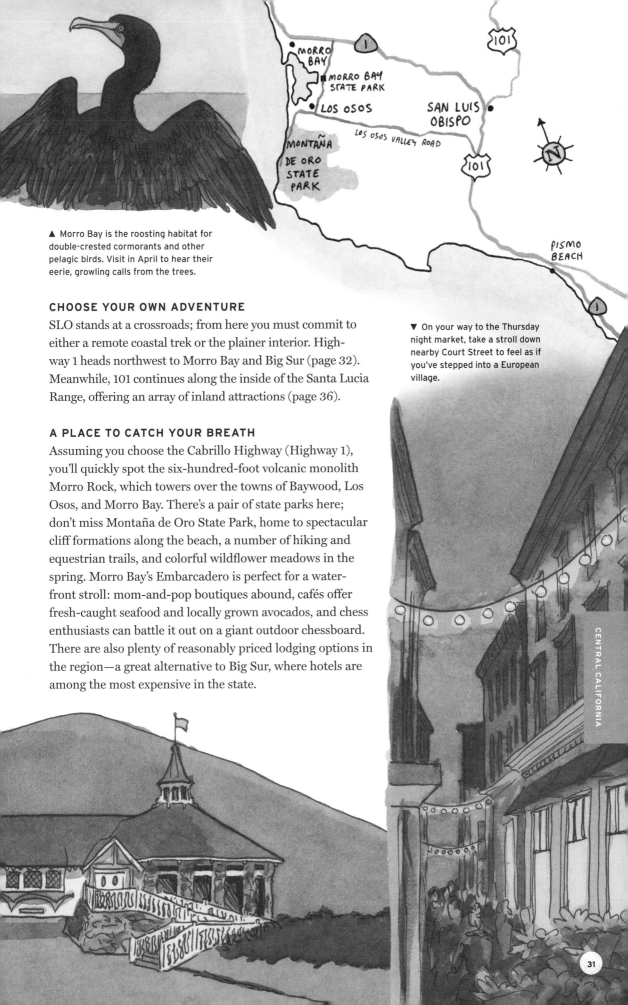

▲ Morro Bay is the roosting habitat for double-crested cormorants and other pelagic birds. Visit in April to hear their eerie, growling calls from the trees.

CHOOSE YOUR OWN ADVENTURE

SLO stands at a crossroads; from here you must commit to either a remote coastal trek or the plainer interior. Highway 1 heads northwest to Morro Bay and Big Sur (page 32). Meanwhile, 101 continues along the inside of the Santa Lucia Range, offering an array of inland attractions (page 36).

A PLACE TO CATCH YOUR BREATH

Assuming you choose the Cabrillo Highway (Highway 1), you'll quickly spot the six-hundred-foot volcanic monolith Morro Rock, which towers over the towns of Baywood, Los Osos, and Morro Bay. There's a pair of state parks here; don't miss Montaña de Oro State Park, home to spectacular cliff formations along the beach, a number of hiking and equestrian trails, and colorful wildflower meadows in the spring. Morro Bay's Embarcadero is perfect for a waterfront stroll: mom-and-pop boutiques abound, cafés offer fresh-caught seafood and locally grown avocados, and chess enthusiasts can battle it out on a giant outdoor chessboard. There are also plenty of reasonably priced lodging options in the region—a great alternative to Big Sur, where hotels are among the most expensive in the state.

▼ On your way to the Thursday night market, take a stroll down nearby Court Street to feel as if you've stepped into a European village.

CENTRAL CALIFORNIA

BIG Picture

THE BIG SUR COAST

The ninety-mile stretch of pristine coastline named Big Sur is the star of Highway 1—and quite possibly the biggest tourist draw on the West Coast. The region is nearly untouched and as sparsely populated as it has ever been. With the possible exception of the Channel Islands (page 24), this is California at its most pure.

WHERE NATURE OUTDOES ITSELF

There is simply nothing quite like Big Sur. Here, the high Santa Lucia Mountains plunge abruptly into the sea, leaving behind a saw-toothed coastline of sheer cliffs and impossible views. California condors soar on the sweeping updrafts of air, while fingers of fog creep their way over the hillsides before obfuscating them entirely. Listen for the barking of sea lions below, their sounds carried upward when the wind is right.

FEATS OF ENGINEERING

It took twenty years (and cost several lives) to complete the Big Sur portion of the highway. The road twists and turns for more than a hundred miles, with each bridge, rock cut, and raised grade representing a feat of engineering. You might find yourself gasping in awe (or cursing in consternation) at the road itself as you pick your way along, hundreds of feet above the water.

THE JOURNEY IS THE REWARD

In truth, it's possible to drive the entire Big Sur road in half a day—but that would be doing yourself a disservice. Take your time here: feel each curve under your wheels; stop frequently to take in the view and explore; remind yourself that this is really happening. You won't regret it, and you'll certainly never forget it.

▼ The 1932 Bixby Creek Bridge, still one of the tallest concrete arch spans in the world, is an essential photo op from every angle.

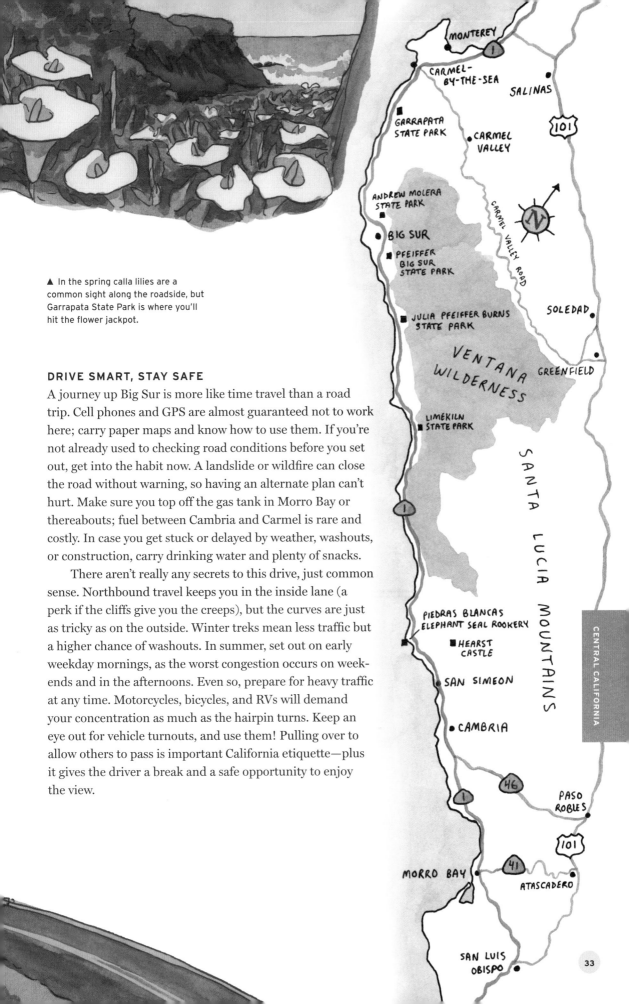

▲ In the spring calla lilies are a common sight along the roadside, but Garrapata State Park is where you'll hit the flower jackpot.

DRIVE SMART, STAY SAFE

A journey up Big Sur is more like time travel than a road trip. Cell phones and GPS are almost guaranteed not to work here; carry paper maps and know how to use them. If you're not already used to checking road conditions before you set out, get into the habit now. A landslide or wildfire can close the road without warning, so having an alternate plan can't hurt. Make sure you top off the gas tank in Morro Bay or thereabouts; fuel between Cambria and Carmel is rare and costly. In case you get stuck or delayed by weather, washouts, or construction, carry drinking water and plenty of snacks.

There aren't really any secrets to this drive, just common sense. Northbound travel keeps you in the inside lane (a perk if the cliffs give you the creeps), but the curves are just as tricky as on the outside. Winter treks mean less traffic but a higher chance of washouts. In summer, set out on early weekday mornings, as the worst congestion occurs on weekends and in the afternoons. Even so, prepare for heavy traffic at any time. Motorcycles, bicycles, and RVs will demand your concentration as much as the hairpin turns. Keep an eye out for vehicle turnouts, and use them! Pulling over to allow others to pass is important California etiquette—plus it gives the driver a break and a safe opportunity to enjoy the view.

BIG SUR *Attractions*

In addition to the drive itself, Big Sur boasts plenty of worth-while places to hike, bike, eat, watch wildlife (bring your binoculars!), or simply take in the view.

▲ Nepenthe is well worth the wait for a table. Here, you can enjoy a midpriced meal with a million-dollar view.

BIG SUR BIG SHOT
The region's best-known landmark is Hearst Castle, the sprawling private estate of newspaper magnate William Randolph Hearst. A larger-than-life hot mess of palatial buildings and priceless antique decor, the place blows right past grandiosity and into megalomania—which, as history paints it, is a fair portrait of Hearst himself. Julia Morgan's architecture is the real star here, particularly in the Roman Pool and the Celestial Suite. The estate is now run as a state park and is accessible only by a series of group tours; advance reservations are crucial.

NITT WITT RIDGE
The nearby town of Cambria, a quiet hamlet with a rich history, is home to another eccentric private estate. Nitt Witt Ridge, nicknamed the Poor Man's Hearst Castle, is the folk-art creation of Arthur Harold Beal, who was the town garbage collector in the 1940s and '50s. The beach flotsam, car parts, and other refuse that make up the property are an amusing and oddly appropriate counterpoint to Hearst's opulent and equally eye-frying fortress.

THE SEALS OF SAN SIMEON
Don't miss the Piedras Blancas Elephant Seal Rookery, easily visible from a roadside overlook near San Simeon. This narrow beach is a haul-out and breeding colony for tens of

◄ In the fields across the highway from the elephant seal overlook, keep an eye out for zebras! The animals are descended from Hearst's exotic menagerie.

▶ You might laugh when you see the yellow warning signs for feral pigs, but the animals are a real roadside pest; drive with care.

thousands of northern elephant seals, which visit the spot annually to mate, duel, and raise their young. February is the ideal time to visit, as the beach is crowded with bellowing bulls, cranky cows, and piles of pups.

A LITTLE R & R

Despite its remote location, Big Sur does offer some services—though many will leave you with serious sticker shock. Big Sur Bakery and Nepenthe are both famous for their flavors, and neither will break the bank; if you have to choose between the two, Nepenthe's views win the day. Big spenders, on the other hand, need only to look for lodging. The Ventana Big Sur resort or the Post Ranch Inn both offer luxury spa treatments. New Age types love the Esalen Institute, which offers meditation workshops and a number of outdoor cliff-top hot springs.

BIG TREES

Big Sur is home to the southernmost groves of redwood trees, which thrive in the narrow gullies fed by coastal fog. Highway 1 twists through a section of redwoods near Big Sur Village, and hiking trails at Pfeiffer Big Sur State Park lead to an old-growth thicket of them.

▼ Adult male elephant seals weigh up to five thousand pounds, but they can move with astonishing speed on the sand.

PRISTINE PARKS

The region is home to a number of stellar state parks, many named for pioneers who settled the area. Andrew Molera State Park preserves a nineteenth-century homestead and former ranch. At Julia Pfeiffer Burns State Park, hike down to the McWay Falls overlook to see an eighty-foot waterfall pour right onto the sand of a secluded cove. Garrapata State Park protects a series of beaches, while Point Sur is home to an 1889 lighthouse.

CENTRAL CALIFORNIA

inland ALTERNATIVES

If the landslide gods lead you to skip the Big Sur coast (or better yet, you have an extra day or two to spend), Highway 101 is worth your time as well. Skirting the Santa Lucia Mountains to the east, the route follows the fertile Salinas Valley for nearly a hundred miles.

WINE AND GUAC

Though still eclipsed by its northern counterparts (page 62), the wine region near Paso Robles is gaining fame and respect. On your way, see the avocado farms that line State Route 41 near Atascadero.

▲ Once extinct in the wild, the California condor gets a wing up at Pinnacles National Park, which was created to protect the bird's nesting habitat.

ON A MISSION

The inland route takes you within reach of four historic missions. San Miguel is still in its original semiruined state, with few tourists to distract from its beauty. San Antonio de Padua requires a detour into the mountains, but its secluded beauty and still-active monastery are worth the trip. Soledad is true to its name, sitting all alone in the middle of a farm field. Finally, San Juan Bautista steals the show. It made a cameo in the Alfred Hitchcock film *Vertigo* and sits directly atop the San Andreas Fault (yikes!), above a preserved original section of El Camino Real. Visit at dawn on the winter solstice to see the sun rise, Stonehenge-style, perfectly framed in the church's front doorway.

▼ The famous mission is not the only attraction in San Juan Bautista. The whole town is a treasure trove of California history.

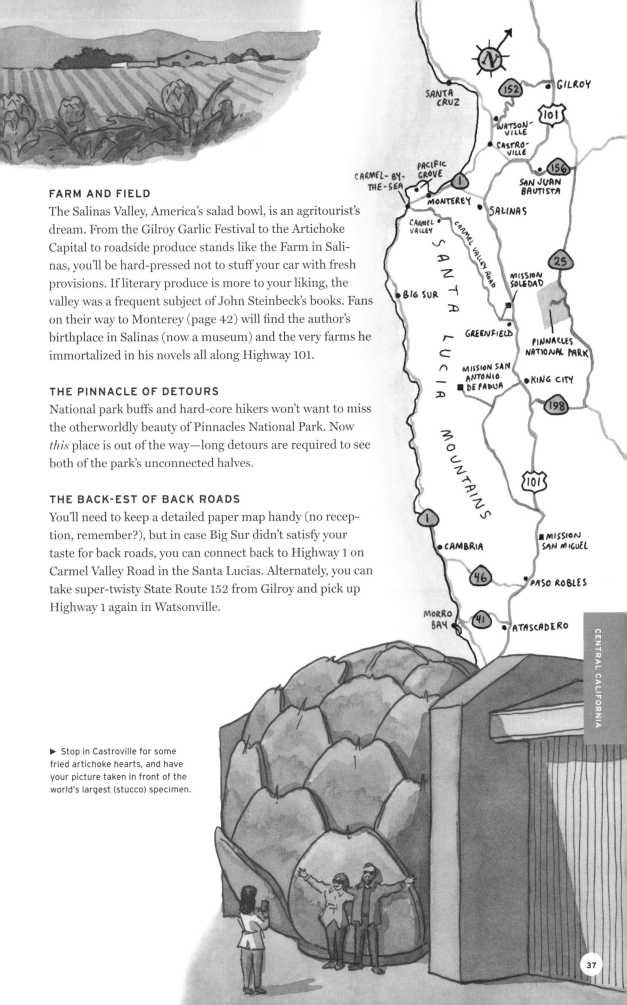

FARM AND FIELD

The Salinas Valley, America's salad bowl, is an agritourist's dream. From the Gilroy Garlic Festival to the Artichoke Capital to roadside produce stands like the Farm in Salinas, you'll be hard-pressed not to stuff your car with fresh provisions. If literary produce is more to your liking, the valley was a frequent subject of John Steinbeck's books. Fans on their way to Monterey (page 42) will find the author's birthplace in Salinas (now a museum) and the very farms he immortalized in his novels all along Highway 101.

THE PINNACLE OF DETOURS

National park buffs and hard-core hikers won't want to miss the otherworldly beauty of Pinnacles National Park. Now *this* place is out of the way—long detours are required to see both of the park's unconnected halves.

THE BACK-EST OF BACK ROADS

You'll need to keep a detailed paper map handy (no reception, remember?), but in case Big Sur didn't satisfy your taste for back roads, you can connect back to Highway 1 on Carmel Valley Road in the Santa Lucias. Alternately, you can take super-twisty State Route 152 from Gilroy and pick up Highway 1 again in Watsonville.

▶ Stop in Castroville for some fried artichoke hearts, and have your picture taken in front of the world's largest (stucco) specimen.

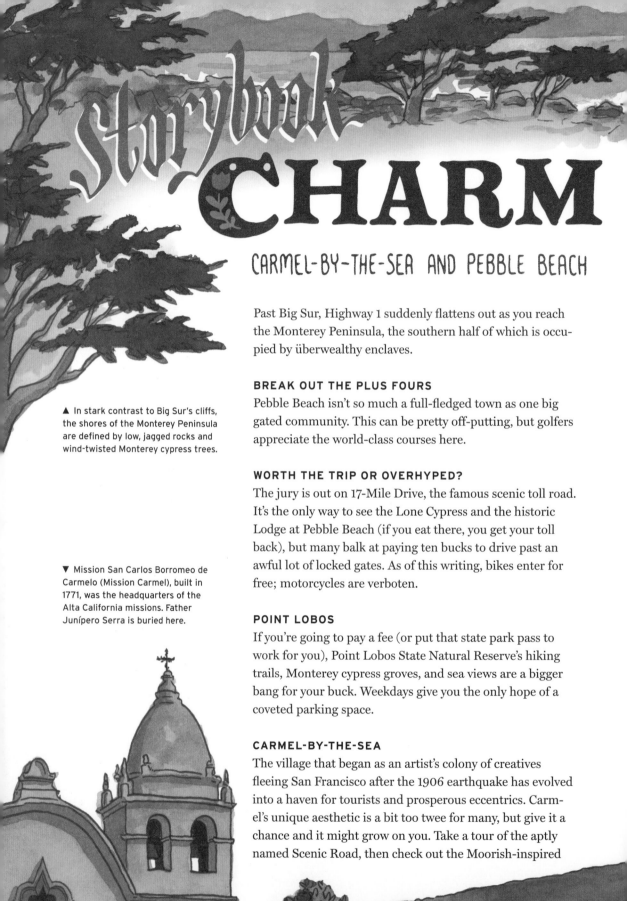

Storybook CHARM

CARMEL-BY-THE-SEA AND PEBBLE BEACH

Past Big Sur, Highway 1 suddenly flattens out as you reach the Monterey Peninsula, the southern half of which is occupied by überwealthy enclaves.

BREAK OUT THE PLUS FOURS
Pebble Beach isn't so much a full-fledged town as one big gated community. This can be pretty off-putting, but golfers appreciate the world-class courses here.

WORTH THE TRIP OR OVERHYPED?
The jury is out on 17-Mile Drive, the famous scenic toll road. It's the only way to see the Lone Cypress and the historic Lodge at Pebble Beach (if you eat there, you get your toll back), but many balk at paying ten bucks to drive past an awful lot of locked gates. As of this writing, bikes enter for free; motorcycles are verboten.

POINT LOBOS
If you're going to pay a fee (or put that state park pass to work for you), Point Lobos State Natural Reserve's hiking trails, Monterey cypress groves, and sea views are a bigger bang for your buck. Weekdays give you the only hope of a coveted parking space.

CARMEL-BY-THE-SEA
The village that began as an artist's colony of creatives fleeing San Francisco after the 1906 earthquake has evolved into a haven for tourists and prosperous eccentrics. Carmel's unique aesthetic is a bit too twee for many, but give it a chance and it might grow on you. Take a tour of the aptly named Scenic Road, then check out the Moorish-inspired

▲ In stark contrast to Big Sur's cliffs, the shores of the Monterey Peninsula are defined by low, jagged rocks and wind-twisted Monterey cypress trees.

▼ Mission San Carlos Borromeo de Carmelo (Mission Carmel), built in 1771, was the headquarters of the Alta California missions. Father Junípero Serra is buried here.

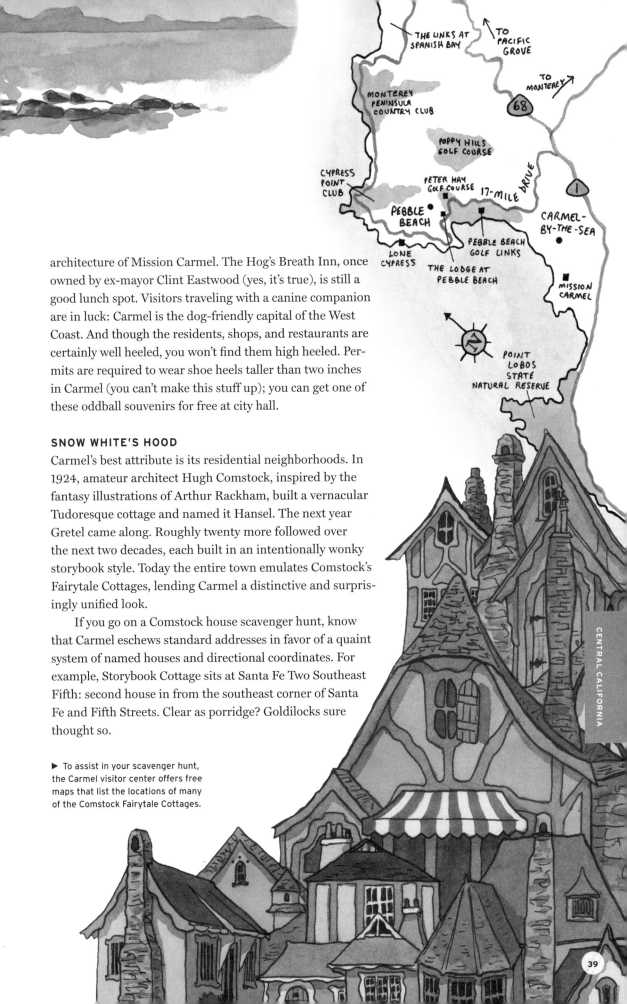

architecture of Mission Carmel. The Hog's Breath Inn, once owned by ex-mayor Clint Eastwood (yes, it's true), is still a good lunch spot. Visitors traveling with a canine companion are in luck: Carmel is the dog-friendly capital of the West Coast. And though the residents, shops, and restaurants are certainly well heeled, you won't find them high heeled. Permits are required to wear shoe heels taller than two inches in Carmel (you can't make this stuff up); you can get one of these oddball souvenirs for free at city hall.

SNOW WHITE'S HOOD

Carmel's best attribute is its residential neighborhoods. In 1924, amateur architect Hugh Comstock, inspired by the fantasy illustrations of Arthur Rackham, built a vernacular Tudoresque cottage and named it Hansel. The next year Gretel came along. Roughly twenty more followed over the next two decades, each built in an intentionally wonky storybook style. Today the entire town emulates Comstock's Fairytale Cottages, lending Carmel a distinctive and surprisingly unified look.

If you go on a Comstock house scavenger hunt, know that Carmel eschews standard addresses in favor of a quaint system of named houses and directional coordinates. For example, Storybook Cottage sits at Santa Fe Two Southeast Fifth: second house in from the southeast corner of Santa Fe and Fifth Streets. Clear as porridge? Goldilocks sure thought so.

▶ To assist in your scavenger hunt, the Carmel visitor center offers free maps that list the locations of many of the Comstock Fairytale Cottages.

CENTRAL CALIFORNIA

COASTAL microcosm
PACIFIC GROVE

At the northern tip of the Monterey Peninsula lies the town of Pacific Grove. Picturesque and unassuming, Pacific Grove feels like a mental palate cleanser between Pebble Beach and Monterey.

A SEASIDE FREE-FOR-ALL
Unlike Pebble Beach, which feels like one giant Keep Out sign, the entire shore within the Pacific Grove city limits is accessible to the public. On the bay side are Shoreline and Lovers Point Parks; Pacific Grove Marine Gardens protects the tide pools and kelp beds at Point Pinos. On the ocean side is the mile-long Asilomar State Beach—even (leashed) dogs are welcome here.

GINGERBREAD COTTAGES
Pacific Grove got its start in the 1870s as a vacation retreat for Methodist revivalists. Many stayed and built houses, creating a collection of ornate Victorian architecture that still stands. Today's Pagrovians take pride in their historic stewardship; look for plaques listing the homes' original owners and dates.

THE BUTTERFLY EFFECT
The West Coast is characterized by its microclimates, created by hyperlocalized temperature zones and weather conditions. Pacific Grove is the perfect example, home to the finest of many coastal-California spots where monarch butterflies overwinter to escape the cold. Drawn to the calm air and just-right temperatures, the insects gather by the thousands in a single grove of eucalyptus and evergreen trees. Here's the amazing thing: the migration route is longer than a

▲ Visit the Monarch Grove Butterfly Sanctuary between October and February for the best chance of seeing the insects up close.

▼ The most famous lightkeeper at Point Pinos was Emily Fish, posted there from 1893 to 1914. Her niece, Juliet Nichols, stayed in the family business and tended the light at Point Knox on Angel Island near San Francisco.

single butterfly can complete in its lifetime—the insects that return to Pacific Grove are the great-great-grandchildren of the ones that left the year before. Visit these beauties at the Monarch Grove Butterfly Sanctuary. Bring your binoculars, but keep your hands to yourself—touching the delicate insects is a misdemeanor that comes with a hefty fine.

THAR SHE PUTTS

If Pebble Beach didn't slake your thirst for golf courses, you'll find a lovely municipal specimen at Point Pinos. Instead of a big clubhouse, the centerpiece of the course is Point Pinos Lighthouse, the oldest continuously operating beacon on the West Coast. The lighthouse is open to the public on certain afternoons year-round.

ENVIRONMENTAL ENCLAVE

Before she spent twenty-eight years at William Randolph Hearst's beck and call (page 34), Julia Morgan designed a beachfront women's retreat for the YWCA from 1913 to 1929, gradually adding buildings as donations and land parcels accumulated. A masterpiece of environmentally responsive design and arts-and-crafts architecture, the Asilomar Conference Grounds' wood-and-stone buildings exist harmoniously among the site's scrub savanna and pebbly shores. California State Parks now manages the place as a conference center and lodging complex, but the grounds are open to the public.

▲ The name "Asilomar," a portmanteau of the Spanish words for "refuge" and "sea," was coined by Stanford University student Helen Salisbury.

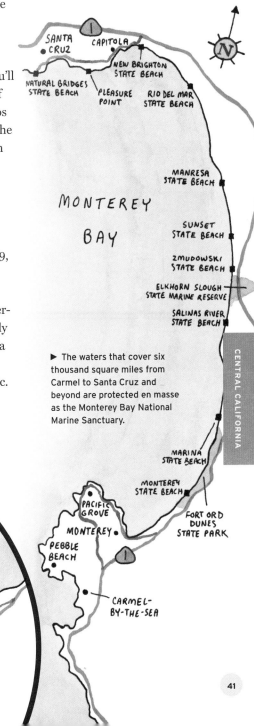

▶ The waters that cover six thousand square miles from Carmel to Santa Cruz and beyond are protected en masse as the Monterey Bay National Marine Sanctuary.

Steinbeck's
STOMPING GROUNDS

It took a twentieth-century author to show us what makes Monterey special. John Steinbeck is the city's most famous son, though he was born in Salinas (page 37) and mostly resided in Pacific Grove. Before he became a writer, he worked on local ranches alongside migrant farmhands and even helped build Highway 1. Later, he immortalized Monterey in his novels *Sweet Thursday*, *East of Eden*, *Tortilla Flat*, and *Cannery Row*—and Monterey honors him at the National Steinbeck Center.

THE FISH DISTRICT
Cannery Row, the waterfront strip originally known only as Ocean View Boulevard, served as the industrial heart of Monterey. It was dominated by commercial canneries that packed sardines into tins as an inexpensive seafood product. Monterey Bay had seemed like a teeming, inexhaustible resource—until overfishing decimated the sardines, and the industry collapsed in the 1950s. Today Cannery Row, restored and officially renamed for Steinbeck's novel, preserves many of the original buildings as a number of pedestrian-friendly shops and restaurants.

THE LIVING OCEAN
We have the Monterey Bay Aquarium to thank for the revitalization of Cannery Row. Housed in the old Hovden

▼ In addition to its aquatic wildlife exhibits, the Monterey Bay Aquarium also contains an excellent interactive exhibit about the city's sardine industry.

42

Cannery, this world-class aquarium focuses on its pioneering conservation programs—which is what that hefty admission fee supports. Don't miss the sea otter exhibit (especially at feeding time!) or the kelp forest display. And if you're looking to make environmentally conscious restaurant choices on your road trip, the aquarium also maintains a list of sustainably fished or harvested seafood.

FOOD AND FUN PIER

After the sardine industry collapsed, nearby Old Fisherman's Wharf rebranded itself as a tourist destination. This pedestrian-only municipal pier is lined with restaurants that pass out free seafood samples to entice diners. After your meal, candy shops and whale-watching tours await. On your return stroll, check out the nearby Old Whaling Station, built in 1847 and home to a diamond-pane sidewalk made entirely of whale vertebrae.

OTHER ATTRACTIONS

Many of the original structures and adobes built in Monterey during the Alta California period are preserved at Monterey State Historic Park. Visit in September to attend the world-famous Monterey Jazz Festival. Cycling enthusiasts will love the Sea Otter Classic, a bike race and outdoor sports festival held each April.

▲ In addition to the restored Cannery Row, the ruins of several canneries that burned down in the 1970s are also preserved along the water's edge.

CENTRAL CALIFORNIA

43

Sunny, Funny Santa Cruz

▲ The banana slug, that giant yellow gastropod emblematic of the Pacific Northwest, is also common near Santa Cruz–it's even the UC Santa Cruz team mascot.

▲ Originally built in 1869, the Mark Abbott Memorial Lighthouse was moved and remodeled several times over the years, before it became the Surfing Museum in 1986.

North of Monterey, Highway 1 hugs the curving shore of Monterey Bay, passing a number of wetlands and state beaches along the way (map on page 41). Each of these places is a good wildlife-watching spot, from shorebirds at the beaches to, with a bit of luck, baby sea otters at Elkhorn Slough. As the road curves westward toward the city, the Santa Cruz Mountains appear, along with redwoods at the higher elevations.

OUT WITH THE OLD

Very little of old Santa Cruz remains, thanks to a series of devastating earthquakes. The Mission Hill neighborhood still contains some Victorian buildings, and a single building from the original Spanish mission remains at Santa Cruz Mission State Historic Park.

PASS THE COTTON CANDY

The main event here is the Santa Cruz Beach Boardwalk, the oldest surviving amusement park in California. The Giant Dipper, a 1924 wooden roller coaster, is such an icon that it's a national historic landmark all by itself. At the north end of the Beach Boardwalk is the archaically spelled Cocoanut Grove conference center, an art deco pavilion that once hosted major big-band acts. The Beach Boardwalk's vintage arcade was featured heavily in the 1980s cult-classic horror film *The Lost Boys*.

OLD-SCHOOL SURFING

Santa Cruz is home to the world's first surfing museum, housing artifacts like solid redwood boards used by Hawaiian princes. The museum is housed inside a lighthouse perched directly above the famous Steamer Lane surf location. On the east end of town is Pleasure Point, a name shared by another surf spot and a neighborhood steeped in surf culture.

EDUCATIONAL ACROPOLIS

The wooded hills above the city are home to the University of California, Santa Cruz. A large swath of the two-thousand-acre campus is undeveloped open space with sweeping views of the sea and the city.

ROADSIDE HEAD SCRATCHER

Built in the grand tradition of the freak-show tent, the Mystery Spot is one of many West Coast attractions designed around disorienting optical illusions where natural physics need not apply. Confused yet? That's the whole point.

SLOW COAST PREVIEW

Before Highway 1 takes you out of town, check out the spectacular scenery at Natural Bridges State Beach and the historic farmhouse and dairy buildings at Wilder Ranch State Park.

▲ Highway 1 is a freeway around Santa Cruz; a scenic alternative is West Cliff Drive, which hugs the shore from downtown to Natural Bridges State Beach.

▼ Also at the Beach Boardwalk is one of six remaining Charles Looff carousels. Built in 1911, it features hand-carved wooden horses and a rare brass ring-toss game.

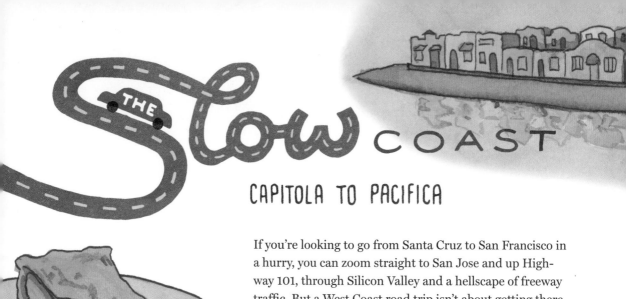

THE Slow COAST

CAPITOLA TO PACIFICA

If you're looking to go from Santa Cruz to San Francisco in a hurry, you can zoom straight to San Jose and up Highway 101, through Silicon Valley and a hellscape of freeway traffic. But a West Coast road trip isn't about getting there at all costs; it's about enjoying the ride. This is where the Slow Coast—the sixty or so miles of Highway 1 south of San Francisco—comes in.

THE ULTIMATE ALTERNATE ROUTE

The actual distances here are deceptive. Driving straight through could get you to Pacifica in about ninety minutes. Yet with so many beaches, vista points, hiking trails, farm stands, and parks to tempt you along the way, the Slow Coast can easily become a full-day adventure.

THE SOUTHERN SECTION

The Davenport Roadhouse makes for a great leisurely breakfast to start your day. Afterward, visit Waddell Beach, where you might meet hard-core hikers arriving from Big Basin Redwoods State Park along the twenty-five-mile Skyline-to-the-Sea Trail. Just down the road is Año Nuevo State Park, where a three-mile guided walk (reservations required) leads to an elephant seal rookery even larger than the one at San Simeon (page 34).

▲ Duarte's Tavern in Pescadero has been serving Portuguese American fare since 1894. Famed specialties include cream of artichoke soup and a host of homemade pies.

▼ The Fitzgerald Marine Reserve, near Pillar Point and Mavericks Beach, is home to delicate tide pools accessible only at minus tides.

▲ Located just east of Santa Cruz, the colorful Capitola Venetian Hotel feels like the gateway to the Slow Coast.

CENTRAL SPLENDOR

The middle third of the Slow Coast is crowned by the slender form of Pigeon Point Lighthouse. Built in 1871, it's the tallest beacon on the West Coast—and maybe the most spectacular, with its dramatic, rocky promontory surrounded by fields of buttercup oxalis flowers. Keep an eye out for the gray and humpback whales that sometimes venture near the shore here. If you can tear your eyes away, continue down the road to Pescadero for a dose of bucolic, rolling farmland. Beyond that is Half Moon Bay, home to a restored Victorian-era downtown.

THE NORTHERN REACHES

North of Montara, there used to be a stretch of Highway 1 that rivaled the terror of Big Sur, clinging to the cliffs in a notorious section called Devil's Slide. After an endless succession of washouts and rockslides, the state finally completed a bypass and opened the twin Tom Lantos Tunnels in 2013. The tunnels dump you out into Pacifica, the last town outside greater San Francisco.

THE CITY LIMITS

Before you know it, the city has sprung up around you, and the highway becomes a jumble of choices. Staying on Highway 1 will bring you to Golden Gate Park; if you'd rather continue hugging the shore, take State Route 35 toward Ocean Beach and the 49-Mile Scenic Drive (overview map on page 49).

▶ The keeper's quarters at Pigeon Point Lighthouse are now a hostel operated by Hostelling International, offering affordable lodging for travelers of all ages.

CENTRAL CALIFORNIA

San Francisco

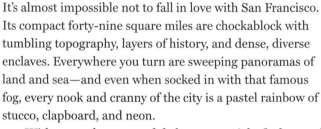

▲ The art deco Coit Tower, which stands atop Telegraph Hill, is visible from nearly everywhere in the northern half of San Francisco.

▼ Grant Avenue is the main street of Chinatown and shows the neighborhood's character and liveliness in one glance.

It's almost impossible not to fall in love with San Francisco. Its compact forty-nine square miles are chockablock with tumbling topography, layers of history, and dense, diverse enclaves. Everywhere you turn are sweeping panoramas of land and sea—and even when socked in with that famous fog, every nook and cranny of the city is a pastel rainbow of stucco, clapboard, and neon.

With so much to see and do here, you might find yourself paralyzed over the choices available. Give yourself the gift of a little extra planning, and don't sweat the stuff you miss on your first visit. (Reason to return, right?) To avoid overwhelming yourself, try thinking of San Francisco on a human scale, and do your exploring in small pieces, one neighborhood or quadrant at a time. The city is certainly walkable—and besides, driving here is not for the faint of heart. It takes skill to navigate the hills and traffic, and chutzpah to so much as park or turn left. Consider leaving the car in a parking garage and using public transit (MUNI, BART), ride-share services, or your own two feet to get around.

SEE THE CITY BY SCENIC LOOP

If you *do* decide to navigate San Francisco by car, a self-guided auto tour via the 49-Mile Scenic Drive is the perfect introduction to the city. Created in 1938 for a world's fair, the tour hits nearly every major landmark in town. While full of quick turns, the tour is well marked (look for the iconic seagull signs) and even avoids the steepest hills. The route runs counterclockwise, starting and ending at city hall—though you can actually begin anywhere. Avoid driving during peak traffic times (seven to ten a.m. and four to seven p.m.). Pro tip: skip the short stretch that runs along Interstate 280, in favor of Third Street through Dogpatch, toward the Embarcadero.

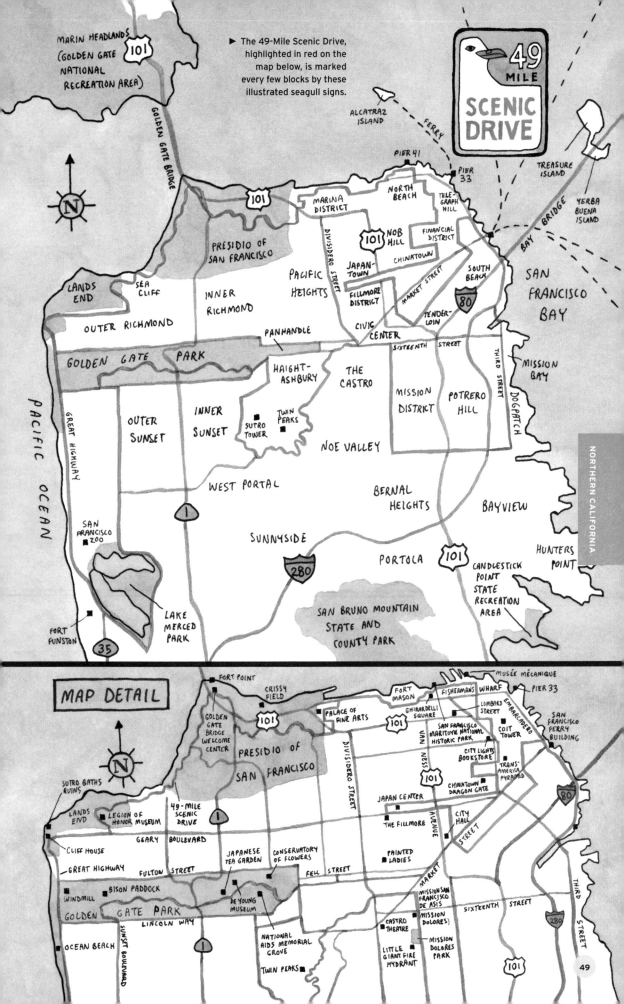

► The 49-Mile Scenic Drive, highlighted in red on the map below, is marked every few blocks by these illustrated seagull signs.

49 MILE

SCENIC DRIVE

MARIN HEADLANDS (GOLDEN GATE NATIONAL RECREATION AREA)

101

GOLDEN GATE BRIDGE

ALCATRAZ ISLAND

FERRY

PIER 41

PIER 33

TREASURE ISLAND

YERBA BUENA ISLAND

BAY BRIDGE

101

MARINA DISTRICT

NORTH BEACH

TELE-GRAPH HILL

PRESIDIO OF SAN FRANCISCO

DIVISIDERO STREET

101

NOB HILL

FINANCIAL DISTRICT

JAPAN-TOWN

CHINATOWN

SOUTH BEACH

SAN FRANCISCO BAY

LANDS END

SEA CLIFF

INNER RICHMOND

PACIFIC HEIGHTS

FILLMORE DISTRICT

MARKET STREET

80

OUTER RICHMOND

PANHANDLE

CIVIC CENTER

TENDER-LOIN

GOLDEN GATE PARK

HAIGHT-ASHBURY

THE CASTRO

SIXTEENTH STREET

THIRD STREET

MISSION BAY

PACIFIC OCEAN

GREAT HIGHWAY

OUTER SUNSET

INNER SUNSET

SUTRO TOWER

TWIN PEAKS

MISSION DISTRICT

POTRERO HILL

DOGPATCH

NOE VALLEY

WEST PORTAL

1

SAN FRANCISCO ZOO

BERNAL HEIGHTS

BAYVIEW

NORTHERN CALIFORNIA

SUNNYSIDE

280

PORTOLA

101

HUNTERS POINT

CANDLESTICK POINT STATE RECREATION AREA

LAKE MERCED PARK

FORT FUNSTON

35

SAN BRUNO MOUNTAIN STATE AND COUNTY PARK

MAP DETAIL

FORT POINT

CRISSY FIELD

FORT MASON

MUSÉE MÉCANIQUE

FISHERMANS WHARF

PIER 33

GOLDEN GATE BRIDGE WELCOME CENTER

101

PALACE OF FINE ARTS

101

GHIRARDELLI SQUARE

LOMBARD STREET

SAN FRANCISCO MARITIME NATIONAL HISTORIC PARK

COIT TOWER

EMBARCADERO

SAN FRANCISCO FERRY BUILDING

PRESIDIO OF SAN FRANCISCO

DIVISIDERO STREET

VAN NESS AVENUE

CITY LIGHTS BOOKSTORE

TRANS-AMERICA PYRAMID

SUTRO BATHS RUINS

LANDS END

LEGION OF HONOR MUSEUM

49-MILE SCENIC DRIVE

101

JAPAN CENTER

CHINATOWN DRAGON GATE

80

1

THE FILLMORE

CITY HALL

CLIFF HOUSE

GEARY BOULEVARD

GREAT HIGHWAY

JAPANESE TEA GARDEN

CONSERVATORY OF FLOWERS

PAINTED LADIES

MARKET STREET

WINDMILL

FULTON STREET

FELL STREET

BISON PADDOCK

DE YOUNG MUSEUM

MISSION SAN FRANCISCO DE ASIS (MISSION DOLORES)

SIXTEENTH STREET

THIRD STREET

GOLDEN GATE PARK

LINCOLN WAY

CASTRO THEATRE

MISSION DOLORES PARK

280

OCEAN BEACH

SUNSET BOULEVARD

NATIONAL AIDS MEMORIAL GROVE

TWIN PEAKS

1

LITTLE GIANT FIRE HYDRANT

101

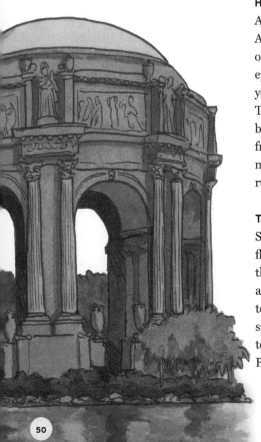

▲ Candy-hued Victorian row houses dominate many of the city's steep hillsides, creating colorful, scenic views in every direction.

▼ The lagoon that surrounds the Palace of Fine Arts, the last remnant of the 1915 Panama-Pacific International Exposition, is the perfect spot for a quiet early-morning stroll.

START IN THE CENTER

Assuming you *do* start the 49-Mile Scenic Drive at city hall, you'll find yourself in the Civic Center District. This massive Beaux-Arts dome was built in 1915 after the 1906 earthquake destroyed the original structure. Just down the road is the Fillmore District, which has been home to a dynamic African American enclave since the end of World War II. A little farther on is the Japan Center, marked by its distinctive 1960s pagoda. Continue on to Nob Hill—home to the famous cable cars—and the oldest and largest Chinatown in North America. For the perfect snack, grab a Chinese egg tart or three at the Golden Gate Bakery on Grant Avenue.

HILLS AND VALLEYS

Adjacent to Chinatown is North Beach, home to an Italian American enclave and a number of sidewalk cafés. Nearby, on Columbus Avenue, is the iconic City Lights Bookstore, an epicenter of the Beat writers and poets of the 1950s. To stretch your legs, hike the wooded pedestrian staircase that runs up Telegraph Hill. Coit Tower awaits you at the top, but an even bigger reward is a rare glimpse of the wild green parrots that frequent the area. The switchbacks of Lombard Street, while not directly on the route, are worth a short detour. The drive runs one way, from the top of the hill to the bottom.

THE MARITIME EFFECT

San Francisco's waterfront is a major ingredient in its flavor. No visit is complete without a drive (or walk) along the Embarcadero, the shoreline promenade that replaced a freeway damaged in the 1989 quake. If you can stand the tourist mobs, the Fisherman's Wharf area is a riot of neon signs, street performers, fishing boats, and fresh seafood. To tour Alcatraz, the historic island prison, catch the ferry from Pier 33.

RECREATIONAL GARRISON

The Presidio, a former military installation, occupies the area around Golden Gate Bridge. Now an enormous park, its labyrinth of wooded roads is a great place to get lost for a while. At the northwestern tip of the peninsula is Lands End, a rugged cliff-side park traversed by the spectacular Coastal Trail. Between is the excellent Legion of Honor museum, which features world-class art exhibits. The whole area lies within the sprawling Golden Gate National Recreation Area. Including Fort Point, Crissy Field, the Marin Headlands (page 58), and more, Golden Gate NRA paints a fascinating picture of the city.

ZIGZAG ALONG THE PACIFIC SHORE

The tour makes a sharp turn at the Cliff House (page 55), then heads south on the Great Highway, the thoroughfare that runs along Ocean Beach. At its southernmost point, the 49-Mile Scenic Drive hooks around Lake Merced. Then you'll zip back north on Sunset Boulevard, doubling back to Golden Gate Park (whose famous Dutch windmills are visible from the Great Highway).

WHERE NATURE AND CULTURE INTERTWINE

Not to be confused with the bridge (page 54), Golden Gate Park contains many points of interest. Best are the Japanese Tea Garden, the bison paddock, the National AIDS Memorial Grove, and the Conservatory of Flowers. Before you leave the park, take in the view from the Hamon Observation Tower at the de Young Museum.

▼ In 1922, eight switchbacks were added to this famous block of Lombard Street, the world's crookedest thoroughfare, to make it navigable by car.

▲ The San Francisco Ferry Building opened on the Embarcadero in 1898. Its sturdy construction carried it through both the 1906 and 1989 earthquakes with minimal damage.

▼ A military installation from 1776 to 1994, the Presidio is now a 1,500-acre park known for its wooded hillsides, miles of trails, and historic buildings.

THE SQUIGGLY SECTION

After winding through Golden Gate Park, the scenic drive skirts the neighborhood of Haight-Ashbury, long a haven of hippies and iconoclasts. Just northeast of the route is Pacific Heights—home to many of the city's famous Victorian residences, each adorned with ornate gingerbread detailing. The tour then heads south again to twist its way up to Twin Peaks. A steep footpath to the top of the park provides a 360-degree view of the city.

BACK TOWARD CIVILIZATION

The Mission, increasingly hipster these days, is an epicurean mecca—don't miss Tartine (either the bar or the bakery) or the homemade ice cream at Bi-Rite. The district has a three-hundred-year Latino history, centered around Mission Dolores, one of the twenty-one original California missions (page 5). The Castro, nearby, is the epicenter of LGBTQ culture past and present. The neighborhood hosts the nation's largest Pride celebration each June, with more than a quarter of a million attendees.

END WHERE YOU BEGIN

If you skip the interstate portion of the 49-Mile Scenic Drive, you'll catch the up-and-coming residential neighborhoods of Potrero Hill and Dogpatch—both have a rich working-class history and many architectural relics, despite recent gentrification. Brake for the tiny Victorian Pelton cottages along Tennessee and Minnesota Streets, and stop for brunch at the Just for You Cafe (best beignets outside of Louisiana!). Third Street will connect you back to the Embarcadero and the busy Financial District. Finally, zoom down Market Street and complete your tour where you started, back at city hall.

SAN FRANCISCO ICONS

▲ While the Painted Ladies are the most famous of San Francisco's houses, they are a fraction of Pacific Heights' dazzling inventory of ornate Victorian architecture.

▲ Mission San Francisco de Asís (also called Mission Dolores) is the oldest building in the city. Don't miss the ornate painted ceiling inside the church.

▲ The Japanese Tea Garden in Golden Gate Park uses features like winding paths and evocative structures to create a meditative experience for the visitor.

▶ Sourdough bread has been a San Francisco foodie icon since the 1849 gold rush—it makes the perfect edible vessel for both clam chowder and cioppino.

◀ The "Little Giant" hydrant at Twentieth and Church Streets, repainted gold each year in tribute, saved the Mission District from the fires following the 1906 earthquake.

▲ The Musée Mécanique displays hundreds of historic mechanical toys and penny-arcade games. You can visit the museum in its new location at Fisherman's Wharf.

▼ On your way up to Coit Tower, keep your eyes peeled for the strangest denizens of Telegraph Hill: feral cherry-headed conures, descended from escaped pet parrots.

▲ Japantown is dotted with a trio of *koban* police kiosks, modeled after the one-room police stations commonly found in Japan, China, and Korea.

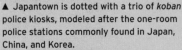

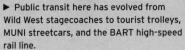

▶ Public transit here has evolved from Wild West stagecoaches to tourist trolleys, MUNI streetcars, and the BART high-speed rail line.

THE GATE & THE GHOST

▼ Each of the bridge's suspension cables is three feet in diameter. Look for the cable cross section on display among the visitor plaza exhibits.

The Golden Gate Bridge is a city icon that deserves special mention. Named for the natural entrance to San Francisco Bay, the bridge carries the merged routes of Highways 1 and 101. At the time of its completion in 1937, it was the longest suspension bridge in the world. Today it has become one of San Francisco's top tourist destinations—as well as a defining symbol of the city itself and the West Coast as a whole.

INTERNATIONAL ORANGE

When the Pennsylvania factory provided the steel for the bridge, it arrived coated in a vermilion primer. Irving Morrow, consulting architect on the project, was pleased by how the color looked against blue skies, gray fog, and the greenish-gold hills. So international orange became the permanent, perfect paint color.

PUT YOUR WALKING SHOES ON

Parking at the Bridge Plaza is limited, but the nearby Presidio also has options. Pedestrian crossing is free (no pets or skateboards), as are the many informational exhibits. The crossing is nearly two miles to Vista Point on the north side of the Gate; expect high winds, cold air, and possibly fog or rain. Cars are charged a toll, which is collected on inbound traffic only (another vote for a northbound road trip).

▶ Visiting the Cliff House and ruins also puts you within easy reach of Lands End, Golden Gate Park, Ocean Beach, and the Great Highway.

NOT YOUR ORDINARY SWIMMING POOL

If this book had been published in 1900, the Sutro Baths would have been on the must-see list. As the world's largest indoor swimming pool, the tide-fed saltwater baths were *the* recreation hot spot for Victorian San Franciscans. Despite its popularity, the attraction was too expensive to maintain, and the baths finally closed in 1965, after nearly seventy years. The complex burned to the ground just six months later.

IN MEMORIAM

Few remain who remember the baths firsthand, but the place still captures the imagination. The ruins of the pools are still there, complete with hiking trails. The combination of eerie history and seaside beauty makes for an unforgettable visit.

WORKING UP AN APPETITE

After you explore the ruins, visit the Cliff House, perched on the rocks above. Now owned and operated by the National Park Service as part of Golden Gate National Recreation Area, the restaurant displays historic photos and a few original artifacts from the baths.

▼ Historic photos and postcards of the Sutro Baths still grace shops and restaurants all over San Francisco. These images remain city icons to this day.

NORTHERN CALIFORNIA

◀ A single bridge rivet weighs about half a pound, and each tower contains six hundred thousand of them. Replica souvenir rivets are available in the gift shop.

Across the BRIDGE

MARIN COUNTY

Just across the Golden Gate is a labyrinth of bays, inlets, and tide flats that defines the eastern half of Marin County. The region has become a playground for celebrities and the wealthy, yet there are still regular folks here, too—as well as plenty of activities to suit every budget.

OVER, UNDER, AND AROUND THE BAY

Sausalito, the first city across the bridge, fills every nook and cranny of the steep hillsides and waterfront around Richardson Bay. It also occupies the land *under* the bay, with theoretical streets demarcated on nineteenth-century maps, should Sausalito ever resort to landfill development the way San Francisco did. For now, though, visitors will need to content themselves to attractions above sea level, like the Bridgeway Promenade, the Spaulding Marine Center, the houseboat district, or the famous music recording studio called the Record Plant.

INSULAR AND PENINSULAR

The twin communities of Belvedere and Tiburon occupy the peninsula on the other side of Richardson Bay. Belvedere is fiercely residential and secluded, with no shops or restaurants allowed in town. Luckily Tiburon has an array of both, as well as an excellent walking path occupying its portion of the San Francisco Bay Trail. For an alternative to Alcatraz (page 50), hop a ferry to Angel Island. Once a military installation and immigration station, the entire island is now a state park.

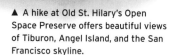

▲ A hike at Old St. Hilary's Open Space Preserve offers beautiful views of Tiburon, Angel Island, and the San Francisco skyline.

▼ The houseboat community at Sausalito's Waldo Point Harbor inspired Otis Redding to pen his classic hit "(Sittin' on) the Dock of the Bay."

▲ Privately operated ferries out of Tiburon run to both Angel Island State Park and San Francisco.

MAINLAND MUNICIPALITIES

Heading inland from Richardson Bay are a number of small communities tucked into the Marin Hills. Larkspur retains vestiges of its Wild West roots in its restored buildings. San Anselmo features a tidy downtown and a variety of great antique shops. Equally picturesque Novato is close to many parks around San Pablo Bay, such as the Hamilton Wetlands and China Camp State Park.

AN ANGELIC ART TOWN

San Rafael, the county seat and largest city in Marin County, features walkable streets, restaurants of all stripes, and one of the best farmers' markets in America. Stop by Mission San Rafael Arcángel, or visit in June for Italian Street Painting Marin, a festival of sidewalk-chalk art. Nearby are the futuristic spire and rotunda of Frank Lloyd Wright's landmark design, the Marin County Civic Center. A more offbeat (and politically charged) destination is the gift shop at San Quentin State Prison, which features souvenirs handcrafted by inmates.

From San Rafael it's easy to zip up Highway 101 to Wine Country (page 62) or east toward Berkeley and Oakland via the impressive Richmond–San Rafael Bridge.

Marin Heaven

STINSON BEACH

MUIR WOODS NATIONAL MONUMENT

RED ROCK BEACH **MOUNT TAMALPAIS STATE PARK**

STEEP RAVINE

1

N

MUIR BEACH

101

MARIN HEADLANDS (GOLDEN GATE NATIONAL RECREATION AREA)

ROBIN WILLIAMS TUNNEL

BUNKER ROAD LOOP

POINT BONITA LIGHTHOUSE

GOLDEN GATE BRIDGE

▲ On your way to pick up the thread, once more, of Highway 1, note the rainbow-arched gateway recently renamed the Robin Williams Tunnel.

While many city dwellers have to travel long distances to escape to the natural world, Bay Area residents have thousands of acres of undeveloped, pristine wonderland right at their doorstep.

HIKE THE HEADLANDS

Golden Gate National Recreation Area, the park that preserves huge swaths of San Francisco, continues on to encompass much of Marin County, including the Marin Headlands, the bare hills visible across the Golden Gate Bridge from the city. After the excitement of the bridge, it's easy to miss the entrance; it's the first exit immediately after the Vista Point overlook. Within the park is a jaw-dropping loop road leading to the visitor center and several historic buildings, along with myriad opportunities to hike and bike your way around the hills. Bring your own water and snacks; despite your proximity to the city, you could be hours from the nearest restaurant.

HUG THE CURVES

Highway 1 picks up again near Mill Valley, where it obtains the new moniker the Shoreline Highway. This is a spectacular stretch of road, but proceed with caution. Between the sharp curves, frequent closures due to weather, city-slicker motorcycles zooming around you at hair-raising speeds, and impatient locals heading home, you'll need to have your wits about you.

◄ For better or worse, the ubiquitous stands of introduced eucalyptus trees are nearly as emblematic of the Bay Area as the redwood trees at Muir Woods.

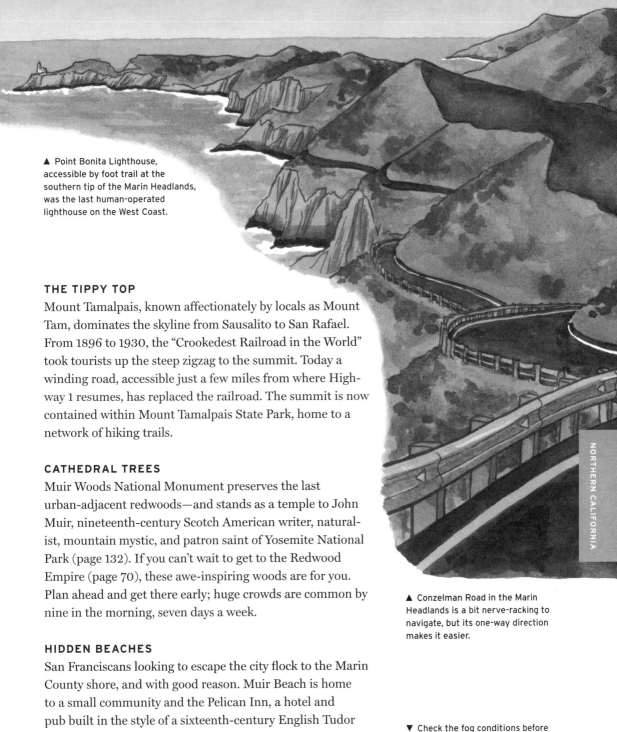

▲ Point Bonita Lighthouse, accessible by foot trail at the southern tip of the Marin Headlands, was the last human-operated lighthouse on the West Coast.

THE TIPPY TOP

Mount Tamalpais, known affectionately by locals as Mount Tam, dominates the skyline from Sausalito to San Rafael. From 1896 to 1930, the "Crookedest Railroad in the World" took tourists up the steep zigzag to the summit. Today a winding road, accessible just a few miles from where Highway 1 resumes, has replaced the railroad. The summit is now contained within Mount Tamalpais State Park, home to a network of hiking trails.

CATHEDRAL TREES

Muir Woods National Monument preserves the last urban-adjacent redwoods—and stands as a temple to John Muir, nineteenth-century Scotch American writer, naturalist, mountain mystic, and patron saint of Yosemite National Park (page 132). If you can't wait to get to the Redwood Empire (page 70), these awe-inspiring woods are for you. Plan ahead and get there early; huge crowds are common by nine in the morning, seven days a week.

HIDDEN BEACHES

San Franciscans looking to escape the city flock to the Marin County shore, and with good reason. Muir Beach is home to a small community and the Pelican Inn, a hotel and pub built in the style of a sixteenth-century English Tudor house. Pristine, sandy Stinson Beach is ideal for swimming, and nearby Steep Ravine boasts a number of rustic ocean-view cabins—if you're lucky enough to snag a reservation. Between the two is Red Rock Beach, a secluded clothing-optional cove (if that's your thing) accessible on foot from Stinson Beach at low tide.

▲ Conzelman Road in the Marin Headlands is a bit nerve-racking to navigate, but its one-way direction makes it easier.

▼ Check the fog conditions before you make the long, winding drive up Mount Tam, so you're assured of a view at the top.

Turn Back the Clock

BOLINAS TO BODEGA BAY

Highway 1 continues north, toward a hook-shaped peninsula with a whole lot of history. It is here that Sir Francis Drake reportedly ended his round-the-world journey in 1579 and made the first European contact with the Coast Miwok people who lived along the shore.

ENTERING THE VALLEY

The tiny town of Bolinas is visible from across the lagoon that begins at Stinson Beach, but requires a bit of doubling back to reach by car. The detour is worth it for the gorgeous views and easy bird-watching. The Bolinas Lagoon is the last glimpse of salt water before Highway 1 continues inland for a time, passing the scrub forests and 1850s-era farms of the Olema Valley.

QUAKE LAND

The northern half of the Point Reyes peninsula is defined by the long, narrow Tomales Bay, which is bisected by the San Andreas Fault. This quiet haven for hiking, fishing, and oyster harvesting is highly susceptible to earthquakes. During the 1906 quake that rocked San Francisco, the peninsula leapt twenty feet to the northwest in a matter of seconds.

HIGHLAND FLING

A quick visit to Point Reyes National Seashore can easily balloon into an all-day adventure. It preserves both the natural ecosystem and the historic industry of the cape, dairy farming. Narrow roads meander over treeless heaths vaguely

▲ Point Reyes Lighthouse requires a steep hike down three hundred steps, but the spot is the ideal place to see migrating gray whales in the winter.

◄ Pierce Point Ranch is one of many nineteenth-century dairies that still operate near Point Reyes. The region is the heart of California's first dairy industry.

AWARD

DAIRY OF MERIT

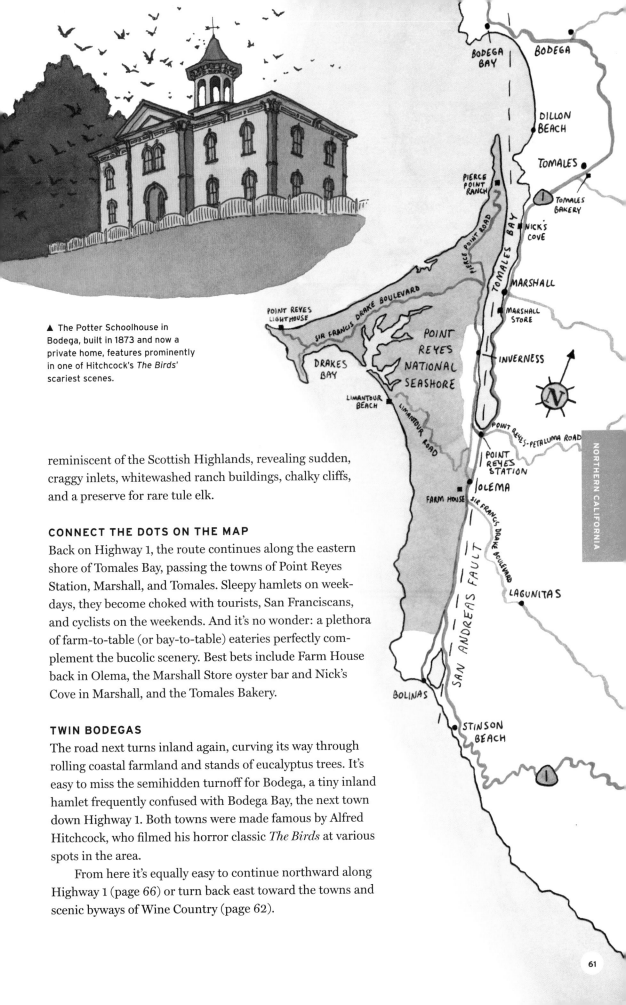

▲ The Potter Schoolhouse in Bodega, built in 1873 and now a private home, features prominently in one of Hitchcock's *The Birds'* scariest scenes.

reminiscent of the Scottish Highlands, revealing sudden, craggy inlets, whitewashed ranch buildings, chalky cliffs, and a preserve for rare tule elk.

CONNECT THE DOTS ON THE MAP

Back on Highway 1, the route continues along the eastern shore of Tomales Bay, passing the towns of Point Reyes Station, Marshall, and Tomales. Sleepy hamlets on weekdays, they become choked with tourists, San Franciscans, and cyclists on the weekends. And it's no wonder: a plethora of farm-to-table (or bay-to-table) eateries perfectly complement the bucolic scenery. Best bets include Farm House back in Olema, the Marshall Store oyster bar and Nick's Cove in Marshall, and the Tomales Bakery.

TWIN BODEGAS

The road next turns inland again, curving its way through rolling coastal farmland and stands of eucalyptus trees. It's easy to miss the semihidden turnoff for Bodega, a tiny inland hamlet frequently confused with Bodega Bay, the next town down Highway 1. Both towns were made famous by Alfred Hitchcock, who filmed his horror classic *The Birds* at various spots in the area.

From here it's equally easy to continue northward along Highway 1 (page 66) or turn back east toward the towns and scenic byways of Wine Country (page 62).

NORTHERN CALIFORNIA

SIDE TRIP

Wine Country

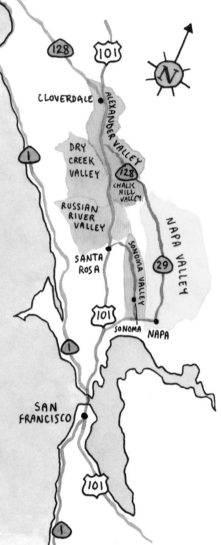

▼ California has far too many wine regions to name individually, so this section focuses on a few adjacent regions within reach of Highway 101.

Whether you're a wine buff or you're just here for the scenery, there is nothing like a trip to Northern California's world-renowned wine regions. There's also no such thing as a direct trip here, so leisurely meandering is the way to go. Still, not all is lighthearted here. In 2017 the region was devastated by a series of unprecedented wildfires—yet the wineries and communities, already well versed in viticulture's long game, are well equipped to bounce back. Traveling to postfire Wine Country is a boon to the recovery effort—and an opportunity to watch the landscape regrow in real time.

The lesser-known valleys, highlighted on this spread, are a great place to start. These regions are often overlooked by the tourist crowd, but their beauty is unparalleled, and their wines are growing in reputation and prestige.

Western Sonoma County

HEAD FOR HEALDSBURG
This lovely, historic town is the perfect place to start your sojourn. Located at the confluence of three distinct wine regions, Healdsburg boasts several cafés and bakeries—as well as fancy groceries for an alfresco picnic.

PASTORAL WONDERLAND: ALEXANDER VALLEY
Stretching from Healdsburg to Cloverdale, this region is slightly warmer and less susceptible to temperature extremes than other valleys. Vineyards here are best known for their merlot and cabernet sauvignon grapes.

▼ There are subtle differences in landscape and climate that separate each valley from the next. Many establishments offer free winery guides to help you orient yourself.

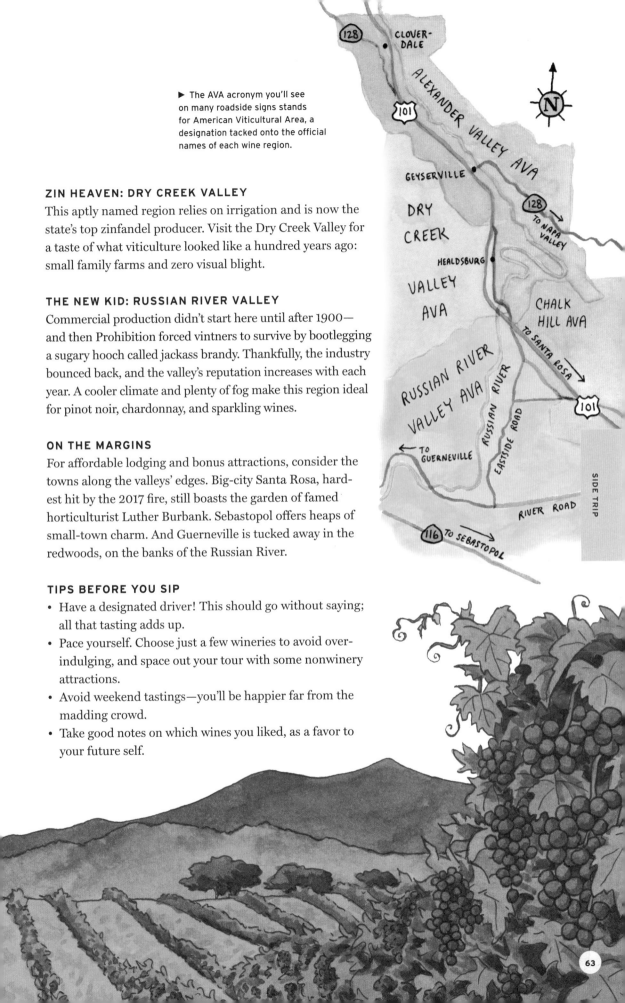

▶ The AVA acronym you'll see on many roadside signs stands for American Viticultural Area, a designation tacked onto the official names of each wine region.

ZIN HEAVEN: DRY CREEK VALLEY

This aptly named region relies on irrigation and is now the state's top zinfandel producer. Visit the Dry Creek Valley for a taste of what viticulture looked like a hundred years ago: small family farms and zero visual blight.

THE NEW KID: RUSSIAN RIVER VALLEY

Commercial production didn't start here until after 1900— and then Prohibition forced vintners to survive by bootlegging a sugary hooch called jackass brandy. Thankfully, the industry bounced back, and the valley's reputation increases with each year. A cooler climate and plenty of fog make this region ideal for pinot noir, chardonnay, and sparkling wines.

ON THE MARGINS

For affordable lodging and bonus attractions, consider the towns along the valleys' edges. Big-city Santa Rosa, hardest hit by the 2017 fire, still boasts the garden of famed horticulturist Luther Burbank. Sebastopol offers heaps of small-town charm. And Guerneville is tucked away in the redwoods, on the banks of the Russian River.

TIPS BEFORE YOU SIP

- Have a designated driver! This should go without saying; all that tasting adds up.
- Pace yourself. Choose just a few wineries to avoid over-indulging, and space out your tour with some nonwinery attractions.
- Avoid weekend tastings—you'll be happier far from the madding crowd.
- Take good notes on which wines you liked, as a favor to your future self.

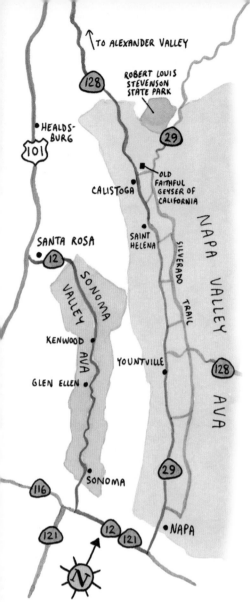

TO ALEXANDER VALLEY

128

ROBERT LOUIS
STEVENSON
STATE PARK

29

HEALDS-
BURG

101

CALISTOGA

OLD
FAITHFUL
GEYSER OF
CALIFORNIA

SANTA ROSA

SAINT
HELENA

12

NAPA VALLEY

SONOMA VALLEY

SILVERADO TRAIL

KENWOOD

AVA

YOUNTVILLE

128

GLEN ELLEN

AVA

SONOMA

29

116

121

12

121

NAPA

N

Napa Valley

Now wine tourism's star diva, Napa Valley has grown from a network of fruit and nut farms into a full-blown agritourism juggernaut. The once-sleepy towns and narrow country highways now burst at the seams on weekends, as tourists and city folk descend upon the region. Wineries run the gamut from simple farmsteads to near theme parks, while the grapes and bottled varietals are equally diverse, thanks to the region's range of microclimates.

Two parallel roads, State Route 29 and the Silverado Trail, form the valley's backbone. For a respite from the traffic, try exploring one of the many cutoff roads between the thoroughfares. Or visit in the off-season (winter and spring), when crowds dwindle and the mustard cover crop is in bloom. For a break from driving, try a bike tour or a ride on the Napa Valley Wine Train.

A CHAIN OF COMMUNITIES

SR 29 connects a series of towns on the valley floor. The city of Napa features the excellent Oxbow Public Market, a variety of live entertainment venues, and the Culinary Institute of America. Yountville is a culinary mecca, with world-class restaurants like the French Laundry. Saint Helena is home to a bustling downtown and the iconic Merryvale Vineyards, the first winery in the region to reopen after Prohibition ended in 1933. Calistoga has the feeling of a spa, with its natural hot springs and trademark mud baths.

◄ The Napa Valley welcome sign has greeted visitors and provided photo ops since 1949. Twin signs mark the northern and southern ends of the valley.

SIDE ATTRACTIONS

For a spectacular and literal overview of Napa, hot-air balloon rides are a popular option. For a bit of kitsch to bring you back down to earth, Old Faithful Geyser of California turns a natural geyser into a roadside attraction. And at the northern extreme of the valley is Robert Louis Stevenson State Park, where the young, then-unknown author spent his honeymoon in 1880.

Sonoma Valley

Thanks to a deep history, a near-perfect climate, and its breathtaking scenery, tiny Sonoma Valley (also called the Valley of the Moon) is the jewel of California's Wine Country. Beyond some of the oldest wineries in the state, the region is known for its artisan cheeses, heirloom fruit, olives, and other crops.

SONOMA'S SIREN CALL

The valley's namesake city was founded as the location of Mission San Francisco Solano, the northernmost of the twenty-one Alta California missions. Home to a number of seasonal restaurants, the town still retains its Spanish vibe, especially around the historic central plaza.

A TRIP UP THE VALLEY

Several of Sonoma Valley's farms also offer lodging, allowing for an up-close view of the vineyards and orchards. Glen Ellen was the residence of Jack London, who canonized the region in his book *The Valley of the Moon*. His former estate is now a state historic park. Nearby is the spectacular Quarryhill Botanical Garden, which highlights endangered Asian plant species.

▲ Mary Ellen Pleasant, a wealthy abolitionist born to Louisiana slaves, designed and built the plantation-style Beltane Ranch in Glen Ellen.

▶ Saint Helena's vibrant central business district is nicknamed Napa Valley's Main Street.

The JOY Is in the Details

JENNER TO FORT BRAGG

▼ Just north of Mendocino is Point Cabrillo Light Station, built in 1909 and still almost completely intact, from its Fresnel lens to its restored wooden beams.

Next to Big Sur (page 32), the remaining 150 miles or so of Highway 1 are the most rugged and remote in California. But don't let the region's small, scattered population fool you: this part of the coast has seen hundreds of years of human influence.

ENDLESS CURVES

Jenner and the mouth of the Russian River mark the start of this long, jagged stretch of coastline. The high cliffs return, and this is your last chance until Fort Bragg to head back inland in any direct fashion. Make sure you keep your tank topped off from now on; around here it's easier to run out of gas than to buy it.

NATURAL WAYSIDES

The Sonoma and Mendocino coasts are home to a large number of state parks and other protected natural areas. Each is worth a stop, but most fascinating are Salt Point State Park—home to the honeycomb-like tafoni rock formations (see illustration, above)—and the historic Point Arena Lighthouse, perched on a windy ridge favored by kite-flying enthusiasts.

CAMOUFLAGED COMMUNITY

Near the town of Gualala is the Sea Ranch, a planned community of site-responsive architecture that began in the 1960s. Here, over 1,800 dynamic shingle-clad homes blend into the trees and cliff sides around them.

▲ Mendocino played the role of the fictional hamlet of Cabot Cove, Maine, in the long-running television series *Murder, She Wrote*.

THE CAPITAL OF QUAINT

Perhaps the most beautiful small town on the California coast is Mendocino. Nearly every building perched on the rocky headland is historic and impeccably preserved—the seemingly endless clapboard houses and storefronts give the place the feel of a New England coastal village. Many of the houses have been converted into bed-and-breakfasts, and the sheer number of upscale shops and restaurants have inspired locals to dub the place Spendocino.

THE BLUE-COLLAR NEIGHBOR

Just down the road is Mendocino's big, burly brother, the lumber and fishing city of Fort Bragg. The highway skirts the town from above, so make sure to descend down to Noyo Harbor to get a real feel for the place. Also worth visiting is MacKerricher State Park, home of Glass Beach, the result of a former seaside dumping ground. Sadly, much of the sea glass here has been illegally harvested by tourists, but sharp eyes can still see the beach glimmer in the sun.

END OF THE LINE

About twenty miles past Fort Bragg, Highway 1 leaves the coast behind, twisting its way through another twenty miles of redwood forest before meeting its end at Highway 101 in Leggett.

▶ Mendocino's architecture is defined by its many wooden water towers. Originally designed to carry the town through seasonal droughts, many are now artist studios or guest lodging.

◀ Fort Ross State Historic Park preserves the southernmost Russian settlement in North America, built in 1812 with the help of Indigenous Siberians, Hawaiians, Alaskans, and Californians.

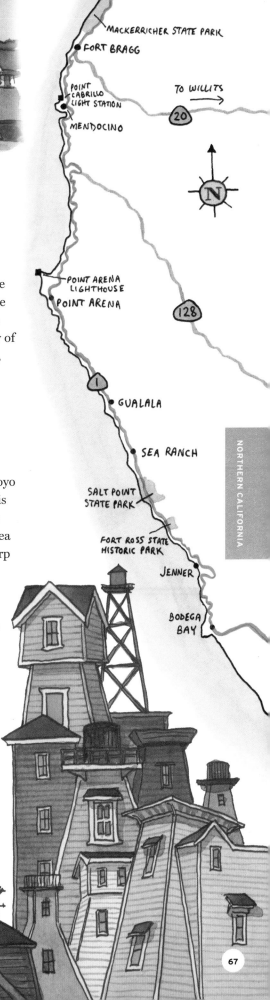

MACKERRICHER STATE PARK
FORT BRAGG

POINT CABRILLO LIGHT STATION
MENDOCINO

TO WILLITS
20

N

POINT ARENA LIGHTHOUSE
POINT ARENA

128

1

GUALALA

SEA RANCH

NORTHERN CALIFORNIA

SALT POINT STATE PARK

FORT ROSS STATE HISTORIC PARK
JENNER

BODEGA BAY

GET Lost

THE LOST COAST

The remote, nearly unpopulated coastal region that Highway 101 skirts on its inland redwood route is known as the Lost Coast. A haven for backcountry hikers, this is one of the West Coast's last truly wild places. A network of primitive roads traverses the region—a rugged coda after the adventure of Highway 1.

OPTION ONE: MATTOLE ROAD

This seventy-mile loop starts in Humboldt Redwoods State Park (page 72), passes through the hamlets of Honeydew and Petrolia, then splits off to Mattole Beach (where a four-mile hiking trail to Punta Gorda Lighthouse begins) before spitting you back out in Ferndale.

OPTION TWO: THE WHOLE ENCHILADA

South of Honeydew, it's actually possible to connect all the way back to Highway 1 on a series of unpaved roads. The only community offering food and lodging is Shelter Cove. Most tourists avoid this route, but hikers and wilderness fans love it. Just do your research beforehand.

SAFETY CONSIDERATIONS

Phones and GPS won't work here, and there are virtually no services of any kind: stock up on maps, rain gear, food, water, and gasoline before you set out. The roads here vary from iffy to harrowing; four-wheel drive is the bare minimum requirement, and a high-clearance vehicle is better still.

▲ Black Sands Beach, which lies just north of Shelter Cove, is composed not of volcanic sand but of particles of graywacke, a dark-colored sandstone.

FERNDALE MEAT CO.

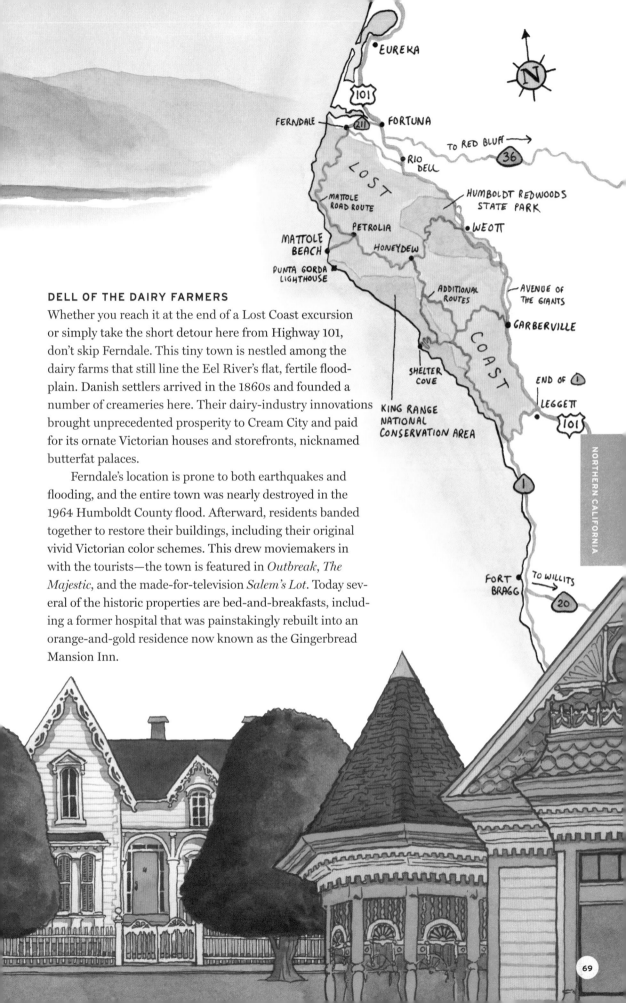

EUREKA

101

FERNDALE

211 FORTUNA

TO RED BLUFF →

RIO DELL

36

L O S T

MATTOLE
ROAD ROUTE

HUMBOLDT REDWOODS
STATE PARK

PETROLIA

WEOTT

MATTOLE
BEACH

HONEYDEW

PUNTA GORDA
LIGHTHOUSE

ADDITIONAL
ROUTES

AVENUE OF
THE GIANTS

GARBERVILLE

C O A S T

END OF 1

SHELTER
COVE

LEGGETT

101

KING RANGE
NATIONAL
CONSERVATION AREA

1

FORT
BRAGG

TO WILLITS →

20

DELL OF THE DAIRY FARMERS

Whether you reach it at the end of a Lost Coast excursion
or simply take the short detour here from Highway 101,
don't skip Ferndale. This tiny town is nestled among the
dairy farms that still line the Eel River's flat, fertile floodplain. Danish settlers arrived in the 1860s and founded a
number of creameries here. Their dairy-industry innovations
brought unprecedented prosperity to Cream City and paid
for its ornate Victorian houses and storefronts, nicknamed
butterfat palaces.

Ferndale's location is prone to both earthquakes and
flooding, and the entire town was nearly destroyed in the
1964 Humboldt County flood. Afterward, residents banded
together to restore their buildings, including their original
vivid Victorian color schemes. This drew moviemakers in
with the tourists—the town is featured in *Outbreak*, *The
Majestic*, and the made-for-television *Salem's Lot*. Today several of the historic properties are bed-and-breakfasts, including a former hospital that was painstakingly rebuilt into an
orange-and-gold residence now known as the Gingerbread
Mansion Inn.

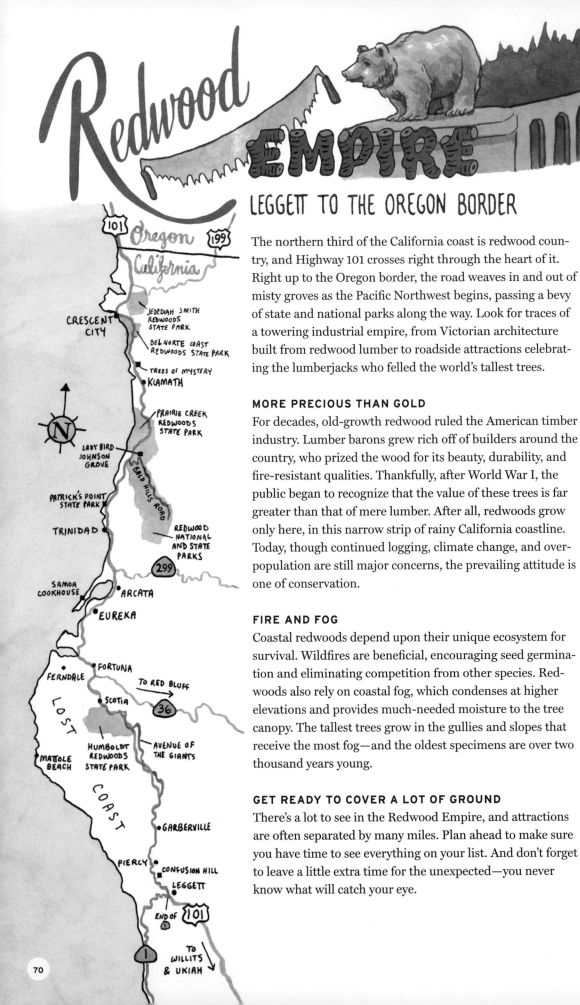

Redwood EMPIRE

LEGGETT TO THE OREGON BORDER

The northern third of the California coast is redwood country, and Highway 101 crosses right through the heart of it. Right up to the Oregon border, the road weaves in and out of misty groves as the Pacific Northwest begins, passing a bevy of state and national parks along the way. Look for traces of a towering industrial empire, from Victorian architecture built from redwood lumber to roadside attractions celebrating the lumberjacks who felled the world's tallest trees.

MORE PRECIOUS THAN GOLD

For decades, old-growth redwood ruled the American timber industry. Lumber barons grew rich off of builders around the country, who prized the wood for its beauty, durability, and fire-resistant qualities. Thankfully, after World War I, the public began to recognize that the value of these trees is far greater than that of mere lumber. After all, redwoods grow only here, in this narrow strip of rainy California coastline. Today, though continued logging, climate change, and overpopulation are still major concerns, the prevailing attitude is one of conservation.

FIRE AND FOG

Coastal redwoods depend upon their unique ecosystem for survival. Wildfires are beneficial, encouraging seed germination and eliminating competition from other species. Redwoods also rely on coastal fog, which condenses at higher elevations and provides much-needed moisture to the tree canopy. The tallest trees grow in the gullies and slopes that receive the most fog—and the oldest specimens are over two thousand years young.

GET READY TO COVER A LOT OF GROUND

There's a lot to see in the Redwood Empire, and attractions are often separated by many miles. Plan ahead to make sure you have time to see everything on your list. And don't forget to leave a little extra time for the unexpected—you never know what will catch your eye.

◀ Keep a sharp eye out for the golden grizzlies that guard the bridge on Highway 101 in Klamath.

▶ Company towns, wholly owned and governed by lumber companies, were common in redwood country. Scotia is noteworthy for its Greek-revival redwood buildings and identical workers' cottages.

SYLVAN CITY

Eureka was California's timber capital, as evidenced by its huge inventory of ornate Victorian buildings. When Highway 101 was completed in 1922, it connected the remote community to the outside world. The resulting trade and tourism boom led the city to give itself the grand nickname Queen City of the Ultimate West. The Eureka of today is somewhat grittier, but the city still features a lively and well-preserved downtown.

HIPPIE HAVEN

Arcata is a liberal stronghold of artists, organic farmers, and marijuana growers. It's no surprise, then, that on Memorial Day weekend, Arcata hosts the Kinetic Grand Championship, a human-powered, amphibious kinetic sculpture competition. The event begins with a parade in downtown Arcata, splashes across Humboldt Bay twice, and finishes with a footrace on Main Street in Ferndale.

TINY TRINIDAD

One of the smallest towns in California is also one of the most beautiful. Perched high above a small harbor, Trinidad is centered around a small lighthouse. It also serves as one of five gateway communities to California Coastal National Monument, which protects the offshore rocks and reefs along the entire length of the California coast.

TSUNAMI CENTRAL

Crescent City is where you'll bid farewell to California. If time and tide are on your side, visit the museum at Battery Point Lighthouse. The structure sits on an island that is accessible only by foot and only at low tide. Also of note is the town's susceptibility to tsunamis. Thanks to the unusual seafloor topography that somehow focuses tidal waves, the town has experienced tsunami conditions more than thirty times since 1933.

▼ Eureka's sixteen-thousand-square-foot Carson Mansion is the most-photographed Victorian home in the United States yet sadly is not open to the public.

Forest ADVENTURES

The founding of the Save the Redwoods League in 1918 led to the establishment of a number of public parks centered around forest and wildlife conservation (map on page 70). Most lie within easy reach of Highway 101, but be sure to build in time for hiking or exploring local back roads, as many of the best groves and park highlights require a side trip.

AVENUE OF THE GIANTS

The best place to kick off your redwood adventure is the Avenue of the Giants, an older alignment of Highway 101 that threads under and around the modern high-speed freeway. The Avenue is lined with scenic viewpoints, named groves, and roadside oddities from the heyday of midcentury road trips (page 74). But the best part is simply the experience of meandering through the trees on the old road.

HUMBOLDT REDWOODS STATE PARK

The best known of the redwood parks is one of the prime attractions along the Avenue of the Giants. This park is home to some of the oldest and tallest redwoods in California. Most noteworthy is the Rockefeller Forest, easily reached by an ADA-accessible loop trail. At over ten thousand acres in size, this grove is one of the largest old-growth forests on earth.

LAND OF THE YUROK

Patrick's Point State Park, near Trinidad, features Sumeg Village, built in 1990 by the Yurok tribe to preserve its culture for future generations. The village includes replica redwood plank houses and occasionally hosts ceremonial dances. The town of Klamath, located within the Yurok Reservation, sits at the mouth of the Klamath River, the lifeblood of traditional Yurok culture.

THE NORTHERN TRIO

Closer to Crescent City are Prairie Creek, Jedediah Smith, and Del Norte Coast Redwoods State Parks. These parks receive fewer visitors than those farther south, allowing for quieter time with the trees. Keep an eye out for rare wildlife, like northern spotted owls, flying squirrels, and the endangered fisher, a small weasel-like mammal.

REDWOOD NATIONAL PARK

Despite the efforts of the Save the Redwoods League, by 1968, 90 percent of the redwoods had been logged. That year, Redwood National Park was established to protect the trees that remained. Very little of the park is old-growth forest, but don't miss a stop at the Lady Bird Johnson Grove or a drive down the gravel Bald Hills Road (four-wheel drive recommended), which in May affords stunning views of wild lupine meadows in bloom.

▼ The meadows in redwood country are grazing haunts for Roosevelt elk, but don't approach them! Rutting bulls and mother cows can be dangerously aggressive.

MAP NOT TO SCALE

EXIT 674

PEPPERWOOD

DRURY-CHANEY GROVE

Avenue of the Giants 101

REDCREST

CHANDLER GROVE

DYERVILLE OVERLOOK

TO ROCKEFELLER FOREST & LOST COAST

TO FOUNDERS GROVE

DYERVILLE LOOP ROAD

MATTOLE ROAD

WEOTT

HUMBOLDT REDWOODS STATE PARK

VISITOR CENTER

SHRINE DRIVE-THRU TREE

BOLLING GROVE

MYERS FLAT

MIRANDA

F.K. LANE GROVE

N

PHILLIPS-VILLE

EXIT 645

GARBER-VILLE 101

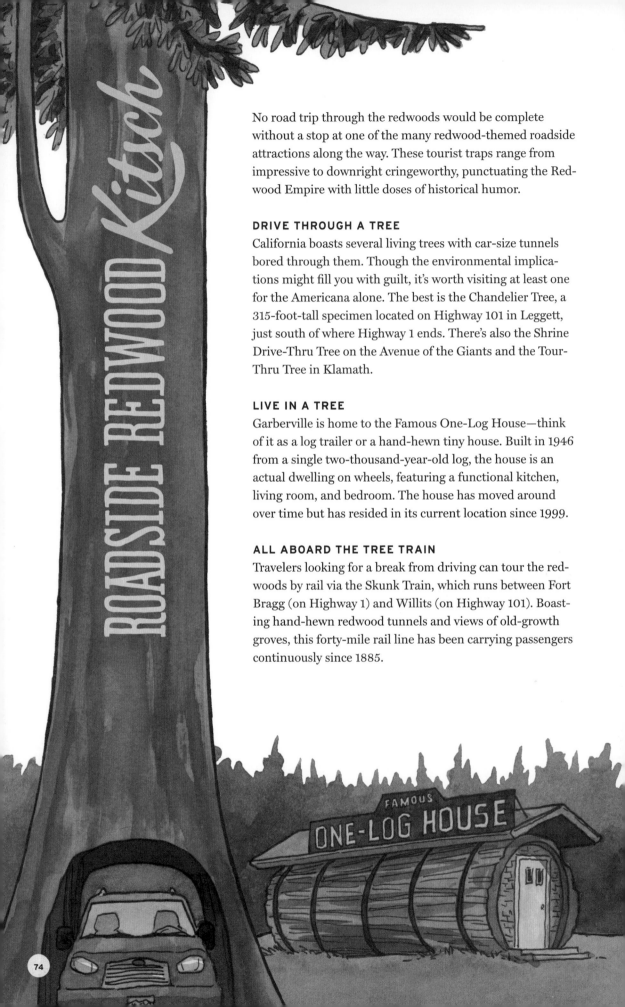

ROADSIDE REDWOOD *Kitsch*

No road trip through the redwoods would be complete without a stop at one of the many redwood-themed roadside attractions along the way. These tourist traps range from impressive to downright cringeworthy, punctuating the Redwood Empire with little doses of historical humor.

DRIVE THROUGH A TREE
California boasts several living trees with car-size tunnels bored through them. Though the environmental implications might fill you with guilt, it's worth visiting at least one for the Americana alone. The best is the Chandelier Tree, a 315-foot-tall specimen located on Highway 101 in Leggett, just south of where Highway 1 ends. There's also the Shrine Drive-Thru Tree on the Avenue of the Giants and the Tour-Thru Tree in Klamath.

LIVE IN A TREE
Garberville is home to the Famous One-Log House—think of it as a log trailer or a hand-hewn tiny house. Built in 1946 from a single two-thousand-year-old log, the house is an actual dwelling on wheels, featuring a functional kitchen, living room, and bedroom. The house has moved around over time but has resided in its current location since 1999.

ALL ABOARD THE TREE TRAIN
Travelers looking for a break from driving can tour the redwoods by rail via the Skunk Train, which runs between Fort Bragg (on Highway 1) and Willits (on Highway 101). Boasting hand-hewn redwood tunnels and views of old-growth groves, this forty-mile rail line has been carrying passengers continuously since 1885.

FAMOUS ONE-LOG HOUSE

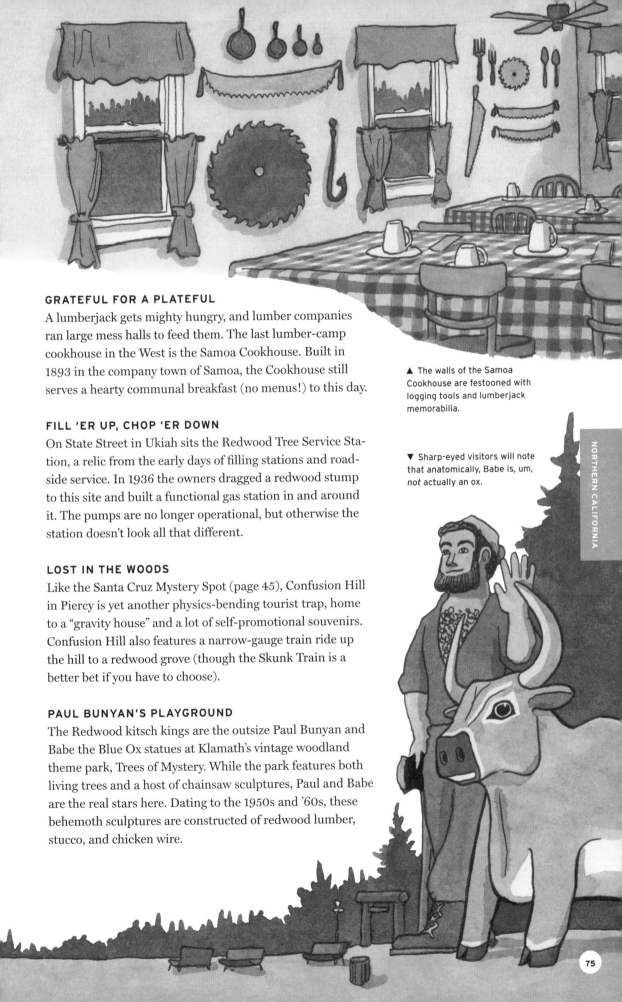

GRATEFUL FOR A PLATEFUL

A lumberjack gets mighty hungry, and lumber companies ran large mess halls to feed them. The last lumber-camp cookhouse in the West is the Samoa Cookhouse. Built in 1893 in the company town of Samoa, the Cookhouse still serves a hearty communal breakfast (no menus!) to this day.

▲ The walls of the Samoa Cookhouse are festooned with logging tools and lumberjack memorabilia.

FILL 'ER UP, CHOP 'ER DOWN

On State Street in Ukiah sits the Redwood Tree Service Station, a relic from the early days of filling stations and roadside service. In 1936 the owners dragged a redwood stump to this site and built a functional gas station in and around it. The pumps are no longer operational, but otherwise the station doesn't look all that different.

▼ Sharp-eyed visitors will note that anatomically, Babe is, um, *not* actually an ox.

LOST IN THE WOODS

Like the Santa Cruz Mystery Spot (page 45), Confusion Hill in Piercy is yet another physics-bending tourist trap, home to a "gravity house" and a lot of self-promotional souvenirs. Confusion Hill also features a narrow-gauge train ride up the hill to a redwood grove (though the Skunk Train is a better bet if you have to choose).

PAUL BUNYAN'S PLAYGROUND

The Redwood kitsch kings are the outsize Paul Bunyan and Babe the Blue Ox statues at Klamath's vintage woodland theme park, Trees of Mystery. While the park features both living trees and a host of chainsaw sculptures, Paul and Babe are the real stars here. Dating to the 1950s and '60s, these behemoth sculptures are constructed of redwood lumber, stucco, and chicken wire.

Welcome to Oregon

The *People's* Coast

After all those miles of California, it's easy to forget you're only halfway up the West Coast. The crossing into Oregon is a subtle one: the redwoods disappear immediately after the border, but the Douglas firs and myrtles of the Oregon rain forests fill in seamlessly. Still, there's no mistaking it: this is officially the Pacific Northwest.

▲ The beaver—representing intelligence, industry, and ingenuity—is the state animal and is featured on the Oregon flag.

▼ The Natural Bridges Viewpoint is one of many overlooks not visible from the road; make sure to heed the signs so you don't miss it.

LEARN TO LOVE YOUR GALOSHES

Odds are that it'll be raining when you arrive in Oregon (note the homemade wooden school-bus shelters along the road-side). Yet water is the source of the Northwest's beauty. The winter rains create all that lush greenery, and colors seem impossibly jewel bright on a gray day. If you visit during the dry season—July through September—coastal fogs make for mild temperatures and spectacular light effects. Whatever the weather, the Oregon coast will capture your heart.

Now that you're on Oregon time, take a moment to thank Highway 101 for bringing you here. Until the route was built in the 1930s, the Oregon shore was completely cut off, with many of the communities reachable only by sea. It took twenty years to complete, but the Oregon Coast Highway opened the shore to pleasure seekers. It took another thirty to make the state's coastline open for all to enjoy, free of charge.

THIS LAND IS YOUR LAND

In the late 1960s a hotel in Cannon Beach closed the beach in front of its property, barring the public from access. The hotelier was just one of many developers who wanted the Oregon coast to follow the example of California and the East Coast states, with their many private beaches and limited or fee-based public access. Then-governor Tom McCall led a grassroots campaign of beachside protests and rallies at the state legislature to fight the developers, and the public won out. In 1967, McCall signed the Oregon Beach Bill into law, preserving all 363 miles of the state's coastline under public ownership. The law defines the extent of public coastline as the stretch between the waterline and sixteen vertical feet beyond the low-tide mark. So if a likely stretch of sand calls to you, have at it—walking, exploring, and playing anywhere along the shore is your right, courtesy of the good people of Oregon.

MORE THAN MEETS THE EYE

Highway 101 through Oregon bears the load of both tourism and industry; as it's the one and only north-south coastal thoroughfare, the road is designed to keep traffic moving as best it can. Unlike along Highway 1 in California, in many places the shore here is obscured by trees, or else the road leaves the coast for a bit to skirt an inlet or cape. As you mosey along, take note of the many scenic viewpoints, loop detours, state parks, and roadside turnoffs along the way. These are important because passing them by will cause you to miss many of the Oregon coast's best attributes, and you'll start to wonder what all the hype was about. The beauty is certainly there; you just have to go out to meet it. Learn to trust the wayside signage—if it tells you something is worth turning off the road to see, believe it!

▼ The Oregon coast is home to eleven lighthouses (plus two just across the bridge in Washington); the majority are open to the public.

OREGON

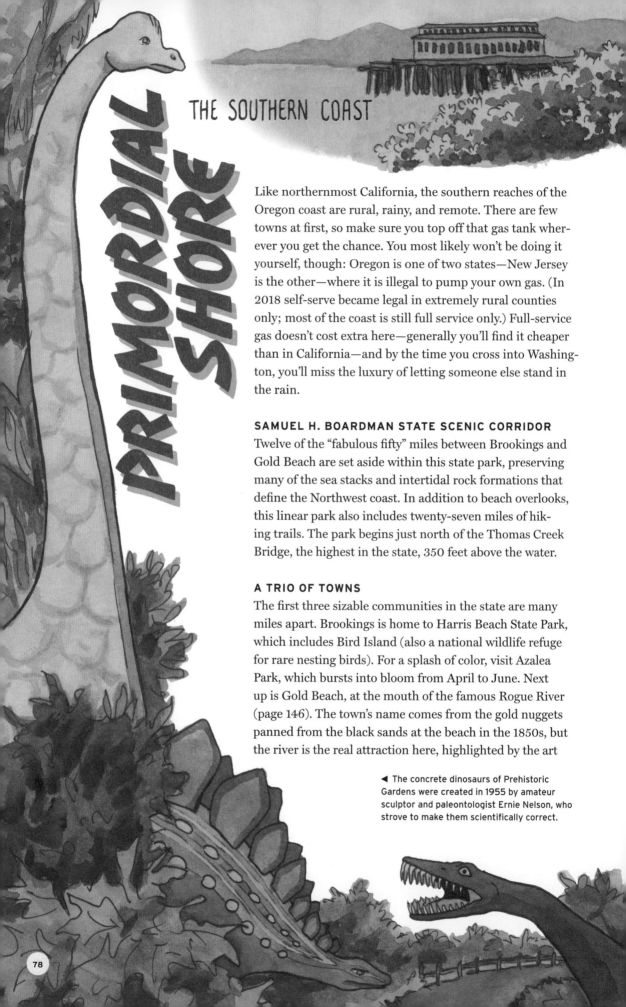

THE SOUTHERN COAST

PRIMORDIAL SHORE

Like northernmost California, the southern reaches of the Oregon coast are rural, rainy, and remote. There are few towns at first, so make sure you top off that gas tank wherever you get the chance. You most likely won't be doing it yourself, though: Oregon is one of two states—New Jersey is the other—where it is illegal to pump your own gas. (In 2018 self-serve became legal in extremely rural counties only; most of the coast is still full service only.) Full-service gas doesn't cost extra here—generally you'll find it cheaper than in California—and by the time you cross into Washington, you'll miss the luxury of letting someone else stand in the rain.

SAMUEL H. BOARDMAN STATE SCENIC CORRIDOR

Twelve of the "fabulous fifty" miles between Brookings and Gold Beach are set aside within this state park, preserving many of the sea stacks and intertidal rock formations that define the Northwest coast. In addition to beach overlooks, this linear park also includes twenty-seven miles of hiking trails. The park begins just north of the Thomas Creek Bridge, the highest in the state, 350 feet above the water.

A TRIO OF TOWNS

The first three sizable communities in the state are many miles apart. Brookings is home to Harris Beach State Park, which includes Bird Island (also a national wildlife refuge for rare nesting birds). For a splash of color, visit Azalea Park, which bursts into bloom from April to June. Next up is Gold Beach, at the mouth of the famous Rogue River (page 146). The town's name comes from the gold nuggets panned from the black sands at the beach in the 1850s, but the river is the real attraction here, highlighted by the art

◄ The concrete dinosaurs of Prehistoric Gardens were created in 1955 by amateur sculptor and paleontologist Ernie Nelson, who strove to make them scientifically correct.

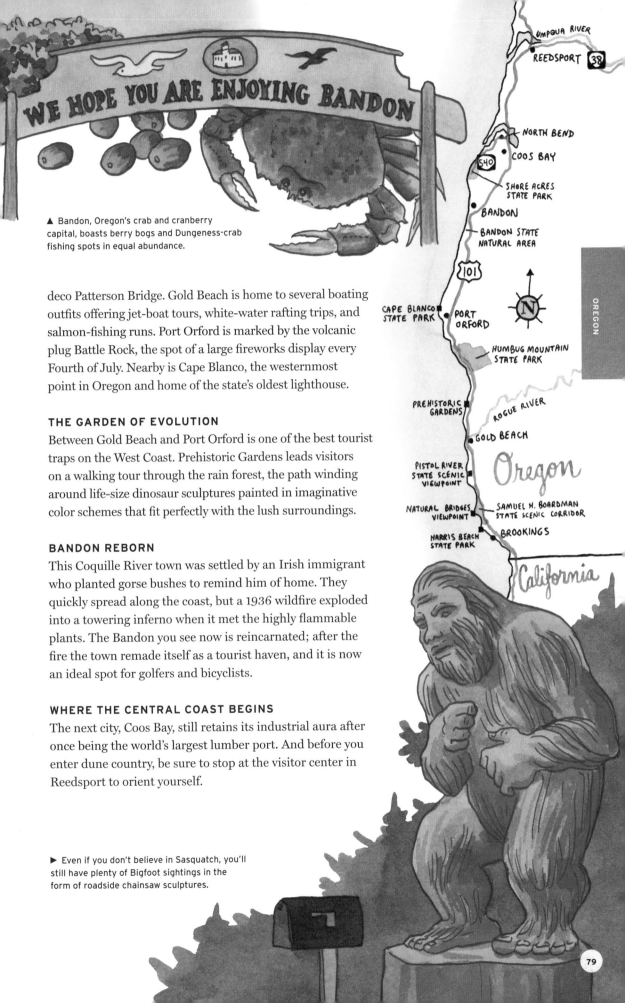

WE HOPE YOU ARE ENJOYING BANDON

▲ Bandon, Oregon's crab and cranberry
capital, boasts berry bogs and Dungeness-crab
fishing spots in equal abundance.

UMPQUA RIVER
REEDSPORT 38
NORTH BEND
COOS BAY
540
SHORE ACRES
STATE PARK
BANDON
BANDON STATE
NATURAL AREA
101
N
CAPE BLANCO
STATE PARK
PORT
ORFORD
HUMBUG MOUNTAIN
STATE PARK
PREHISTORIC
GARDENS
ROGUE RIVER
GOLD BEACH
PISTOL RIVER
STATE SCENIC
VIEWPOINT
Oregon
NATURAL BRIDGES
VIEWPOINT
SAMUEL H. BOARDMAN
STATE SCENIC CORRIDOR
BROOKINGS
HARRIS BEACH
STATE PARK
California

OREGON

deco Patterson Bridge. Gold Beach is home to several boating
outfits offering jet-boat tours, white-water rafting trips, and
salmon-fishing runs. Port Orford is marked by the volcanic
plug Battle Rock, the spot of a large fireworks display every
Fourth of July. Nearby is Cape Blanco, the westernmost
point in Oregon and home of the state's oldest lighthouse.

THE GARDEN OF EVOLUTION

Between Gold Beach and Port Orford is one of the best tourist
traps on the West Coast. Prehistoric Gardens leads visitors
on a walking tour through the rain forest, the path winding
around life-size dinosaur sculptures painted in imaginative
color schemes that fit perfectly with the lush surroundings.

BANDON REBORN

This Coquille River town was settled by an Irish immigrant
who planted gorse bushes to remind him of home. They
quickly spread along the coast, but a 1936 wildfire exploded
into a towering inferno when it met the highly flammable
plants. The Bandon you see now is reincarnated; after the
fire the town remade itself as a tourist haven, and it is now
an ideal spot for golfers and bicyclists.

WHERE THE CENTRAL COAST BEGINS

The next city, Coos Bay, still retains its industrial aura after
once being the world's largest lumber port. And before you
enter dune country, be sure to stop at the visitor center in
Reedsport to orient yourself.

▶ Even if you don't believe in Sasquatch, you'll
still have plenty of Bigfoot sightings in the
form of roadside chainsaw sculptures.

Natural WONDERS

With more parks per mile than any other shoreline, the big draw of the Oregon coast is the natural scenery. With viewpoints and landmarks around every corner, especially along the south-central coast, it can be a little overwhelming. Just get used to pulling over every few minutes, and give yourself plenty of time to explore.

MYRTLE ACRES
Oregon myrtle trees, a type of laurel, are endemic to this part of the coast. Humbug Mountain State Park is a great place to see them in the wild, and nearly every beach town sports at least one Myrtlewood gift shop.

A SHORE THING
Take a twelve-mile detour west on the Cape Arago Highway to visit Shore Acres State Park, home to the formal gardens that once belonged to a private mansion, which burned down in 1921. Nearby are Cape Arago Lighthouse (not open to the public) and Simpson Reef, a haul-out site for thousands of seals and other pinnipeds.

THE SAHARA OF THE NORTHWEST
The Oregon Dunes, now protected as a national monument, stretch along nearly fifty miles of the central coast, from North Bend to Florence. The dunes reach heights of up to five hundred feet in places and even *move*, threatening to swallow anything in their path. In the 1950s the US Forest Service planted grasses along the roadsides to stabilize the slopes, but the dunes still loom over the roadbed. You might even see construction cones announcing an impending sand slide.

▼ After a bank crisis in 1933, North Bend minted its own Myrtlewood coins in place of cash. These now-rare coins are still legal tender here.

▼ It might be possible to spot pinnipeds from the roadside above Sea Lion Caves, but nothing beats seeing them up close inside the cave.

While the dunes hug the highway, you have to get off the main drag to see them in detail. Jessie M. Honeyman Memorial State Park near Florence is a great place to walk or picnic on the sand. There's also an overlook just off 101, about five miles south of Dunes City. If off-road vehicles are your thing, there are lots of places to rent a dune buggy, particularly in Reedsport and Florence.

▲ The Oregon Dunes were the inspiration for Frank Herbert's landmark science-fiction epic, *Dune*.

THE DEVIL'S COAST

The central coast is home to a number of spectacular and dangerous tidal features named for demons and deities (map on page 83). Near Depoe Bay is Devils Punchbowl, a circular rock hollow that fills with turbulent "punch" to match the tide. Cape Perpetua has three: Devils Churn refers to a narrow rock gash, while Spouting Horn shoots a geyser of foam with each crashing wave. Best of the three is Thor's Well, a deep hole just offshore running with cascading water at high tide. Cape Perpetua also boasts a stone viewing shelter eight hundred feet above the water, accessible by a side road and short trail.

▼ At Thor's Well you might catch a glimpse of rare tufted puffins, along with sea stars in a rainbow of colors.

PILES OF PINNIPEDS

If you missed Simpson Reef, you'll have another chance to see pinnipeds at Sea Lion Caves, located just before Heceta Head. This privately owned tourist attraction is worth the admission fee (dress warmly, as you'll be mostly outside). An elevator descends two hundred feet to a large natural sea cave home to the world's only known mainland rookery for Steller sea lions. Fall and winter are the best times to see, hear, and smell them by the hundreds.

SEASIDE HEARTLAND

THE CENTRAL COAST

When Captain James Cook (yes, *that* Captain Cook) first laid eyes on the Oregon coast in 1778 on a search for the mythical Northwest Passage, his only comments were about the weather. He dubbed the headland at his voyage's northern limit Cape Foulweather, a name that still persists for the spot, near modern-day Depoe Bay. He might have been right about the rain, but that's no reason to shy away—this is the heart of the Oregon coast, with plenty to see and lots to love.

SANDY BANKS

This sleepy village of Winchester Bay sits on the Umpqua River, at the center of dune country. Take a detour down Salmon Harbor Drive to see the Umpqua River Lighthouse, perched on a bluff southwest of town.

BRIDGING THE GAP

The dunes peter out around Florence, and you cross the Siuslaw ("sigh-YEW-slaw") River on the most ornate of Conde McCullough's bridges (see caption, left). Old town Florence is home to a number of riverfront businesses and historic buildings. About twelve miles north of town, just past Sea Lion Caves, is Heceta Head Lighthouse, part of Carl G. Washburne Memorial State Park.

A RIVER RUNS THROUGH IT

Just past Cape Perpetua (page 81) is tiny Yachats, pronounced "YA-hots." Its size is part of the appeal: travelers flock here for its quiet vibe and big beauty. A pair of short loop roads, Yachats Ocean Road and Ocean View Drive, offers public oceanfront overlooks like Agate Point and Yachats Recreation Area. The town itself features a surprising number of reasonable lodging options, from hotels to vacation cottages. About nine miles east of town, on Yachats River

▲ From 1927 to 1940, master engineer Conde McCullough designed eleven magnificent bridges along the Oregon coast, featuring Egyptian-style obelisks, art deco fluted columns, and graceful arches.

◄ Lincoln City's colorful orbs are an homage to the glass floats that once steadied fishermen's nets. Antique floats still wash ashore occasionally, from as far away as Japan.

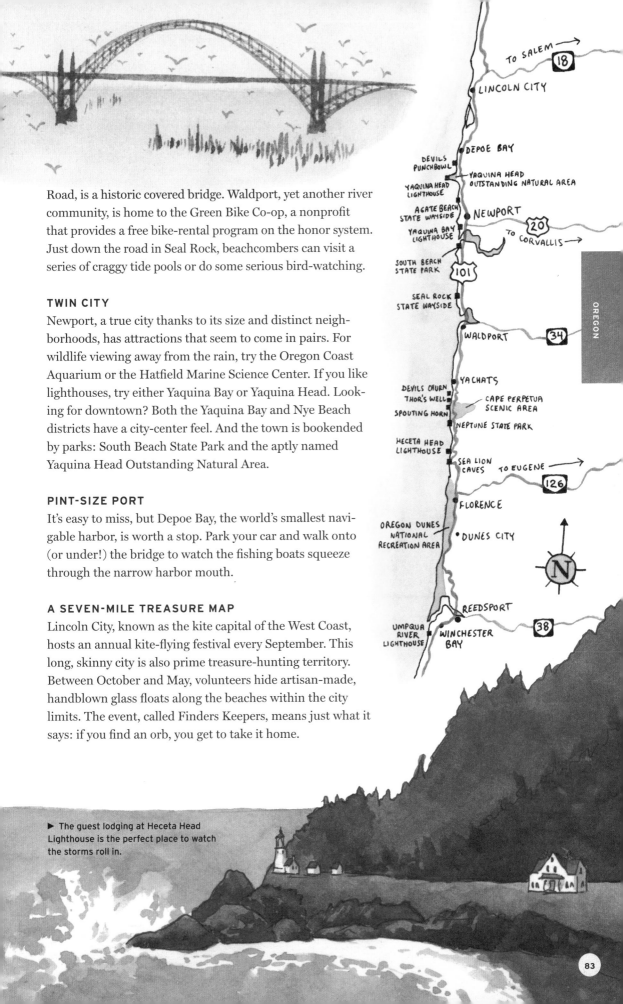

Road, is a historic covered bridge. Waldport, yet another river community, is home to the Green Bike Co-op, a nonprofit that provides a free bike-rental program on the honor system. Just down the road in Seal Rock, beachcombers can visit a series of craggy tide pools or do some serious bird-watching.

TWIN CITY

Newport, a true city thanks to its size and distinct neighborhoods, has attractions that seem to come in pairs. For wildlife viewing away from the rain, try the Oregon Coast Aquarium or the Hatfield Marine Science Center. If you like lighthouses, try either Yaquina Bay or Yaquina Head. Looking for downtown? Both the Yaquina Bay and Nye Beach districts have a city-center feel. And the town is bookended by parks: South Beach State Park and the aptly named Yaquina Head Outstanding Natural Area.

PINT-SIZE PORT

It's easy to miss, but Depoe Bay, the world's smallest navigable harbor, is worth a stop. Park your car and walk onto (or under!) the bridge to watch the fishing boats squeeze through the narrow harbor mouth.

A SEVEN-MILE TREASURE MAP

Lincoln City, known as the kite capital of the West Coast, hosts an annual kite-flying festival every September. This long, skinny city is also prime treasure-hunting territory. Between October and May, volunteers hide artisan-made, handblown glass floats along the beaches within the city limits. The event, called Finders Keepers, means just what it says: if you find an orb, you get to take it home.

► The guest lodging at Heceta Head Lighthouse is the perfect place to watch the storms roll in.

Drop Anchor

THE NORTHERN COAST

Just past Lincoln City, Highway 101 turns inland for a time. While the small farms and valleys that dominate the landscape here are lovely, know that the main event lies west of here, along a winding shoreline detour.

LOOP THE LOOP

Weather and road conditions permitting, make sure you allow time to drive the forty-mile Three Capes Scenic Loop, which takes in the triple promontories of Cape Kiwanda, Cape Lookout, and Cape Meares. Cape Lookout is a two-mile-long headland that juts straight out to sea and is accessible by hiking trail. The seaside villages of Netarts and Oceanside are postcard perfect, as is the hike out to Cape Meares Lighthouse. Near the lighthouse is the Octopus Tree, a massive, outlandish Sitka spruce. At the northern end of the Three Capes Scenic Loop is Bayocean Peninsula Park, the remains of a historical oddity. In the early 1900s, developers turned this narrow sandspit into "the Atlantic City of the West." However, severe storms immediately wiped out the homes, shops, and hotel and carved a half-mile lagoon into the spit.

BUILDING A BETTER CHEDDAR

The Three Capes Scenic Loop and the main highway intersect in downtown Tillamook, home of one of the largest cooperative dairies in the United States. The Tillamook Cheese Factory opened a new interpretive visitor center in 2018, featuring a viewing area overlooking the cheese-making process, cheesy (literally) souvenirs, and—most important of all—free cheese samples.

▲ In 1906 the *Peter Iredale* ran aground near what is now Warrenton. The bones of the prow are easily accessible at Fort Stevens State Park.

◀ In Gearhart you're likely to meet the town's most famous residents: a bold-as-brass herd of Roosevelt elk.

SEASIDE STOPS

The highway then skirts around Tillamook Bay to the east, passing the picturesque fishing village of Garibaldi. After that you meet the open ocean again at Rockaway Beach. The town's contribution to Americana is the Pronto Pup, the original corn dog, invented at a beachfront stand in the 1930s (though many credit the invention to the Cozy Dog Drive In on Route 66 in Illinois).

THE HIGH POINT, IN MORE WAYS THAN ONE

Don't miss the charming resort village of Manzanita, named for the twisty, delicate trees that grow in the region. North of town, the highway climbs up Neahkahnie Mountain; the road over the 1,600-foot summit was a Works Progress Administration project in the 1930s and the last section of Highway 101 to be completed.

PASS THE SALTWATER TAFFY

After Cannon Beach (page 86), you'll pass sizable Seaside and tiny Gearhart. Seaside is the quintessential beach town, with the 1920s-era Promenade and a clutch of historic summer homes. Gearhart is far sleepier and downright bucolic, with a number of arts-and-crafts cottages and the oldest golf course west of the Mississippi. Its original clubhouse has been restored as a hotel by the Oregon historic hotel-brewpub chain McMenamins.

THE OTHER COAST HIGHWAY

Before Highway 101 cut its way along the coast, residents along the northern Oregon coast used the beach as their motorway. There are still a few places where you can legally drive on the beach; the longest stretch is the ten miles between the Tenth Street beach entrance in Gearhart and the *Peter Iredale* in Warrenton. (How often do you get to use a *shipwreck* as a landmark?) Four-wheel drive is essential; open year-round. Proceed slowly and with great caution—and watch for pedestrians!

▶ Cape Kiwanda State Natural Area, on the Three Capes Scenic Loop, is home to golden sandstone cliffs weathered into hoodoos, arches, and sea caves.

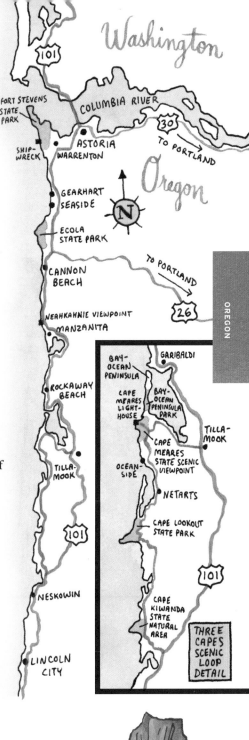

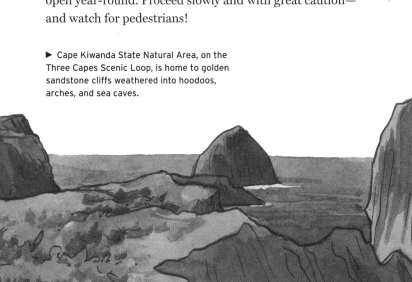

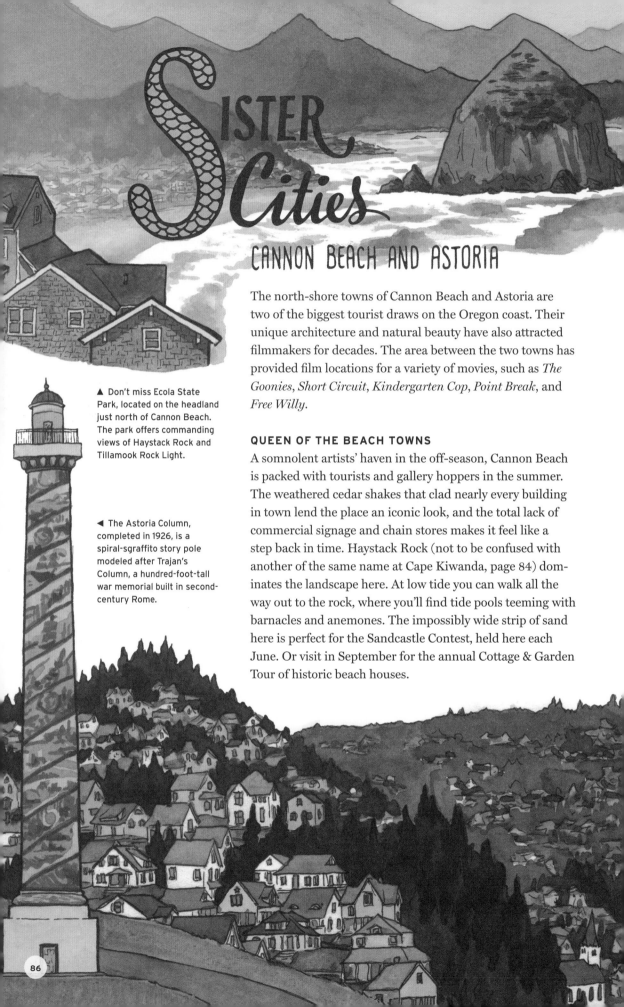

Sister Cities

CANNON BEACH AND ASTORIA

The north-shore towns of Cannon Beach and Astoria are two of the biggest tourist draws on the Oregon coast. Their unique architecture and natural beauty have also attracted filmmakers for decades. The area between the two towns has provided film locations for a variety of movies, such as *The Goonies*, *Short Circuit*, *Kindergarten Cop*, *Point Break*, and *Free Willy*.

QUEEN OF THE BEACH TOWNS

A somnolent artists' haven in the off-season, Cannon Beach is packed with tourists and gallery hoppers in the summer. The weathered cedar shakes that clad nearly every building in town lend the place an iconic look, and the total lack of commercial signage and chain stores makes it feel like a step back in time. Haystack Rock (not to be confused with another of the same name at Cape Kiwanda, page 84) dominates the landscape here. At low tide you can walk all the way out to the rock, where you'll find tide pools teeming with barnacles and anemones. The impossibly wide strip of sand here is perfect for the Sandcastle Contest, held here each June. Or visit in September for the annual Cottage & Garden Tour of historic beach houses.

▲ Don't miss Ecola State Park, located on the headland just north of Cannon Beach. The park offers commanding views of Haystack Rock and Tillamook Rock Light.

◄ The Astoria Column, completed in 1926, is a spiral-sgraffito story pole modeled after Trajan's Column, a hundred-foot-tall war memorial built in second-century Rome.

THE GRAND DAME OF THE WEST COAST

Located at the mouth of the Columbia River and named for New York fur magnate John Jacob Astor, Astoria is the oldest American settlement west of the Rockies. Canneries line the riverfront while an endless tangle of Victorian houses clings to the steep hillsides. The town is picturesque from every angle, and the ever-changing weather makes for almost-daily rainbow sightings.

For a bird's-eye view, start at the Astoria Column. Perched on Coxcomb Hill, six hundred feet above the river, it provides a stunning 360-degree view. If you're brave enough, you can climb the 164 steps up the claustrophobic spiral staircase to the observation deck above.

Get an even bigger dose of regional history at the Flavel House Museum or else the Hanthorn Cannery Museum, housed in a former Bumble Bee salmon cannery. The Garden of Surging Waves honors Astoria's Chinese immigrant history, and the annual Scandinavian Midsummer Festival celebrates the city's Finnish and Nordic heritage. Round out your historic tour with Maritime Memorial Park, which honors those lost at sea, past and present.

As you continue on your way and leave the state of Oregon, you'll cross the Astoria–Megler Bridge. At four miles in length, it is a marvel of engineering—and the longest continuous truss bridge in North America.

▲ The old Clatsop County Jail, beloved since *The Goonies*, now houses the Oregon Film Museum, commemorating movies shot in the Beaver State.

▼ The Astoria Column, weather permitting, offers a view of Cape Disappointment on the Washington side of the river (page 89).

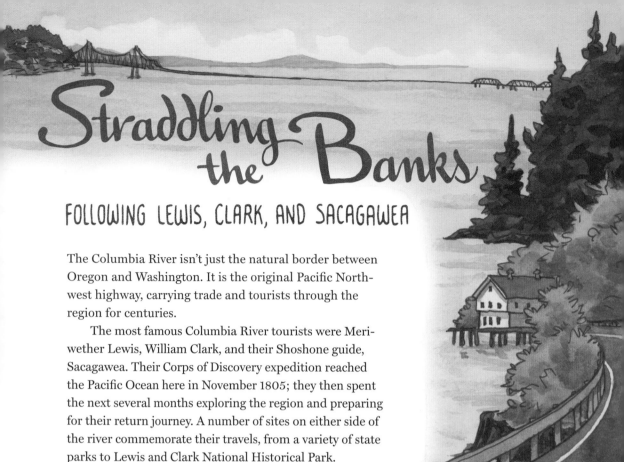

Straddling the Banks

FOLLOWING LEWIS, CLARK, AND SACAGAWEA

The Columbia River isn't just the natural border between Oregon and Washington. It is the original Pacific Northwest highway, carrying trade and tourists through the region for centuries.

The most famous Columbia River tourists were Meriwether Lewis, William Clark, and their Shoshone guide, Sacagawea. Their Corps of Discovery expedition reached the Pacific Ocean here in November 1805; they then spent the next several months exploring the region and preparing for their return journey. A number of sites on either side of the river commemorate their travels, from a variety of state parks to Lewis and Clark National Historical Park.

THE OREGON SIDE

Start at the Fort Clatsop Visitor Center, south of Astoria, home of an interpretive museum and a convincing replica of the fort where the Corps spent their winter. From there head south to Seaside to see the replica salt cairn that marks the place where the party boiled seawater to produce salt for preserving food. Then stop at Ecola State Park in Cannon Beach to walk in Lewis and Clark's footsteps to the southernmost point of their Oregon coast sojourn.

▲ Scenic highways line both sides of the river, with US Highway 30 along the Oregon shore and State Route 4 on the Washington side.

▼ Cape Disappointment gets its name from an eighteenth-century fur trader who missed finding the mouth of the river when a storm forced him to turn back.

▲ Though they never painted Sacagawea's portrait, Lewis and Clark sketched everything else on their travels, from local flora and fauna to incredibly accurate maps.

Map labels:
Washington
4
101
CAPE DISAPPOINTMENT STATE PARK
NORTH HEAD LIGHTHOUSE
ILWACO
401
CAPE DISAPPOINTMENT LIGHTHOUSE
FORT COLUMBIA HISTORICAL STATE PARK
LEWIS AND CLARK INTERPRETIVE CENTER
DISMAL NITCH
COLUMBIA RIVER
ASTORIA-MEGLER BRIDGE
COLUMBIA RIVER MARITIME MUSEUM
ASTORIA COLUMN
30
FORT STEVENS STATE PARK
WARRENTON ASTORIA
FORT CLATSOP VISITOR CENTER
SUNSET BEACH STATE RECREATION SITE
FORT TO SEA TRAIL
Oregon
SEASIDE
SEASIDE HISTORICAL SOCIETY MUSEUM
SALT WORKS
101
N
CANNON BEACH
OREGON

THE RIVER

On your way back northward, stop at the Columbia River Maritime Museum in Astoria. Though it doesn't deal specifically with Lewis and Clark, it does give you a sense of the dangers of the Columbia River Bar, nicknamed the Graveyard of the Pacific for the hundreds of vessels that have sunk there. Exhibits center on the Columbia River Bar Pilots, who since 1846 have guided ships through one of the most dangerous water passages on earth—first in rowboats and now in helicopters.

THE WASHINGTON SIDE

As soon as you cross the Astoria–Megler Bridge, turn right to see the pull-off that marks the site of Dismal Nitch, where the Corps camped for ten miserable nights during a storm. From there head back west along the river toward Ilwaco. Along the way, Fort Columbia Historical State Park, a pre–World War I military installation, sits at Chinook Point, where Clark surveyed the land on his way to a side survey of the Long Beach Peninsula.

Continue past Ilwaco to reach Cape Disappointment State Park (you'll need to switch to your Washington State park pass), and stop for a picnic at one of two historic lighthouses. Complete your excursion at the Lewis and Clark Interpretive Center, which features an extensive museum and panoramic views of the river's mouth.

▼ The replica outpost at Fort Clatsop was painstakingly reconstructed to scale using sketches drawn by Clark on the elk-hide cover of his journal.

► In 2011, Clark's descendants presented a traditional wooden canoe to the Chinook people, to replace the one stolen from them by the Corps in 1806.

Washington

THE RAIN COAST

Highway 101 makes its grand finale with a 360-mile Washington loop around the Olympic Peninsula. You're never far from seawater on this route, from the Pacific Ocean on the west side to the Strait of Juan de Fuca on the north to Hood Canal on the east. As if that weren't enough, a series of back roads and scenic detours loops you along the complex bays and spits that make up the southwestern shore.

PUT ON YOUR CLAM DIGGERS

Twenty-eight miles of sand make Long Beach (Washington, not California), well, the longest beach in the world (and another place where you can drive on the beach). In addition to having a kite festival even larger than Lincoln City's (page 83), this is prime territory for razor clams—if you're quick enough to nab the lightning-fast mollusks, that is. If you miss your chance, you can still sample some at the Razor Clam Festival each April.

▲ Despite its rainy reputation, the Washington coast benefits from the typical Pacific Northwest dry season, giving visitors many flawless, sunny days from July through September.

OYSTER COUNTRY

Thanks to the shallow waters of Willapa Bay, South Bend is the self-proclaimed oyster capital of the world. You can watch the speedy shuckers firsthand with a tour of Goose Point Oysters in nearby Bay Center. Then head back to the Tim Chester Club in South Bend, the world's best down-home oyster bar.

THE CRANBERRY COAST

The all-American cranberry, which grew wild in the marsh flats of coastal Oregon and Washington, has become an important cash crop from Ilwaco to Aberdeen. If you make the drive in early to mid October, you'll see a sea of vivid red berry bogs.

▼ Ilwaco and Grayland host cranberry festivals every October, and Long Beach is home to the Pacific Coast Cranberry Research Foundation Museum.

▲ The world's largest frying pan is a mere statue these days, but in the 1930s and '40s it was actually used for cooking razor clams and even eggs (page 169)!

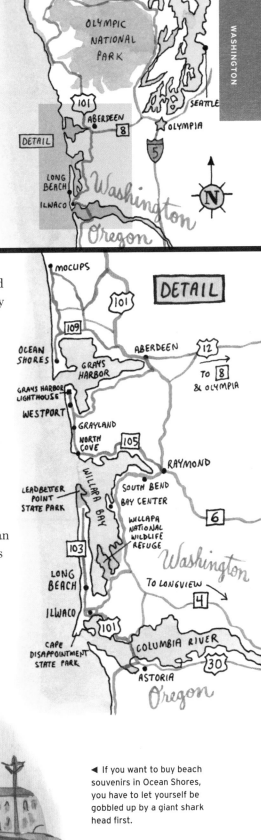

THE SCENIC SLOW ROAD

After Raymond, Highway 101 plows through heavily logged forests all the way to Aberdeen. For a more scenic route, try looping around on State Route 105. At North Cove you'll be able to see across Willapa Bay to Leadbetter Point, and Westport is home to Grays Harbor Lighthouse.

SMELLS LIKE GRUNGE ROCK

Located on Grays Harbor, working-class Aberdeen is the birthplace of Kurt Cobain, lead singer of grunge band Nirvana. Recently the town changed its welcome signage to read "Come as You Are," in tribute to his life.

ONE MO' SANDY BEACH

Before you reach Olympic National Park (page 94), there's one more tempting loop detour, which takes in sandy Ocean Shores and the start of the sea stacks at Moclips, which lies south of the Quinault Reservation.

◀ If you want to buy beach souvenirs in Ocean Shores, you have to let yourself be gobbled up by a giant shark head first.

NORTHWEST Hospitality

The western shore of the Olympic Peninsula is one of the remotest corners of Washington—and of the West Coast itself. There aren't a whole lot of lodging options in this neck of the woods, but the quality here makes up for the quantity.

THE OLD-SCHOOL LODGE

Built in 1926 in the tradition of the WPA park lodges (page 133, 158, and 175), Lake Quinault Lodge is the most hotel-like of the area's accommodations. Located just outside one of Olympic National Park's three rain forests, the lodge is privately run by a concessionaire to the park. Don't miss the totem-style rain gauge that measures precipitation in *feet*, the nearby world's largest spruce tree, or the Roosevelt Dining Room, where President Franklin D. Roosevelt visited in 1937, just before creating the national park.

THE PLACE TO UNPLUG

Perhaps best known of the Olympic National Park lodges is Kalaloch (pronounced "CLAY-lock"), a midcentury rustic property perched on a sea cliff. The place offers three lodging types, depending on your needs: the inn-like Main Lodge, built in 1953; the apartment-style Seacrest House on the other end of the property; or a number of single-family cabins built in a ring around the cliff top. Whichever you choose, Kalaloch Lodge's main draws are its beachfront location and its rural seclusion. To minimize modern life's intrusions, there's no cell service, television, Wi-Fi, or internet access on site (nor for miles around, as it turns out).

▼ Kalaloch Lodge also offers ADA-accessible cabins, pet-friendly rooms, and a group campsite for tent campers or small RVs.

NEAH BAY
HOBUCK BEACH
SHI SHI BEACH
POINT OF THE ARCHES
112
OZETTE LAKE
113
RIALTO BEACH
110
FORKS
FIRST BEACH
LA PUSH
SECOND BEACH
101
THIRD BEACH
RUBY BEACH
OLYMPIC NATIONAL PARK
KALALOCH LODGE
QUEETS
SOUTH BEACH
LAKE QUINAULT
LAKE QUINAULT LODGE
101
ABERDEEN

17 FT
16 FT
15 FT
14 FT
13 FT
12 FT
11 FT
10 FT
9 FT
8 FT
7 FT
6 FT
5 FT
4 FT
3 FT
2 FT

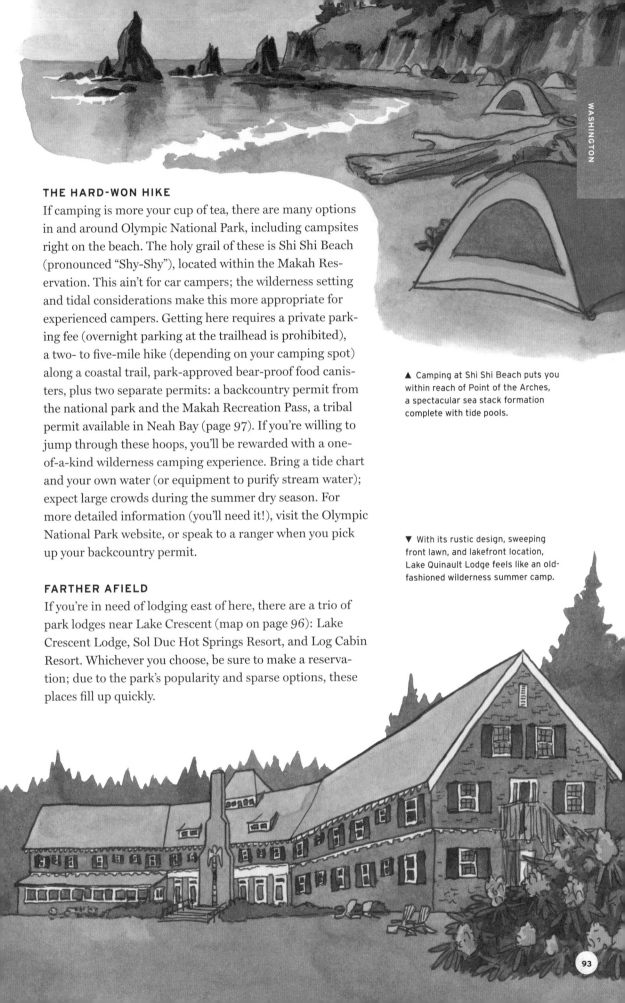

THE HARD-WON HIKE

If camping is more your cup of tea, there are many options in and around Olympic National Park, including campsites right on the beach. The holy grail of these is Shi Shi Beach (pronounced "Shy-Shy"), located within the Makah Reservation. This ain't for car campers; the wilderness setting and tidal considerations make this more appropriate for experienced campers. Getting here requires a private parking fee (overnight parking at the trailhead is prohibited), a two- to five-mile hike (depending on your camping spot) along a coastal trail, park-approved bear-proof food canisters, plus two separate permits: a backcountry permit from the national park and the Makah Recreation Pass, a tribal permit available in Neah Bay (page 97). If you're willing to jump through these hoops, you'll be rewarded with a one-of-a-kind wilderness camping experience. Bring a tide chart and your own water (or equipment to purify stream water); expect large crowds during the summer dry season. For more detailed information (you'll need it!), visit the Olympic National Park website, or speak to a ranger when you pick up your backcountry permit.

▲ Camping at Shi Shi Beach puts you within reach of Point of the Arches, a spectacular sea stack formation complete with tide pools.

FARTHER AFIELD

If you're in need of lodging east of here, there are a trio of park lodges near Lake Crescent (map on page 96): Lake Crescent Lodge, Sol Duc Hot Springs Resort, and Log Cabin Resort. Whichever you choose, be sure to make a reservation; due to the park's popularity and sparse options, these places fill up quickly.

▼ With its rustic design, sweeping front lawn, and lakefront location, Lake Quinault Lodge feels like an old-fashioned wilderness summer camp.

A WORLD Apart

OLYMPIC NATIONAL PARK

When you look at a map of the Olympic Peninsula, you'll see a massive, mountainous interior with zero through roads. This wilderness was set aside in 1937 as Olympic National Park, and hikers come from all over the world to explore the park's interior. You don't have to be a wilderness expert to get a taste of the park, though; many natural wonders lie within reach of Highway 101. The park is vast, with long distances between sites (maps on pages 92 and 96); allow ample time to explore. The main visitor center is located in Port Angeles.

TEMPERATE RAIN FORESTS

The Olympic Peninsula receives wildly varied amounts of precipitation annually, from fewer than twenty inches in the rain shadow (page 100) to more than twenty *feet* on Mount Olympus. The temperate rain forests that lie beneath the windward slopes of the mountains get twelve to fourteen feet of rain each year, resulting in the impossibly lush forests now designated as a UNESCO World Heritage Site. The national park protects three rain forests: the Quinault, the Queets, and the Hoh. Most popular is the Hoh, with its visitor center and easy trails.

▲ The Hall of Mosses Trail in the Hoh Rain Forest is one of the park's top destinations, featuring old-growth groves and roving elk herds.

ROCKY BEACHES

Almost all of the peninsula's western coastline, extending one mile inland, is preserved as part of the park. There are countless beaches and sea stacks to explore, but highlights include Ruby and Rialto Beaches. There are several coastal trails as well, but some require scrambling over rock formations at low tide. Carry a tide chart and time your hike carefully to avoid getting trapped and waiting hours for the tide to go back out again.

LAKE COUNTRY

The park is home to several large lakes, the most famous of which are Ozette Lake and Lake Crescent. Ozette is an archaeological wonder, site of a Pompeii-like village buried centuries ago in a mudslide. Over fifty thousand artifacts found here now reside at the Makah Museum (page 97). Lake Crescent, closer to Port Angeles, is a deep freshwater channel carved by glaciers and filled with jewel-bright water reminiscent of Crater Lake in Oregon (page 148). Recreational opportunities abound here, either on foot or by boat; most popular is the mile-long spur trail to Marymere Falls.

MOUNTAIN WONDERLAND

The Hurricane Ridge district is one of the most popular destinations within the park and the perfect finale for your visit. This alpine region is accessible via a seventeen-mile mountain road leading upward from Port Angeles. The road is ostensibly open year-round, but heavy snows in winter lead to frequent closures, particularly on weekdays. Winter visitors enjoy the snowshoeing prospects, while in the spring and summer the subalpine meadows bloom with wildflowers. Either way, the ridge itself is the main attraction here—various trails and overlooks offer jaw-dropping, panoramic views of the saw-toothed peaks and steep glacial valleys.

▲ Highway 101 twists around the southern shore of Lake Crescent, the 1930s-era roadbed perched directly on the lakeshore in places.

▼ If you hike the steep trail to Hurricane Hill, you might catch a glimpse of the Olympic marmot, the state endemic mammal of Washington.

The North Shore

FORKS TO PORT ANGELES

As you curve around the Olympic Peninsula, you're faced with yet another choice: continue on the "fast" road of Highway 101 or take a slow spur to Cape Flattery. (Hint: take the detour, if time and weather allow.)

▲ The Black Ball Ferry provides service between Port Angeles and Victoria, British Columbia (page 104), perfect for bringing your car over to Vancouver Island.

FICTIONAL FORKS

Twilight fans will want to make a pilgrimage to the setting of the teen vampire franchise, while their parents (or spouses, let's be honest) might enjoy the Forks Timber Museum. The most cheeseball attractions (*Twilight* firewood!) have faded away in recent years, but there are still plenty of fan-worthy spots. Despite many problematic cultural inaccuracies in the books and films, the Quileute people have been remarkably good sports about *Twilight* tourism. The boundary of their reservation near La Push is marked with a sign that reads: "Treaty Line: No Vampires beyond This Point!"

THE SHORE ROAD

Just east of Forks is, well, a fork in the road. State Route 113 (and then 112) leads to Neah Bay along a breathtaking two-lane shoreline road. The route is susceptible to mudslides and washouts, but the rewards are bald eagle sightings and panoramic views of Vancouver Island. Stop in Sekiu to see a bizarre roadside statue depicting a sort of reverse mermaid: a human-legged fish wearing a sports bra and jogging sneakers.

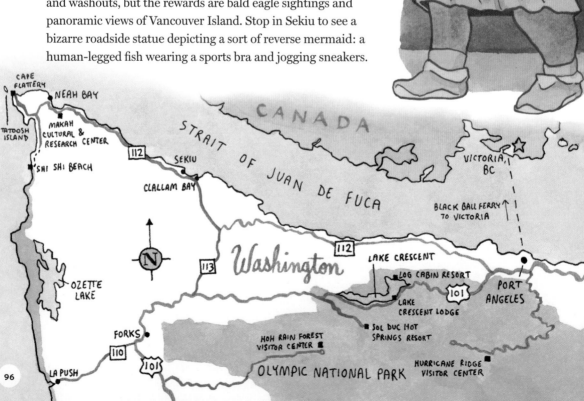

CULTURAL OUTPOST

The last town on the peninsula is Neah Bay, part of the Makah Reservation. Still an active fishing port, the town is also the gateway to Shi Shi Beach (page 93). Don't miss the Makah Cultural & Research Center, home of one of the best cultural museums in the Northwest.

EDGE OF THE EARTH

The northwesternmost tip of the contiguous United States, Cape Flattery is accessible by a well-maintained three-quarter-mile wooden boardwalk trail on the Makah Reservation. Here, you'll feel like you're standing on the edge of the world—and at the apex of your West Coast journey. Note the sea stacks to the south and the lighthouse on Tatoosh Island across the channel. A Makah Recreation Pass, available at several locations in Neah Bay, is required to park at the Cape Flattery trailhead.

THE BIG CITY

The largest city on the peninsula is Port Angeles, home of the Olympic National Park headquarters—as well as the gateway to Hurricane Ridge (page 95). Highway 101, through the outskirts, is occupied with strip malls and other less scenic spots, but head downtown for more pleasant sights. First and Front Streets are home to a number of shops and restaurants, and the City Pier is the lively heart of the waterfront. The Waterfront Trail runs throughout the city, part of the sixty-mile path called the Olympic Discovery Trail—which eventually will stretch from Port Townsend (page 100) to the Pacific shore.

▲ At Cape Flattery, keep an eye out for elusive wildlife like sea otters, gray whales, marbled murrelets, or even rare snowy owls.

▼ A pair of male and female figures guards the entrance to the Makah Museum. These traditional welcome figures are a common motif in Coast Salish carvings.

Totems

THE WEST COAST'S BORROWED CULTURE

The West Coast is studded with Indigenous cultural icons—many of which turn out to be imported or even fake. Learning to spot the difference can help you make informed choices about what to see on your road trip.

TOTEM TERRITORY

The Pacific Northwest evokes mental images of totem poles, yet these Coast Salish icons are mostly endemic to Alaska and upper British Columbia. The totem poles so commonly found in Seattle and the Puget Sound region were either carved by non-Alaskans or imported—often unethically—from up north. Yet the tourist appeal is undeniable; even some of the modern tribal hotels and casinos are marked with totem poles.

In addition to the Makah Museum (page 97), Washington is home to a number of authentic Indigenous cultural experiences. The Seattle Art Museum, the Burke Museum, the Hibulb Cultural Center, and the Suquamish Museum have excellent exhibits on Coast Salish culture. And several towns are home to traditional nontotem carvings, such as a Puyallup welcome figure in downtown Tacoma.

And then there are the mixed bags. Tillicum Village, a dinner-theater experience on Blake Island in the Puget Sound, is a hodgepodge of different Salish cultures from Washington to Alaska. And Ye Olde Curiosity Shop, Seattle's old-fashioned waterfront tourist trap, began in the nineteenth century as an actual trading post for area tribes—yet now is an odd mix of authentic souvenirs, cheap knockoffs, and historical artifacts that probably ought to be repatriated back to their respective tribes.

▲ Indigenous peoples from around the Salish Sea travel by canoe to a large summer gathering hosted by a different tribe each year.

◄ The famous totem pole in Seattle's Pioneer Square is a replica of one stolen from an Alaskan Tlingit village in 1899.

▶ At Tillicum Village, enjoy fresh salmon prepared in the traditional method, roasted on cedar spits over an open fire.

TIKI TOURIST TRAPS

Tiki culture, on the other hand, is entirely fabricated, more of a restaurant theme than an actual reflection of Polynesian culture. In 1934 white Louisianan Ernest Beaumont-Gantt changed his name and opened Don the Beachcomber, a theme bar in Hollywood. His decor, mostly a vague mish-mash of tropical motifs and nautical bric-a-brac, inspired a generation of pop-culture eateries, programmatic architecture, and souvenir cocktails.

Tiki culture is making something of a comeback among hipsters and nostalgic types, keeping several midcentury establishments alive. The Alibi in Portland is beloved by locals, and the Bali Hai restaurant in San Diego still serves Polynesian fare. Many tiki bars and even South Pacific–themed apartment buildings still exist in California, including the flagship Trader Vic's in Emeryville (the one in Portland closed in 2016). Most spectacular of all is the Tonga Room & Hurricane Bar, a lavish affair located inside the Fairmont Hotel in San Francisco's Nob Hill neighborhood.

STRANGE COINCIDENCES

There are also a couple of Highway 101 landmarks that seem like a bizarre combination of tiki *and* totems—but that actually belong to different categories altogether. In Lincoln City, Oregon, a set of four Korean *jang seung* wishing statues sits in front of the Palace Inn. These were carved in 2002 for the World Cup soccer match in Seoul, then brought back by the hotel's owners. Down the road in Astoria is an eighteen-foot wooden head, carved in 1987 by white artist Peter Toth as part of his *Whispering Giants* sculpture series, possibly in tribute to the Clatsop chief Comcomly.

▲ San Diego's Shelter Island is almost entirely tiki-themed, from hotels and restaurants to apartment buildings and even a tiki picnic shelter.

▶ At the Tonga Room, sip your mai tai while a live band floats by on a barge and indoor monsoons "rain" down every half hour.

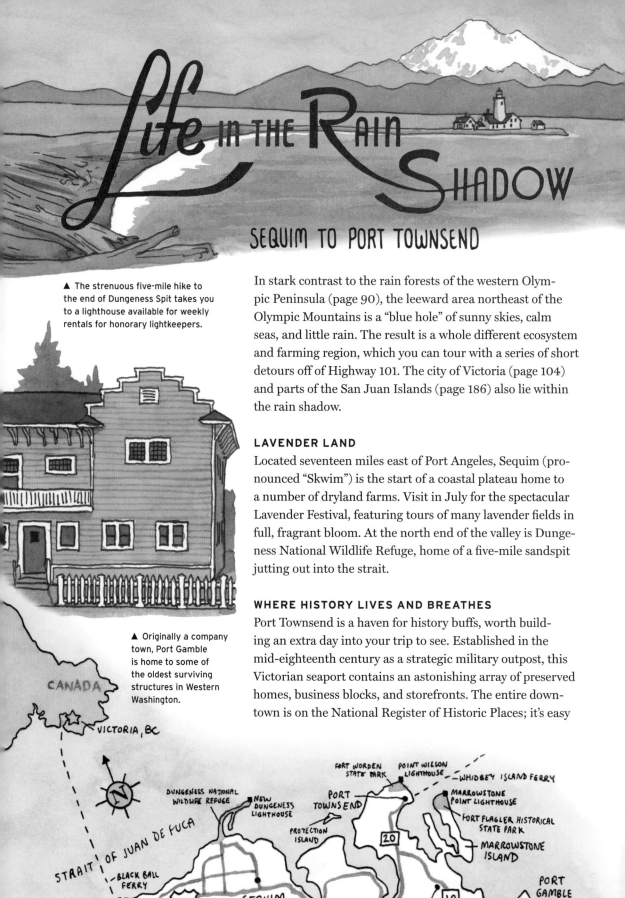

Life in the Rain Shadow

SEQUIM TO PORT TOWNSEND

▲ The strenuous five-mile hike to the end of Dungeness Spit takes you to a lighthouse available for weekly rentals for honorary lightkeepers.

▲ Originally a company town, Port Gamble is home to some of the oldest surviving structures in Western Washington.

In stark contrast to the rain forests of the western Olympic Peninsula (page 90), the leeward area northeast of the Olympic Mountains is a "blue hole" of sunny skies, calm seas, and little rain. The result is a whole different ecosystem and farming region, which you can tour with a series of short detours off of Highway 101. The city of Victoria (page 104) and parts of the San Juan Islands (page 186) also lie within the rain shadow.

LAVENDER LAND

Located seventeen miles east of Port Angeles, Sequim (pronounced "Skwim") is the start of a coastal plateau home to a number of dryland farms. Visit in July for the spectacular Lavender Festival, featuring tours of many lavender fields in full, fragrant bloom. At the north end of the valley is Dungeness National Wildlife Refuge, home of a five-mile sandspit jutting out into the strait.

WHERE HISTORY LIVES AND BREATHES

Port Townsend is a haven for history buffs, worth building an extra day into your trip to see. Established in the mid-eighteenth century as a strategic military outpost, this Victorian seaport contains an astonishing array of preserved homes, business blocks, and storefronts. The entire downtown is on the National Register of Historic Places; it's easy

to spend a whole day just exploring the shops and peering up at ornate architectural details.

At the north end of town is Fort Worden State Park, a historic army base perched at the entrance of Admiralty Inlet. The parade grounds and officers' quarters were featured in the film *An Officer and a Gentleman*. At the northeastern tip of the park is Point Wilson Lighthouse, the tallest on Puget Sound.

Port Townsend is home to a vibrant seafaring culture. The Northwest Maritime Center features a boat workshop and a world-class pilot simulator. Visit the Boat Haven to see hundred-year-old vessels in storage, or take a walk around the Point Hudson Marina. The city hosts the Wooden Boat Festival every September and is also the starting point for the Race to Alaska (R2AK), a human-powered-vessel dash to Ketchikan.

OTHER DESTINATIONS

Just beyond Port Townsend is bucolic Marrowstone Island, connected to the mainland by a narrow isthmus. At the tip is Fort Flagler Historical State Park, great for a beachside stroll. Farther south, though technically just outside the rain shadow boundary, is Port Ludlow, home of a luxurious modern resort. Finally, a quick jaunt across the floating Hood Canal Bridge will take you to Port Gamble. This tiny community is chock-full of impeccably restored Victorian buildings. From here, if you choose not to continue along Highway 101, it's easy to head south along the Kitsap Peninsula to catch ferries to Seattle (page 176) from Bainbridge Island or Bremerton.

▲ One of the most popular ways to see the lavender fields is by hot-air balloon; tours depart from Sequim.

▶ Port Townsend's historic district includes about seven hundred homes and sixty commercial and civic buildings.

THE Home Stretch

QUILCENE TO OLYMPIA

After Sequim, Highway 101 makes one last big right turn, forcing you to head south in order to complete your northward journey. This last stretch of historic highway doesn't get the visitors that the rest of the peninsula does, but it's well worth a closer look.

FJORDELIGHTFUL

Most of the eastern side of the Olympic Peninsula is dominated by Hood Canal, an honest-to-goodness fjord. The only path across is the Hood Canal Bridge at the northern end—so if you're thinking of cutting over and catching a ferry to Seattle (page 176), you'll need to decide before Port Townsend. Meanwhile, the last leg of Highway 101 is squeezed precariously between the water and the mountainside, offering unforgettable views of the canal and its wetlands from a number of WPA-era bridges and hairpin turns. Watch out for logging trucks, a common sight here, and make use of the vehicle turnouts to avoid traffic piling up behind you.

PLAY THE NAME GAME

As you head south, you'll pass a number of places with unusual names: Quilcene (pronounced "QUILL-seen"), Dosewallips ("doe-see-WALL-ups"), Duckabush, Lilliwaup. If you're hungry for oysters, there's only one name you need remember: the famous Hama Hama Company. Look for the monster middens of oyster shells piled high by the roadside near Lilliwaup.

STRAIT OF JUAN DE FUCA

SEQUIM

PORT TOWNSEND

20

19

PUGET SOUND

104

PORT GAMBLE

N

101

305

QUILCENE

HOOD CANAL BRIDGE

OLYMPIC NATIONAL PARK

3

BAINBRIDGE ISLAND

TO SEATTLE FERRY

BRINNON

HOOD CANAL

HAMA HAMA COMPANY

KITSAP PENINSULA

BREMERTON

STAIRCASE

LAKE CUSHMAN

LILLIWAUP

SEATTLE FERRY

3

16

HOODSPORT

BELFAIR

106

3

TACOMA

SHELTON

DETAIL

5

OLYMPIA (END OF 101)

ELD INLET

101

DETAIL

BUDD INLET

8

OLD 101 ROUTE TERMINUS

OLYMPIA

FOURTH AVENUE (OLD 99)

MUD BAY ROAD EXIT

HARRISON AVENUE (OLD 101)

CAPITOL WAY (OLD 99)

101

5

STAIRWAY TO HEAVEN

Near the elbow of Hood Canal lies a nearly unknown corner of Olympic National Park (page 94). This section of the park, called Staircase, features a number of subalpine hiking trails and campsites in the old-growth forests surrounding Mount Ellinor. Adjacent Lake Cushman was originally referred to by the Quinault people as "the lake with the monster." Whether or not you spot any water monsters, you'll want to take care on the road in. Staircase can be reached only by the mostly unpaved Lake Cushman Road, heading west from Hoodsport.

CHRISTMAS TOWN USA

At Shelton, Highway 101 finally turns back into a limited-access freeway for the first time since Northern California. Located on Oakland Bay, the westernmost inlet of Puget Sound, Shelton dubbed itself Christmas Town USA in the 1950s, in honor of the seven million Christmas trees it shipped around the country each year. The star of Shelton's annual Christmas parade is a giant Muffler Man statue (page 21) dressed as Paul Bunyan.

THE LAST MILE

At the end of more than 1,500 road miles through three states, Highway 101 ends rather unceremoniously, swallowed up by modern-day Interstate 5. To end your epic journey with a bit more fanfare, exit at Mud Bay Road and follow the original, prefreeway highway alignment into Olympia (page 170). The terminus of historic Highway 101 is at the intersection of Fourth Avenue and Capitol Way downtown—which, incidentally, connects you directly to old Highway 99, the subject of Part Two of this book (page 106).

▲ Consider a late-night summer kayak outing on Hood Canal. When conditions are right, bioluminescent phytoplankton light up the nighttime waters with an astonishing glow.

▼ Accommodations along the fjord make it easy to explore by boat—in Hoodsport there's even a motel that caters to paddlers.

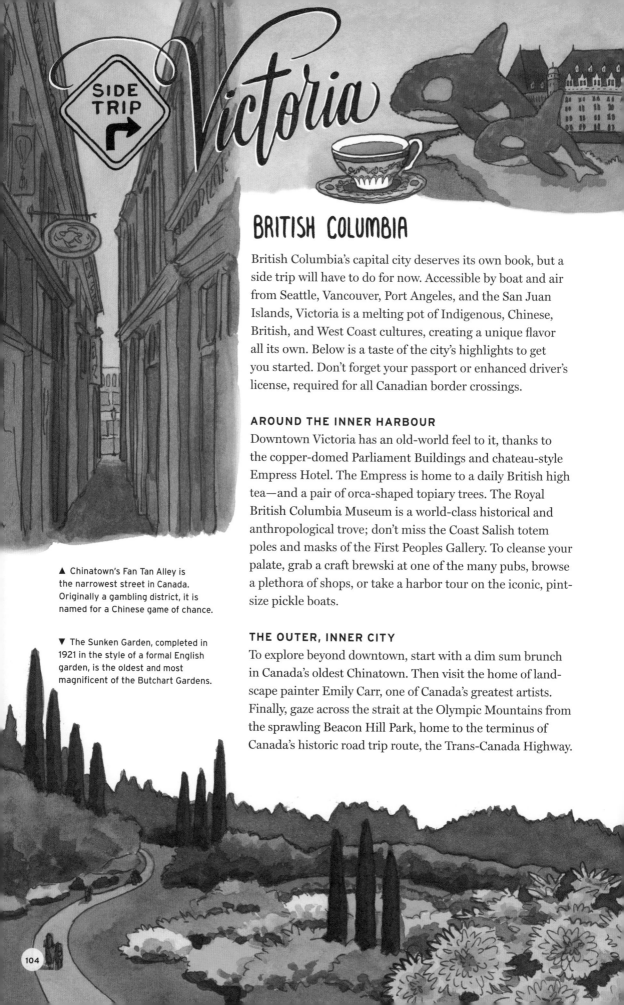

Victoria

BRITISH COLUMBIA

British Columbia's capital city deserves its own book, but a side trip will have to do for now. Accessible by boat and air from Seattle, Vancouver, Port Angeles, and the San Juan Islands, Victoria is a melting pot of Indigenous, Chinese, British, and West Coast cultures, creating a unique flavor all its own. Below is a taste of the city's highlights to get you started. Don't forget your passport or enhanced driver's license, required for all Canadian border crossings.

AROUND THE INNER HARBOUR

Downtown Victoria has an old-world feel to it, thanks to the copper-domed Parliament Buildings and chateau-style Empress Hotel. The Empress is home to a daily British high tea—and a pair of orca-shaped topiary trees. The Royal British Columbia Museum is a world-class historical and anthropological trove; don't miss the Coast Salish totem poles and masks of the First Peoples Gallery. To cleanse your palate, grab a craft brewski at one of the many pubs, browse a plethora of shops, or take a harbor tour on the iconic, pint-size pickle boats.

THE OUTER, INNER CITY

To explore beyond downtown, start with a dim sum brunch in Canada's oldest Chinatown. Then visit the home of land-scape painter Emily Carr, one of Canada's greatest artists. Finally, gaze across the strait at the Olympic Mountains from the sprawling Beacon Hill Park, home to the terminus of Canada's historic road trip route, the Trans-Canada Highway.

▲ Chinatown's Fan Tan Alley is the narrowest street in Canada. Originally a gambling district, it is named for a Chinese game of chance.

▼ The Sunken Garden, completed in 1921 in the style of a formal English garden, is the oldest and most magnificent of the Butchart Gardens.

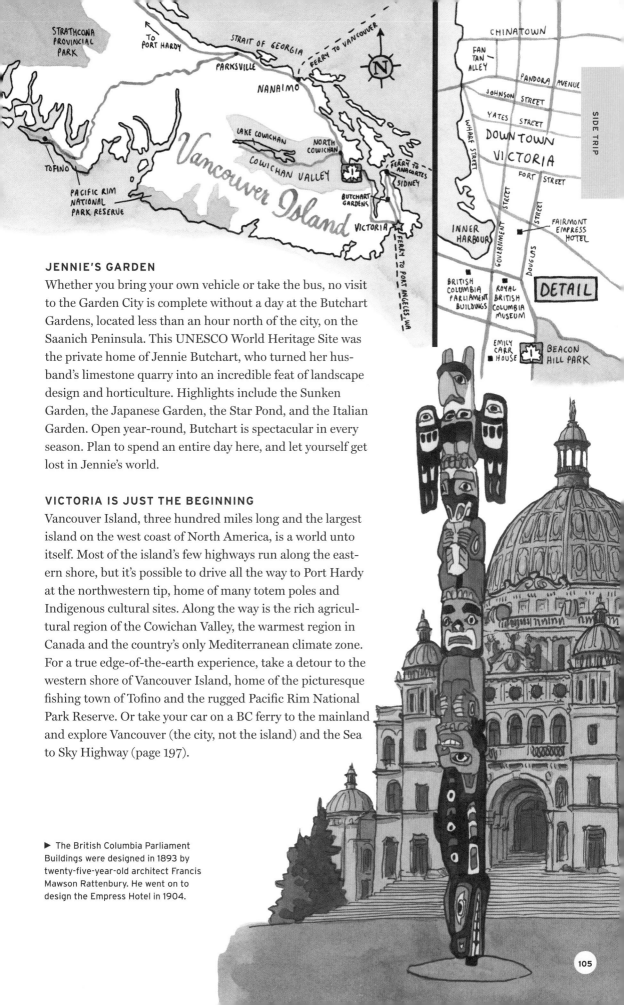

JENNIE'S GARDEN

Whether you bring your own vehicle or take the bus, no visit to the Garden City is complete without a day at the Butchart Gardens, located less than an hour north of the city, on the Saanich Peninsula. This UNESCO World Heritage Site was the private home of Jennie Butchart, who turned her husband's limestone quarry into an incredible feat of landscape design and horticulture. Highlights include the Sunken Garden, the Japanese Garden, the Star Pond, and the Italian Garden. Open year-round, Butchart is spectacular in every season. Plan to spend an entire day here, and let yourself get lost in Jennie's world.

VICTORIA IS JUST THE BEGINNING

Vancouver Island, three hundred miles long and the largest island on the west coast of North America, is a world unto itself. Most of the island's few highways run along the eastern shore, but it's possible to drive all the way to Port Hardy at the northwestern tip, home of many totem poles and Indigenous cultural sites. Along the way is the rich agricultural region of the Cowichan Valley, the warmest region in Canada and the country's only Mediterranean climate zone. For a true edge-of-the-earth experience, take a detour to the western shore of Vancouver Island, home of the picturesque fishing town of Tofino and the rugged Pacific Rim National Park Reserve. Or take your car on a BC ferry to the mainland and explore Vancouver (the city, not the island) and the Sea to Sky Highway (page 197).

▶ The British Columbia Parliament Buildings were designed in 1893 by twenty-five-year-old architect Francis Mawson Rattenbury. He went on to design the Empress Hotel in 1904.

105

PART TWO

The Inland COAST

Though it may not get the attention that the coastal routes do, the inland route along historic Highway 99 takes you to the West Coast's most diverse destinations, including all the wildly varied climate regions—plus all three state capitals. You'll visit searing deserts and alpine peaks, barren plains and inland seas, the largest cities and the smallest towns, from ancient history to the wave of the future.

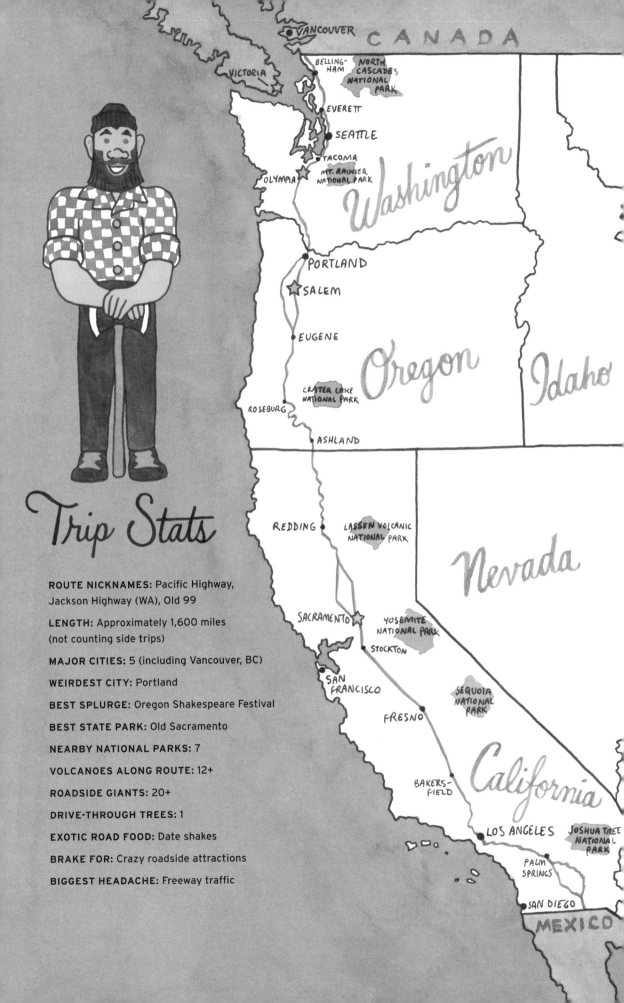

Trip Stats

ROUTE NICKNAMES: Pacific Highway, Jackson Highway (WA), Old 99

LENGTH: Approximately 1,600 miles (not counting side trips)

MAJOR CITIES: 5 (including Vancouver, BC)

WEIRDEST CITY: Portland

BEST SPLURGE: Oregon Shakespeare Festival

BEST STATE PARK: Old Sacramento

NEARBY NATIONAL PARKS: 7

VOLCANOES ALONG ROUTE: 12+

ROADSIDE GIANTS: 20+

DRIVE-THROUGH TREES: 1

EXOTIC ROAD FOOD: Date shakes

BRAKE FOR: Crazy roadside attractions

BIGGEST HEADACHE: Freeway traffic

◀ While the interstate roars past the town of Dunsmuir, California, a stretch of old Highway 99 remains untouched as the town's main thoroughfare.

An Old-School Road Trip

Unlike Highways 1 and 101, traveling the inland coast takes a bit of sleuthing. Much like America's most famous historic highway, Route 66, Old 99 has been decommissioned as a US highway and, in places, subsumed by the modern interstate highway system. While it is no longer possible to travel every mile of the old route from border to border, the vast majority of Highway 99 is still drivable. Map nerds and history buffs will love delving into the intricacies of tracing old highway alignments and variations as they travel between major cities off the beaten path. The reward is a huge number of attractions and landmarks that the interstate would cause you to miss.

For speed and ease of navigation, you may choose to cherry-pick certain sections of road to plan your trip, using major highways to zoom between destinations. Part Two keeps Highway 99 as its main focal point but notes wherever it is difficult or impossible to avoid the interstate. The most notable places are east and north of Los Angeles (pages 118 and 126); northernmost California (page 142); the mountains south of Eugene, Oregon (page 150); southern Washington (page 168); and the military area between Olympia and Tacoma (page 172). For each of these areas, the easiest route is chosen for you and noted in the text. On the maps, the historic highway is highlighted in red, with any interstate freeways or other alternate routes clearly marked. This allows you to pick and choose your route to hit your desired destinations along the way.

A word of caution: though it will guide your inland coast route, this book is not a substitute for a proper map or detailed atlas. The maps in this section are merely a basic overview of the historic routes (there's a list of alternate routes and connectors on page 200). In many places, particularly in major cities and some of the more mountainous regions, you'll need turn-by-turn directions if you want to follow old Highway 99 to the letter.

◀ Keep a sharp eye out for the pine and palm trees near Madera. The trees were planted side by side to mark the symbolic boundary between Northern and Southern California.

THE GOLDEN STATE

Like Part One, this section is oriented from south to north, starting all the way down in Calexico, California, just one block shy of the Mexican border. Highway 99 makes a nine-hundred-mile trek through California, starting in the remote Salton Sink, a desert basin located hundreds of feet below sea level. From there you turn almost due west for more than a hundred miles, from the mirage-like Palm Springs all the way to the immense sprawl of Los Angeles. Then you'll turn north once more, weaving your way through the San Gabriel Mountains and into the Central Valley, California's enormous inland growing region.

For the next four hundred or so miles, Highway 99 cuts a nearly straight line, bisecting the state and creating a major farm-to-market arterial for thousands of families and businesses. Sacramento, the state capital, is the embodiment of this, originally home to a number of vegetable canneries—which earned it the nickname of the Big Tomato. Even the roadside attractions in the Central Valley are agricultural in nature, from giant olives and milk jugs to rural tours of orange blossoms and almond orchards. During the midcentury golden age of family road trips, roadside farm stands were nearly equal in status to amusement parks, and parched travelers quenched their thirst with an ice-cold glass of orange juice from the now-defunct statewide chain Giant Orange. (You can still find a few of these big fruits around, in Riverside, Chowchilla, Shasta Lake, and other places.)

Though most modern road trippers yearn to cross through "boring" places like the Central Valley as quickly as possible, a slight shift of perspective reveals the vast beauty of the landscape and the pleasing geometry of fields and orchards. Highway 99 reveals the best of these things to the observant traveler—as well as a glimpse of what it was like to travel decades ago, during the golden age of American road trips.

▲ California's famous orange groves, long gone from the Los Angeles area, now thrive just east of the Highway 99 corridor, near Tulare.

▶ Despite the restoration of some cult favorites, historic Highway 99 landmarks continue to disappear at an alarming rate, victims of decay or development.

THE PACIFIC NORTHWEST

▼ At the time of this book's publication, the elevated Alaskan Way Viaduct freeway, built in 1953 to carry Highway 99 along the Seattle waterfront, is being replaced by a tunnel.

After Sacramento, you won't see a good-size city again until Portland, Oregon. The area in between is the mountain wonderland of the Cascades, a chain of volcanoes from Mount Shasta in California to southern British Columbia, Canada. Near Eugene, Oregon, Highway 99 spits you out into the fertile Willamette Valley. Welcome to Oregon Trail country, the destination and dream for the many thousands of white settlers who crossed the American West in search of the land of milk and honey. The Oregon Territory was the embodiment of Manifest Destiny, the idea that Americans had the God-given right to extend their boundaries from sea to shining sea. Settlers began flocking to the Northwest shortly after Lewis and Clark found their way to the Pacific Ocean (page 88), so the Willamette Valley has been farmed by white settlers for over two hundred years.

The new-world utopia of Cascadia came with its own host of problems, however—starting with the displacement and genocide of many Indigenous peoples. After statehood, communities expelled the Chinese laborers who had built the railroads that brought white people westward. Oregon was notorious for its exclusion of African Americans: it was illegal for them to live there at all until 1926, and the state didn't ratify 1870's fifteenth amendment of the Constitution (granting Black citizens the right to vote) until 1959. During World War II, the military imprisoned Japanese American families in inland internment camps, while their property was sold out from under them by whites. This history continues to play out today: Portland and Seattle are overwhelmingly white, and old laws continue to make it difficult for minority groups to prosper. Yet while the interstate tears through historic minority enclaves in a destructive swath of eminent domain, Highway 99 connects them—creating a link to the past, as well as a path forward.

THE NORTHERN REACHES

In contrast to the remote Rain Coast along Highway 101, the inland route through western Washington State is positively action packed—and feels even more coastal than the *actual* coastal route. Much of Highway 99 (the Pacific Highway) hugs the shoreline of the Salish Sea, from the state capital of Olympia all the way to the Canadian border. In Seattle you get the sense that the completion of your journey is drawing near—or else that another adventure beckons. If the constant summer presence of cruise ships doesn't give you a clue, Seattle is the gateway to Alaska, and for the remainder of Highway 99 there are numerous chances to expand your trip by car, boat, or plane. If you can resist the call of the far north, though, the Pacific Highway will reward you with mountain vistas, rainbow flower fields, and access to a number of island getaways. Unlike the nondescript southern terminus in California, Highway 99 ends with a celebration, at the Peace Arch on the Canadian border.

▲ With its stone parapets, Highway 99 affords a jaw-dropping view of horseshoe-shaped Willamette Falls, the largest (by volume) waterfall in the Pacific Northwest.

▼ Highway 99 through Seattle is a collage of time, juxtaposing midcentury relics with ultramodern high-rises and a rapidly changing city skyline.

AMERICANA AT YOUR FINGERTIPS

Interstate 5 can speed you from Mexico to Canada in just over twenty-four straight hours. Yet the inland coast has so much to see and discover that you could devote an entire season to exploring every nook and cranny along the way. If you have a little patience and a sense of adventure, Highway 99 can give you a sense of the West Coast the locals know and love. In this way, a Pacific Highway road trip transforms an ordinary vacation into a tribute to the open road.

HEAT
& Hallelujah
THE LOW DESERT

▲ The eastern shore of the Salton Sea is littered with ghosts from its brief heyday as a destination for water-skiers, recreational fishermen, and bird-watchers.

▼ The painted marker on a sugar plant near Brawley is a visceral reminder of just how low the Low Desert lies.

SEA LEVEL

Your trip up historic Highway 99 begins in the Low Desert, an impossibly hot swath of California that lies below sea level. The corner of First Street and Heffernan Avenue in the tiny border town of Calexico is the historic terminus of Highway 99, marked with a small, sun-faded sign. Once the main international crossing to Mexicali, the checkpoint has moved a few blocks west. What remains at this now-sleepy corner is the hundred-year-old Sam Ellis department store, a 1930s-era former customs house, and the traffic noise of cars entering the United States on the other side of the tall wrought-iron fence.

Imperial Avenue will take you northward out of town, along what is now State Route 111, and through a series of Imperial Valley farming towns. If you'd prefer to stick to 99's original path, choose adjacent State Route 86, which zooms up the western shore of the Salton Sea. But the more scenic—and stranger—of the two routes is 111, which meanders along the eastern shore.

HOLY GROUND

The first stop on 111 actually requires a short detour into the desert northeast of Niland. Out here stands one man's personal monument to God, Salvation Mountain: part church, part fantasy, part hallucination. Built entirely of hay bales, sand, car parts, and house paint, Leonard Knight's creation is living folk art. Trails meander over, under, and through the fifty-foot-tall scripture-scrawled hunk of brimstone, but beware: you're being watched. Knight died in 2014, but his spirit (or a caretaker in an RV) rebukes wayward pilgrims over a loudspeaker.

RIVIERA OF THE DAMNED

The centerpiece of the Imperial Valley is the Salton Sea, California's largest lake (actually a man-made mistake). In 1905 engineers cut into the Colorado River to boost an irrigation channel. The diversion overwhelmed the canal, and for two *years* water flowed into the Salton Sink, creating a land-locked salt lake two hundred feet below sea level.

Both aquaculture and tourism followed; by the 1950s the Salton Sea was home to massive fish farms and a booming resort industry. Agricultural runoff and climate change, however, wiped out this new riviera within a few decades. Today the lake is receding fast, with the waterline losing half a foot of height a year. As it shrinks, the Salton Sea increases in salinity, killing the fish and leaving behind a toxic chemical brine. The shore is now lined with abandoned motels and modular homes—and thousands of tilapia skeletons.

BANANA YOUR DREAMS

It may sound odd, but a frozen banana feels like manna from heaven after all this desert hellfire and apocalyptic salt. You can score one of these roadside treats at the International Banana Museum, which also has a huge collection of banana memorabilia and ephemera.

THE MIDDLE EAST OF THE GOLDEN WEST

As you leave the Salton Sea behind, the sudden presence of heavily irrigated farms marks the transition to the Coachella Valley. Most noticeable are the stands of date palms near the aptly named town of Mecca. After all, this is one of the few regions outside the Middle East and North Africa capable of cultivating exotic date crops.

GO WANDERING IN THE DESERT

For even more Low Desert adventures, see the Imperial Sand Dunes (east of Brawley), filming location for *The Return of the Jedi* and *Stargate*. From Mecca, a scenic route leads to the backside of Joshua Tree National Park (page 116). And of course, you could expand your trip into Baja California (it's possible to drive all the way to Cabo San Lucas, another thousand miles, starting in Mexicali—but that's a story for another book).

▶ Salvation Mountain has been the setting of an endless array of music videos. Expect to share your visit with sequin-bedecked rockers and Steadicam filmmakers.

SOUTHERN CALIFORNIA

Midcentury Modern

PALM SPRINGS

Just north of Mecca, Highways 86 and 111 cross. While 86 gets swallowed up by Interstate 10, 111 follows the former Highway 99 alignment through the Coachella Valley, toward Palm Springs. The farms and roadside fruit stands that used to line the highway here have been replaced by twenty-five miles of suburban sprawl and traffic lights, so it's understandable if you want to skip the old route and jump on the interstate for a bit.

CHEAP DATE

Still, sticking to the slow road has its own rewards, including the best place to sample a legendary California date shake (a milkshake made with Medjool or Deglet Noor dates). Shields Date Garden began in 1924 as one of the earliest date farms in the valley. To stand out from the competition, Floyd Shields developed his own date hybrids and invented and sold both date sugar and a powdered version of the fruit he called date crystals.

GARDEN OF DELIGHTS

While the admission fee is slightly outside the cheap-date zone, the Living Desert Zoo and Gardens in Palm Desert is a great place to explore the differences between the High and Low Deserts. Exhibits include North American as well as African plants and animals. The zoo is also close to the start of State Route 74, known as the Palms to Pines Scenic Byway (page 117).

DESERT OASIS

At last, you reach your real destination: the shimmering oasis of Palm Springs. Its hot springs made it a winter settlement for the native Cahuilla people and an early-1900s resort spot for health tourists in need of dry air. By the 1920s it was a playground for movie stars, but the post–World War II development of air-conditioning made the population explode.

▲ Even though the ocean is just a few hours away, Palm Springs has been known for a century as a destination for luxury swimming pools.

▼ While you sip your date shake at Shields Date Garden, stay for a free viewing of Floyd Shields' 1950 film, *Romance & the Sex Life of the Date*.

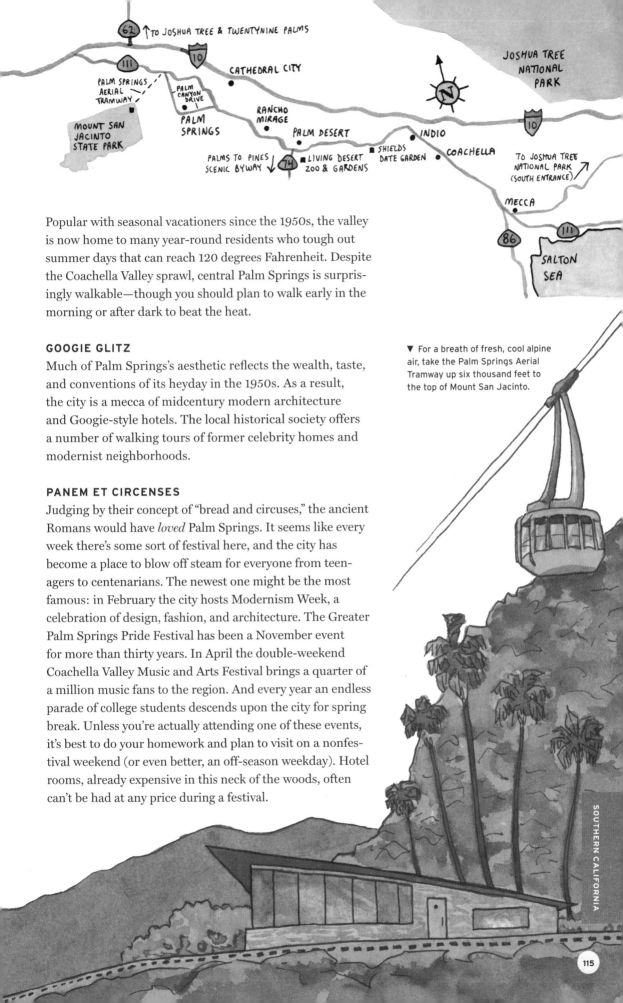

62 ↑TO JOSHUA TREE & TWENTYNINE PALMS

10

111

CATHEDRAL CITY

JOSHUA TREE
NATIONAL
PARK

PALM SPRINGS
AERIAL
TRAMWAY

PALM
CANYON
DRIVE

N

MOUNT SAN
JACINTO
STATE PARK

PALM
SPRINGS

RANCHO
MIRAGE

PALM DESERT

INDIO

10

PALMS TO PINES
SCENIC BYWAY

74

LIVING DESERT
ZOO & GARDENS

SHIELDS
DATE GARDEN

COACHELLA

TO JOSHUA TREE
NATIONAL PARK
(SOUTH ENTRANCE)

MECCA

86

111

SALTON
SEA

Popular with seasonal vacationers since the 1950s, the valley is now home to many year-round residents who tough out summer days that can reach 120 degrees Fahrenheit. Despite the Coachella Valley sprawl, central Palm Springs is surprisingly walkable—though you should plan to walk early in the morning or after dark to beat the heat.

GOOGIE GLITZ

Much of Palm Springs's aesthetic reflects the wealth, taste, and conventions of its heyday in the 1950s. As a result, the city is a mecca of midcentury modern architecture and Googie-style hotels. The local historical society offers a number of walking tours of former celebrity homes and modernist neighborhoods.

PANEM ET CIRCENSES

Judging by their concept of "bread and circuses," the ancient Romans would have *loved* Palm Springs. It seems like every week there's some sort of festival here, and the city has become a place to blow off steam for everyone from teenagers to centenarians. The newest one might be the most famous: in February the city hosts Modernism Week, a celebration of design, fashion, and architecture. The Greater Palm Springs Pride Festival has been a November event for more than thirty years. In April the double-weekend Coachella Valley Music and Arts Festival brings a quarter of a million music fans to the region. And every year an endless parade of college students descends upon the city for spring break. Unless you're actually attending one of these events, it's best to do your homework and plan to visit on a nonfestival weekend (or even better, an off-season weekday). Hotel rooms, already expensive in this neck of the woods, often can't be had at any price during a festival.

▼ For a breath of fresh, cool alpine air, take the Palm Springs Aerial Tramway up six thousand feet to the top of Mount San Jacinto.

SOUTHERN CALIFORNIA

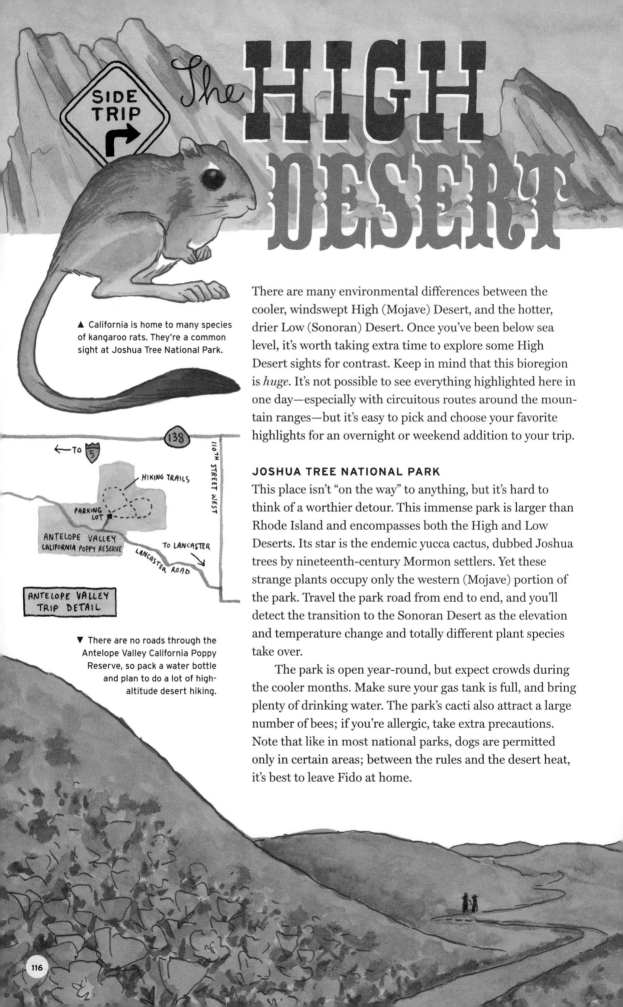

SIDE TRIP →

The HIGH DESERT

▲ California is home to many species of kangaroo rats. They're a common sight at Joshua Tree National Park.

138

← TO 5

110TH STREET WEST

HIKING TRAILS

PARKING LOT

ANTELOPE VALLEY CALIFORNIA POPPY RESERVE

TO LANCASTER

LANCASTER ROAD

ANTELOPE VALLEY TRIP DETAIL

▼ There are no roads through the Antelope Valley California Poppy Reserve, so pack a water bottle and plan to do a lot of high-altitude desert hiking.

There are many environmental differences between the cooler, windswept High (Mojave) Desert, and the hotter, drier Low (Sonoran) Desert. Once you've been below sea level, it's worth taking extra time to explore some High Desert sights for contrast. Keep in mind that this bioregion is *huge*. It's not possible to see everything highlighted here in one day—especially with circuitous routes around the mountain ranges—but it's easy to pick and choose your favorite highlights for an overnight or weekend addition to your trip.

JOSHUA TREE NATIONAL PARK

This place isn't "on the way" to anything, but it's hard to think of a worthier detour. This immense park is larger than Rhode Island and encompasses both the High and Low Deserts. Its star is the endemic yucca cactus, dubbed Joshua trees by nineteenth-century Mormon settlers. Yet these strange plants occupy only the western (Mojave) portion of the park. Travel the park road from end to end, and you'll detect the transition to the Sonoran Desert as the elevation and temperature change and totally different plant species take over.

The park is open year-round, but expect crowds during the cooler months. Make sure your gas tank is full, and bring plenty of drinking water. The park's cacti also attract a large number of bees; if you're allergic, take extra precautions. Note that like in most national parks, dogs are permitted only in certain areas; between the rules and the desert heat, it's best to leave Fido at home.

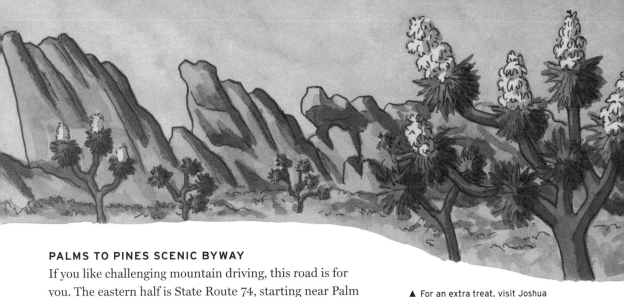

PALMS TO PINES SCENIC BYWAY

If you like challenging mountain driving, this road is for you. The eastern half is State Route 74, starting near Palm Springs; the other half is State Route 243 to Banning. The route covers sixty-seven twisty miles and five thousand feet of elevation over the San Jacinto Mountains, contrasting alpine forests with the desert floor of the Coachella Valley. Bring lots of layered clothing; temperatures can range from over one hundred degrees in the valley to freezing with snow at the highest elevations. Drive with extreme caution here! This is a popular route, and not every driver knows what they're doing; this road averages more than two hundred accidents a year, mostly due to speeding drivers and a handful of sharp curves that lack guardrails.

ANTELOPE VALLEY CALIFORNIA POPPY RESERVE

Located in the western reaches of the Mojave Desert, this state reserve is more of an arid plain than a barren desert. Visit when conditions are right, and you'll be rewarded with a vast landscape carpeted with uncountable wild California poppies, the state flower. Luck is the key factor here, though. The bloom season runs from February to May, but the timing, amount, and duration of the winter rains determine the number of flowers—or whether any appear at all. Check the park website for frequent bloom updates.

▲ For an extra treat, visit Joshua Tree National Park in the spring to see the namesake cacti and other plants in full bloom.

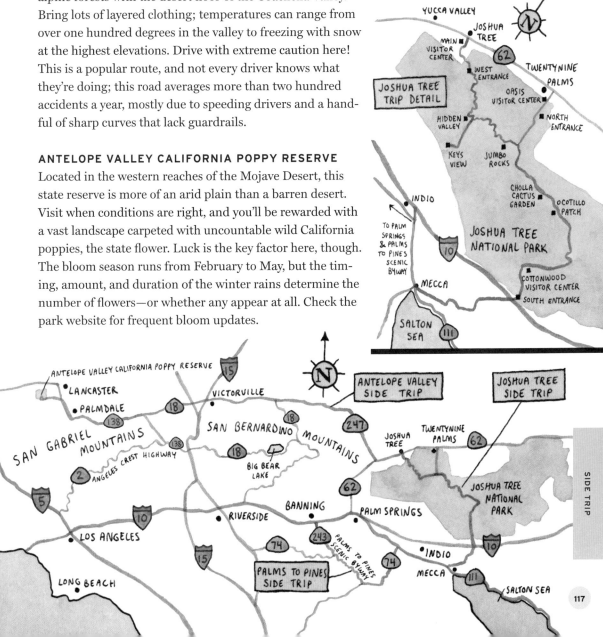

THE INLAND Empire

CABAZON TO RIVERSIDE

West of Palm Springs, the elevation climbs, and the landscape makes a subtle shift from the desert to a succession of fertile, arid valleys. This is the Inland Empire, an eighty-mile swath of urban and suburban sprawl east of Los Angeles that was once home to a vast network of fruit and produce farms. Here, historic Highway 99 paralleled the famous Route 66—though while 66 still survives along Foothill Boulevard, Highway 99 has been subsumed by freeways. Unless you feel like exploring Route 66 all the way to LA (which is worth doing), it's easiest just to take the freeway between attractions.

DINO YOU ARE, BUT WHAT AM I?

Just west of Palm Springs, stop at Cabazon, where a pair of life-size roadside dinosaurs towers over San Gorgonio Pass and marks the entrance to the Inland Empire. These guys are actually buildings designed by Claude Bell, former chief sculptor for the Knott's Berry Farm theme park. The dinos achieved cult status with the 1985 film *Pee-Wee's Big Adventure* and also appeared in the opening credits of 1983's *National Lampoon's Vacation*.

A TREE GROWS IN RIVERSIDE

Before it earned the Inland Empire moniker, the valley stretching between Redlands and Pasadena was known as the Orange Empire for its endless groves of citrus trees. In 1873 some cuttings from a new variety of Brazilian orange tree were shipped to settler Eliza Tibbets. She successfully grafted the branches, and the Washington navel orange was born. The navel launched a second gold rush in California, with growers grabbing land and cashing in on public demand for citrus. Eliza's parent tree, the ancestor of every navel orange ever grown in the state, still stands on Magnolia Avenue in Riverside.

▲ At the entrance to California Citrus State Historic Park is a former Giant Orange stand; another stands on Route 66 in nearby Fontana.

▼ Ironically, the Cabazon Dinosaurs have evolved under new ownership and now house a creationist museum and religious gift shop.

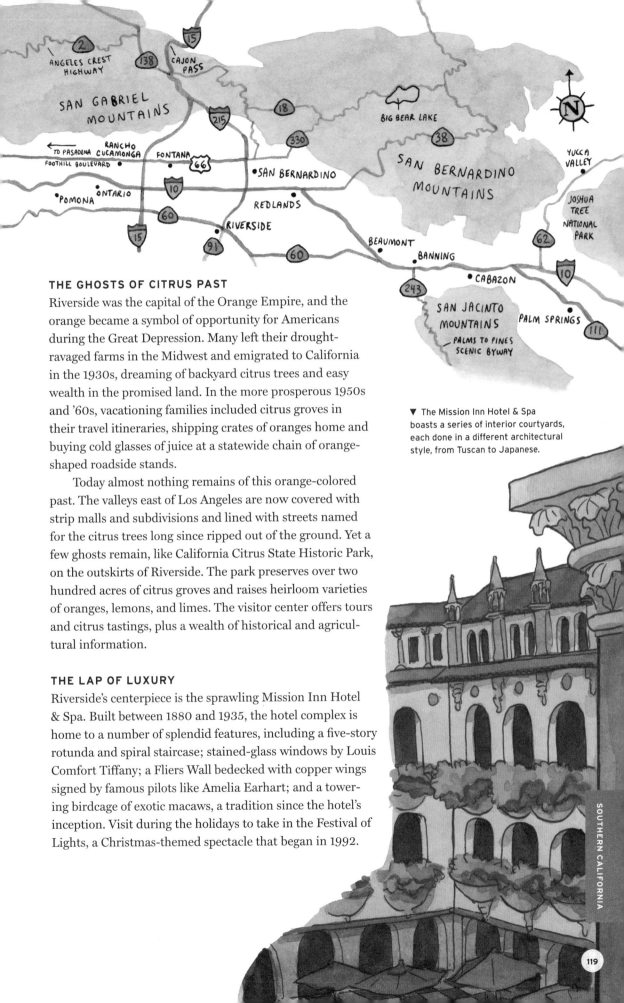

ANGELES CREST HIGHWAY

SAN GABRIEL MOUNTAINS

← TO PASADENA
FOOTHILL BOULEVARD

RANCHO CUCAMONGA FONTANA

CAJON PASS

BIG BEAR LAKE

SAN BERNARDINO MOUNTAINS

YUCCA VALLEY

•SAN BERNARDINO

•POMONA •ONTARIO

REDLANDS

•RIVERSIDE

BEAUMONT

BANNING

•CABAZON

JOSHUA TREE NATIONAL PARK

SAN JACINTO MOUNTAINS

PALM SPRINGS

— PALMS TO PINES SCENIC BYWAY

THE GHOSTS OF CITRUS PAST

Riverside was the capital of the Orange Empire, and the orange became a symbol of opportunity for Americans during the Great Depression. Many left their drought-ravaged farms in the Midwest and emigrated to California in the 1930s, dreaming of backyard citrus trees and easy wealth in the promised land. In the more prosperous 1950s and '60s, vacationing families included citrus groves in their travel itineraries, shipping crates of oranges home and buying cold glasses of juice at a statewide chain of orange-shaped roadside stands.

Today almost nothing remains of this orange-colored past. The valleys east of Los Angeles are now covered with strip malls and subdivisions and lined with streets named for the citrus trees long since ripped out of the ground. Yet a few ghosts remain, like California Citrus State Historic Park, on the outskirts of Riverside. The park preserves over two hundred acres of citrus groves and raises heirloom varieties of oranges, lemons, and limes. The visitor center offers tours and citrus tastings, plus a wealth of historical and agricultural information.

THE LAP OF LUXURY

Riverside's centerpiece is the sprawling Mission Inn Hotel & Spa. Built between 1880 and 1935, the hotel complex is home to a number of splendid features, including a five-story rotunda and spiral staircase; stained-glass windows by Louis Comfort Tiffany; a Fliers Wall bedecked with copper wings signed by famous pilots like Amelia Earhart; and a towering birdcage of exotic macaws, a tradition since the hotel's inception. Visit during the holidays to take in the Festival of Lights, a Christmas-themed spectacle that began in 1992.

▼ The Mission Inn Hotel & Spa boasts a series of interior courtyards, each done in a different architectural style, from Tuscan to Japanese.

SOUTHERN CALIFORNIA

Coming Up ROSES

THE SAN GABRIEL VALLEY

Before you pull into Los Angeles proper, it's worth stopping at a few suburban destinations. If you followed Route 66 into town, you'll find yourself on Colorado Boulevard, the main drag through Pasadena. And while the city gets the most attention in January of each year, there are reasons to visit at any time.

ROSES ON PARADE

If you like a party on the scale of the Thanksgiving Day Parade in New York, Pasadena's Tournament of Roses Parade is for you. Held on New Year's Day each year (or January 2 if the holiday falls on a Sunday) just before the Rose Bowl football game, the Rose Parade is a floral feast for the senses. Sidewalk vantage points are free, but with over half a million fellow visitors camping out on New Year's Eve, it's worth purchasing advance tickets for the grandstand. Even if you can't get here for New Year's, head to the Rose Bowl anyway—the stadium is home to the world's craziest Sunday flea market.

BRICKS AND BUNGALOWS

Pasadena is also home to an impressive array of early-twentieth-century architecture. Downtown boasts a number of art-deco-style commercial buildings, including the Hotel

▲ In order to be included, Rose Parade floats must be decorated only with unaltered natural materials, such as flowers, seeds, nuts, shells, and feathers.

▼ The Gamble House, near Rose Bowl Stadium, stands in as Doc Brown's home in the *Back to the Future* trilogy.

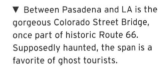

Constance, the Warner Building, and the Royal Laundry building. Bungalow Heaven is a tree-lined residential enclave boasting over eight hundred houses built in the craftsman style. The entire neighborhood is listed on the National Register of Historic Places and hosts a public tour every April.

MANUSCRIPTS AND MAGNOLIAS

If you'd like to spend a day in quiet contemplation, look no farther than San Marino, home of the Huntington Library, Art Collection, and Botanical Gardens. Like J. Paul Getty of the Getty Villa (page 22), Henry Huntington was an industry tycoon who devoted much of his wealth to collecting art and rare manuscripts. Today these collections are open to the public as part of a world-class museum, surrounded by a variety of formal gardens that compose the Huntingtons' two-hundred-acre estate. The Huntington is an engrossing experience—plan to spend some serious time here.

SECRET MISSION

If Highway 101 gave you a taste for the California missions (page 5), you can cross one more off your list at San Gabriel Arcángel, perched near the original alignment of Highway 99. This is, unfortunately, the most overlooked mission in the chain; the earthquake-damaged property hasn't been spruced up the way Mission Carmel or La Purísima have. Still, the Moorish-style structure is worth the visit, and the only crowds you're likely to encounter are regular Sunday churchgoers.

▼ Between Pasadena and LA is the gorgeous Colorado Street Bridge, once part of historic Route 66. Supposedly haunted, the span is a favorite of ghost tourists.

Los Angeles

Equal parts glitz, glamour, and grit, the West Coast's largest city is a constant play between rich and poor, scenic and seedy, celebrity and ordinary. The old highways offer a unique perspective for exploring this vast burg—but whichever path or itinerary you choose, be prepared to meet California's most ferocious traffic.

▼ LA's film industry leaves its mark far beyond the boundaries of Hollywood. Downtown still boasts twelve historic movie palaces that line the length of Broadway.

ALL ROADS LEAD TO LA

Every one of the West Coast's historic highways converges in Los Angeles. Tracing these old routes, though, takes a bit of sleuthing. "The 99" (locals add a "the" in front of highway numbers) has changed its urban alignment so many times over the past century that it's almost impossible to trace at all. Further complicating things is the labyrinthine freeway spaghetti bowl that snakes through the city. To start with a clean slate, pick a route and head downtown. From San Gabriel, Valley Boulevard (Old 99) will feed you right onto Main Street. Or from Pasadena, take Figueroa to Broadway, where Route 66 and Highway 99 share a path for a short distance.

LET'S GO OUT TO THE LOBBY

Broadway is a canyon of neon signs and theater marquees— the first sign that you are in the city that cinema built. While studios made the films out in Hollywood, downtown is where people flocked to see their creations—first at organ-piped silent-movie palaces, and then at the new talkie houses. This strip was once home to the highest concentration of movie theaters on earth, with a capacity of fifteen thousand seats by 1931. After World War II, audiences switched loyalties to the newer movie palaces in Hollywood, and the Broadway Theatre District fell into decline. In recent years, however, preservation efforts have set their sights here.

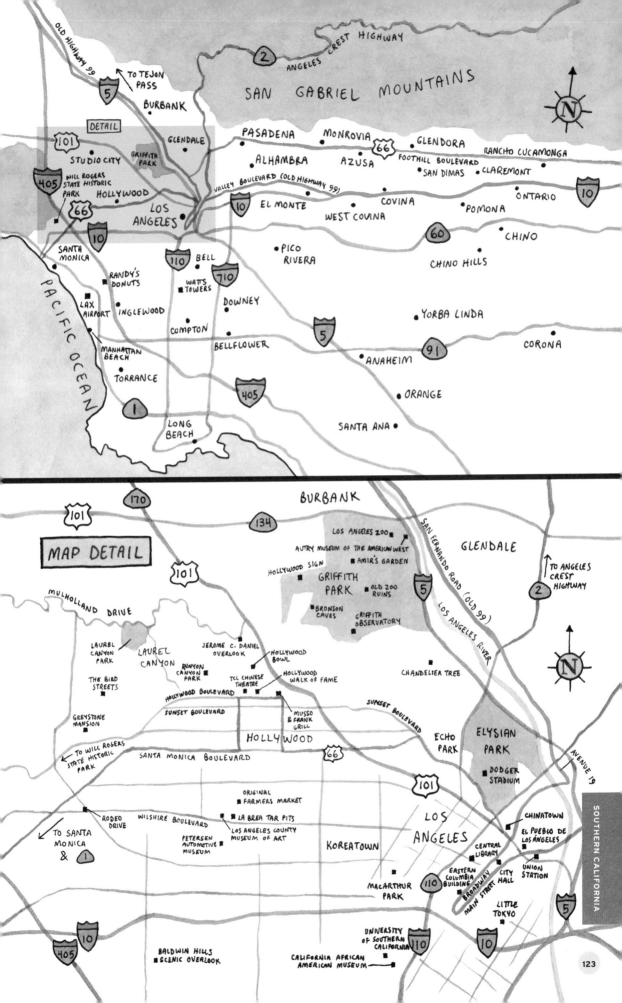

OLD HIGHWAY 99

5 TO TEJON PASS

BURBANK

101 DETAIL

STUDIO CITY

GRIFFITH PARK

405

WILL ROGERS STATE HISTORIC PARK

HOLLYWOOD

66

LOS ANGELES

GLENDALE

2 ANGELES CREST HIGHWAY

SAN GABRIEL MOUNTAINS

PASADENA

MONROVIA

66

GLENDORA

RANCHO CUCAMONGA

ALHAMBRA

AZUSA

FOOTHILL BOULEVARD

SAN DIMAS

CLAREMONT

VALLEY BOULEVARD (OLD HIGHWAY 99)

10

EL MONTE

COVINA

ONTARIO

10

WEST COVINA

POMONA

10

SANTA MONICA

SANTA MONICA

110

BELL

710

RANDY'S DONUTS

WATTS TOWERS

DOWNEY

60

CHINO

CHINO HILLS

PICO RIVERA

LAX AIRPORT

INGLEWOOD

COMPTON

BELLFLOWER

5

YORBA LINDA

CORONA

MANHATTAN BEACH

TORRANCE

1

405

ANAHEIM

91

ORANGE

PACIFIC OCEAN

LONG BEACH

SANTA ANA

MAP DETAIL

170

101

134

BURBANK

LOS ANGELES ZOO

AUTRY MUSEUM OF THE AMERICAN WEST

AMIR'S GARDEN

GLENDALE

TO ANGELES CREST HIGHWAY

2

MULHOLLAND DRIVE

101

HOLLYWOOD SIGN

GRIFFITH PARK

OLD ZOO RUINS

5

SAN FERNANDO ROAD (OLD 99)

LOS ANGELES RIVER

LAUREL CANYON PARK

LAUREL CANYON

JEROME C. DANIEL OVERLOOK

BRONSON CAVES

GRIFFITH OBSERVATORY

THE BIRD STREETS

RUNYON CANYON PARK

HOLLYWOOD BOWL

TCL CHINESE THEATRE

HOLLYWOOD WALK OF FAME

CHANDELIER TREE

GREYSTONE MANSION

HOLLYWOOD BOULEVARD

SUNSET BOULEVARD

MUSSO & FRANK GRILL

SUNSET BOULEVARD

ECHO PARK

ELYSIAN PARK

TO WILL ROGERS STATE HISTORIC PARK

SANTA MONICA BOULEVARD

HOLLYWOOD

66

101

DODGER STADIUM

AVENUE 19

TO SANTA MONICA & 1

RODEO DRIVE

WILSHIRE BOULEVARD

ORIGINAL FARMERS MARKET

LA BREA TAR PITS

LOS ANGELES COUNTY MUSEUM OF ART

KOREATOWN

LOS ANGELES

CHINATOWN

EL PUEBLO DE LOS ÁNGELES

PETERSEN AUTOMOTIVE MUSEUM

CENTRAL LIBRARY

UNION STATION

10

405

MACARTHUR PARK

110

EASTERN COLUMBIA BUILDING

BROADWAY

CITY HALL

MAIN STREET MALL

LITTLE TOKYO

5

BALDWIN HILLS SCENIC OVERLOOK

CALIFORNIA AFRICAN AMERICAN MUSEUM

UNIVERSITY OF SOUTHERN CALIFORNIA

110

10

SOUTHERN CALIFORNIA

ART DECO PROMENADE

While you're downtown, take a good look around you. If art deco is your thing, you are in the right place. Los Angeles is home to more than three dozen art deco masterpieces, and many of them are right here, thanks to the booming film and oil industries of the 1920s.

▼ Art deco highlights include City Hall, the Central Library, Union Station, and the Eastern Columbia Building. Also keep an eye out for small art deco details on many other buildings.

THE CRADLE OF LOS ANGELES

Olvera Street bisects the city's original pueblo, a village that dates back to the Spanish colonial era of the 1780s. Today El Pueblo de Los Ángeles is set aside as Los Angeles Plaza Historic District. The heart of LA's Latino culture is centered here as well; for a bigger taste, visit the food stalls at the nearby Grand Central Market or the museum at the LA Plaza de Cultura y Artes.

A CULTURAL SMÖRGÅSBORD

Los Angeles is a true melting pot, a sum of diverse enclaves. Koreatown, the most densely populated neighborhood, is home to a number of acclaimed restaurants. To sample the city's rich Black history, visit the California African American Museum, then grab dinner at Harold & Belle's, a hub of New Orleans cuisine since 1969. Little Tokyo, birthplace of the California roll, is home to the Japanese American National Museum and Nisei Week, a large festival held every August. Or if you're inspired to try a bit of international cooking yourself, you can pick up fresh ingredients at the original Farmers Market, a fixture at Third and Fairfax since 1934.

MUSEUM ROW

Los Angeles, not surprisingly, has an overwhelming array of museums. Some of the best are concentrated in Museum Row on Wilshire Boulevard. Los Angeles County Museum of Art (LACMA) boasts 120,000 objects from every culture and era. The Craft and Folk Art Museum is a bit more hands on and down to earth but still not to be missed. And the La Brea Tar Pits are not only the site of an incredible Ice Age fossil dig but also a bit of a roadside throwback, with their dramatic life-size diorama of contorted mammoths sinking in prehistoric tar.

▲ The plaza is the focal point of El Pueblo de Los Ángeles and home to a Mexican marketplace and a number of festivals.

VALLEY OF THE STARS

Hollywood's hot spots are well-trodden ground; from the Sunset Strip to the Walk of Fame to celebrity spotting in Beverly Hills, you don't need this book to tell you what to do. But for a slightly offbeat movie-magic experience, try a meal at the Musso and Frank Grill, Hollywood's oldest eatery. Then check out the gleaming lights of the Chandelier Tree in Silverlake, followed by a midnight showing of *The Rocky Horror Picture Show* at the Nuart Theatre in Santa Monica.

PARK YOURSELF AT A PARK

The concrete jungle of Los Angeles also has some world-class green spaces—great for when you need a break from your driving. Best known is the massive Griffith Park, home to the famous observatory, Amir's Garden, and the Bronson Caves. Runyon Canyon is popular with hikers—so popular, in fact, that you might want to try Will Rogers State Historic Park instead. To give your hike the feeling of a treasure hunt, look for the many public staircases that add beauty and mystery to the hilly western neighborhoods.

▲ The jacaranda trees that line many of the city's residential streets experience a rare double bloom each year: once in May and again in October.

▼ Watts Towers, the most recognizable landmark in a historically African American neighborhood, were actually hand built by an Italian American folk artist.

A BIRD'S-EYE VIEW

Don't forget that Los Angeles is surrounded by mountains—even though they're often obscured by the city's infamous smog. When the air is clear, there are many hilltop drives to give you an unforgettable overview of the city and seaside. For a quick jaunt, drive up to the Hollywood Bowl Overlook or do the famous Mulholland Drive. Or, for a full-day skyline adventure, try the challenging Angeles Crest Highway. Pro tip: do your driving during the day, as the tricky business of navigating tight curves in the dark outweighs the twinkling view. It's also illegal to pull over at night on many of the hill roads—theater tickets are a better value than traffic tickets.

GET THEE TO THE BEACH

While Los Angeles proper is landlocked, you're never too far from the ocean. You can even follow Route 66 to its legendary end at the Santa Monica Pier (page 21). Just know that a million other folks might have the same idea. Do your beachcombing on a weekday or early in the morning to avoid the traffic and crowds.

FARTHER AFIELD

Santa Monica will link you to Highway 1 and the rest of the Pacific shore. To continue your inland coast trek along old Highway 99, pick up San Fernando Boulevard north of downtown. That will lead you all the way through Glendale, Burbank, and Santa Clarita (keep a good map handy to navigate the handful of route jogs around the freeways). Eventually, though, you'll need to join Interstate 5 to leave greater LA behind: the freeway is the only route over Tejon Pass, which you'll cross on your way to the massive Central Valley.

LOS ANGELES
ICONS

▶ Doughnuts are a *thing* in this town (LA is even responsible for the "donut" spelling), and Randy's Donuts in Inglewood stands out from the fried-dough pack.

RANDY'S DONUTS

▲ El Día de los Muertos is an important holiday for Latino Los Angeles. Look for sidewalk *ofrendas*, or altars devoted to departed friends and family.

Autographs

▲ At the Hollywood Walk of Fame, bring your autograph book in case you spot living stars among the geometric ones.

◀ While Huntington Beach may have snagged the title of Surf City USA, Los Angeles is awash in surf shops and surfer dudes and dudettes.

▶ The Columbian mammoth, star attraction of the La Brea Tar Pits, roamed the grassy plains of Ice Age Los Angeles.

▲ Chicken and waffles are an adopted staple of LA's soul-food culture. The Roscoe's franchise has been serving them up for more than forty years.

ANGELS FLIGHT

▲ The Angels Flight Railway, a narrow gauge funicular tram in operation since 1901, takes both tourists and commuters up the steep incline of downtown's Bunker Hill.

▲ The Theme Building at LAX Airport is the city's most iconic Googie-style building, designed by African American architect Paul R. Williams.

Larger Than LIFE

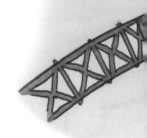

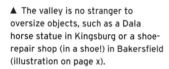

THE SAN JOAQUIN VALLEY

After you climb out of Los Angeles and over Tejon Pass on Interstate 5, Highway 99 resumes once more, this time as a proper freeway. Here, both highways begin the long trek through the San Joaquin Valley, the southern half of the great 450-mile-long flat plain known as the Central Valley. Interestingly, this time Highway 99 is the main route—both highways join again at the state capital of Sacramento, but I-5 is the lonely road this time.

▲ The valley is no stranger to oversize objects, such as a Dala horse statue in Kingsburg or a shoe-repair shop (in a shoe!) in Bakersfield (illustration on page x).

AMERICA'S FOOD BASKET

Originally a seasonal wetland filled with freshwater tule marshes, the Central Valley is now one of the most important agricultural regions in America. The San Joaquin Valley, warmer and drier than the Sacramento Valley to the north, is a major producer of nuts, fruit, vegetables, and feed crops for livestock. On your drive you'll share the road with citrus trucks (though you'll have to head well east of the highway to find the actual orange and lemon groves). As seemingly endless vineyards of table grapes sweep by, look for the Sun-Maid headquarters in Kingsburg. Near Ripon, the nation's almond capital, almond blossoms line the route in pale pink each spring. If all this agricultural splendor has you hankering for more, it's worth taking time to explore the grid of farm roads that stretches along the length of the valley. Family-owned farm stands still sell roadside fruit, nuts, and preserves in many places. And Fresno County offers a well-marked auto tour route called the Blossom Trail, which passes fragrant nut and citrus orchards between Highway 99 and the foothills of the Sierra Nevada.

◄ Also in Kingsburg is a water tower shaped like a Swedish coffeepot. In nearby Tulare is a milk-jug tower—complete with a drinking straw.

▲ Many of the towns in the Central Valley mark their city limits with an ornate typographic archway over the historic Highway 99 alignment through town.

TOWN AND COUNTRY

Punctuating the endless farmland are a series of agricultural towns and cities connected by 99. Rough-and-tumble Bakersfield is equally devoted to oil production, with many oil wells and natural gas reserves nearby. Fresno (page 130) is a geographical hub, with its position near the center of the state giving access to both the coast and the mountains. Stockton's location on the California Delta, a major system of rivers and waterways, made it a major inland port in the nineteenth and twentieth centuries. Even the roadside attractions here are ag related, with giant vegetables, decorated water towers, and farm-stand funhouses surviving from the 1950s until today.

TRAVEL WITH CARE

For the first time since the Low Desert, you'll find yourself on a fast road and a flat plain. It'll be tempting to zoom along at top speed, but be cautious: this is the main highway through the valley, so there's often heavy traffic and a lot of semitrucks to contend with. Also, the weather still treats the valley like the wetland it used to be, with thick bands of tule fog obscuring the region in the colder, wetter months. Tule fog is no joke—it can either creep up in sudden patches or fill the whole valley with an impenetrable soup. The fog has been responsible for many huge accidents over the years, sometimes with pileups of more than a hundred cars. So drive carefully, slow down, and consider hanging out in a coffee shop until the fog burns off.

Raisin THE ROOF

FRESNO

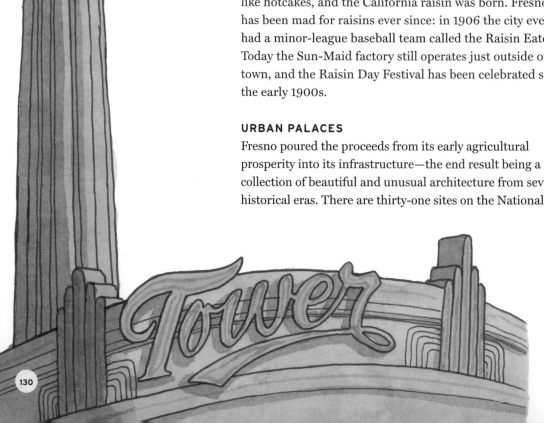

California's sixth-largest city is not exactly synonymous with tourism: it's not on the coast, it's in a firmly flat and agricultural area, and it's a bit rough around the edges. It has the dubious honor of being the city that birthed both the trash landfill and the credit card. Yet look a little closer, and you'll find many things to love. After all, the Highway 99 archway on Van Ness Avenue proclaims Fresno the "Best Little City in the USA."

▼ The Tower Theatre is home to the Fresno Film Festival and is the backdrop for the Tower District's annual Mardi Gras Parade.

THROUGH THE GRAPEVINE

Fresno is not merely California's raisin capital. It's also the place where the raisin was invented—or at least, rediscovered. In the 1870s, cultivation of seedless grapes began here; one hot summer, an entire crop dried up on the vine. To make the best of it, growers brought the fruit to San Francisco and marketed it as a "Peruvian" delicacy. It sold like hotcakes, and the California raisin was born. Fresno has been mad for raisins ever since: in 1906 the city even had a minor-league baseball team called the Raisin Eaters. Today the Sun-Maid factory still operates just outside of town, and the Raisin Day Festival has been celebrated since the early 1900s.

URBAN PALACES

Fresno poured the proceeds from its early agricultural prosperity into its infrastructure—the end result being a collection of beautiful and unusual architecture from several historical eras. There are thirty-one sites on the National

Register of Historic Places and another eighty or so on a local heritage list. Must-see examples include the 1894 Old Fresno Water Tower, the 1924 San Joaquin Light and Power Corporation Building, the art deco Tower Theatre, and the turn-of-the-century agricultural buildings of Warehouse Row.

▲ Some architectural details here need to be seen up close, like the ornate tiled portico over the Fresno City College library.

VALLEY VILLAS

Fresno was home to a number of oil, timber, and agricultural barons—their homes are also worthy of an architecture tour. The most beautiful specimens are the English-cottage-style Einstein Home, the Tuscan-style Brix Mansion, and the French-revival Kearney Mansion. For an interesting mix of indoor and outdoor, public and private, check out the Forestiere Underground Gardens, built in 1906. Sicilian horticulturist Baldassare Forestiere built his home around a series of stone vaults, catacombs, and atria to escape the brutal summer heat—and to cultivate a number of ornamental and edible plants in the underground microclimates he created.

NEON DREAMS

Highway 99 has left its mark on Fresno, too, particularly in the form of neon signs and midcentury motels. Many of these places are in disrepair now, but you can still find a number along Old 99, on Golden State Boulevard and Van Ness Avenue. Some signs—like the iconic Fresno Motel diving girl (page 109)—have been restored and moved to the Fresno Fairgrounds.

▶ The Old Fresno Water Tower was designed in a medieval Romanesque style by Chicago architect George Washington Maher.

SIDE TRIP

SEQUOIA & YOSEMITE

NATIONAL PARKS

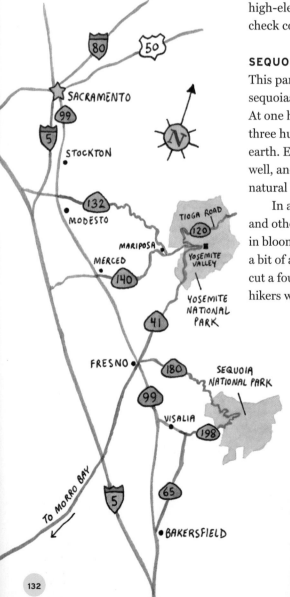

▲ While the giant sequoia is related to the coastal redwood (page 70), this shorter but stouter tree is found only in the Sierra Nevada.

The San Joaquin Valley is next door to two of America's most beloved national parks. Getting there from the valley is fairly easy, but keep in mind that there is no direct road between the parks—depending on time, you may need to choose one or the other. Both parks are in the High Sierra; high-elevation roads usually close in the colder months, so check conditions before you set out.

SEQUOIA NATIONAL PARK

This park protects and highlights rare groves of giant sequoias, the king of which is the General Sherman Tree. At one hundred feet in circumference at its base and nearly three hundred feet in height, it is the largest living tree on earth. Easy hiking trails explore other groves of giant trees as well, and the Giant Forest Museum offers exhibits about the natural history of the trees.

In addition to the groves themselves, Crescent Meadow and other natural clearings are great places to see wildflowers in bloom. Moro Rock is a massive granite dome that offers a bit of a Yosemite preview; the Civilian Conservation Corps cut a four-hundred-step stairway into the rock, providing hikers with a path to the top.

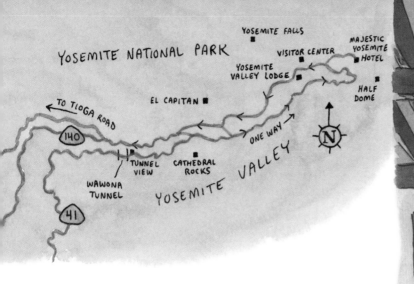

YOSEMITE NATIONAL PARK

YOSEMITE FALLS

VISITOR CENTER

MAJESTIC
YOSEMITE
HOTEL

YOSEMITE
VALLEY LODGE

EL CAPITAN

HALF
DOME

TO TIOGA ROAD

140

ONE WAY

N

TUNNEL
VIEW

CATHEDRAL
ROCKS

YOSEMITE VALLEY

WAWONA
TUNNEL

YOSEMITE VALLEY

41

YOSEMITE NATIONAL PARK

This park, one the oldest and most visited in America, is also
a UNESCO World Heritage Site. Over four million people a
year pour into the Yosemite Valley to feast their eyes upon
El Capitan, Half Dome, and Bridalveil Fall. Arrive early on
a weekday morning to beat the crowds. The drive here is an
experience in itself, with hairpin turns, panoramic vistas,
and the chance to spot wildlife. The Tunnel View pullout
offers a picture-postcard glimpse of the valley, and you can
even see a group of giant sequoias at Mariposa Grove.

THE MAJESTIC AHWAHNEE

One of many national park lodges built in the West during
the 1920s and '30s, the Ahwahnee Hotel (now called the
Majestic Yosemite Hotel) opened in 1927. Snagging a
reservation here requires both luck and a wad of cash, but
you don't have to be a guest to explore the main floor. Each
room boasts a cavernous ceiling, huge windows looking out
onto the valley, and rustic decor inspired by art deco, Middle
Eastern, arts-and-crafts, and Indigenous motifs. Don't miss
the Majestic Yosemite Dining Room, the Great Lounge, or
the exquisite, tapestry-like paintings in the Mural Room.

▲ The Great Lounge of the
Ahwahnee Hotel inspired the interior
sets built for the film *The Shining*
(page 159).

▼ California naturalist John Muir
championed the protection of
Yosemite and Sequoia, leading the
effort that led to their becoming
national parks in 1890.

SIDE TRIP

133

CENTRAL PACIFIC RAILROAD COMPANY

Sacramento

▲ The Big Four House, comprising several attached storefronts, once belonged to merchants like Charles Crocker and Leland Stanford, who went on to become hugely influential statewide.

The state capital sits pretty in the middle of the Central Valley, smack-dab between the Sierra Nevada mountains and the sea. A major hub of commerce and transportation, Sacramento is close to both San Francisco (page 48) and Wine Country (page 62). The freeway portion of Highway 99 ends here, bringing you right downtown.

STEP BACK IN TIME

Sacramento has seen a lot of firsts over the past 150 years. It was the western terminus of the short-lived Pony Express and a major stop on the first transcontinental railroad and telegraph line. Travelers and settlers arrived by train, stagecoach, and riverboat—and tens of thousands of forty-niners poured in to try their luck in the California gold rush.

Visitors can get a hearty glimpse of the city's early days at Old Sacramento State Historic Park. Located along the riverbank, between the interstate, Tower Bridge, and the I Street Bridge, the area was preserved starting in the 1960s as a living history museum and park. The old storefronts are impeccably restored, though choked with a constant flow of tourists. The nearby California State Railroad Museum, though not an old building, is also worth a visit for anyone interested in iron-horse history.

▼ The original Tower Records store is long gone, but its 1949 neon sign has been restored to its former glory at Sixteenth Street and Broadway.

BURYING THE PAST

Sadly, Sacramento's historic Chinatown didn't make the cut. The community, once the country's second-largest Chinese immigrant population (their name for Sacramento was Yee Fow, or "Second City"), the community was subjected to decades of abuse and sabotage by white residents. Today most of the original district now lies under the Interstate 5 roadbed and the Amtrak station.

RECORDS

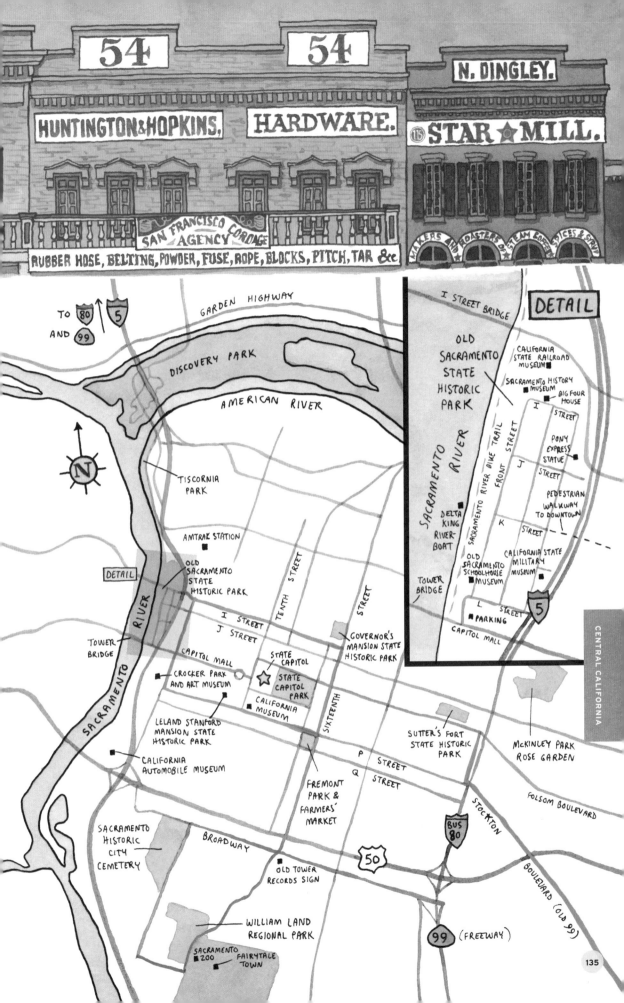

▲ Fairytale Town is a small amusement park located inside William Land Regional Park. To visit, though, you need to arrive with kids—no unattended adults allowed!

▼ The state capitol grounds contain both pine and palm trees to symbolize its location at the junction of Southern and Northern California.

THE BIG TOMATO

Thanks to its agricultural history and a canning industry that preserved all that fresh bounty, Sacramento earned the nickname of the Big Tomato. The old canneries have either been torn down or been converted to offices by now, but the city celebrates its foodie history each September with the Farm-to-Fork Festival. Sacramento is also home to a number of breweries, farmers' markets, farm-to-fork restaurants, and organized agricultural tours.

TOUR YOUR HEART OUT

Old Sacramento is just the start of Sacramento's museums and tour opportunities. Sutter's Fort State Historic Park preserves the city's earliest white settlement, with tours and costumed interpreters to complete the experience. The California State Capitol is free and open to the public, with several exhibits and tours available of the legislative chambers. The Italianate-style governor's mansion, located nearby, is both a state historic park and the official residence of the state governor. Round out your tour circuit at the Crocker Art Museum, the oldest art museum in the West, specializing in Californian and American art.

NATURE CALLS

After all those museums, take a break at Discovery Park, a large green space located on an island at the confluence of the American and Sacramento Rivers. Or if you prefer a park with a lot of amenities and attractions, try the 170-acre William Land Regional Park, on the south side of town. For something a little different (and slightly macabre), pay a visit to Sacramento Historic City Cemetery. Designed in the style of a Victorian garden, the cemetery is the resting place of Sacramento dignitaries. Also buried there is a survivor of the 1846–47 Donner Party disaster, when a group of California-bound pioneers spent the winter trapped in the Sierra Nevada, and several settlers had to resort to cannibalism to survive.

SACRAMENTO ICONS

▶ Pay your respects to the Pony Express statue in Old Sacramento and then buy a postcard or three to mail to your friends back home.

▲ Sutter's Fort hosts a candlelight tour each fall to demonstrate what evenings in the 1830s looked and felt like.

◀ It's not called the Big Tomato for nothing. The city boasts more than ten farmers' markets, where you can buy the freshest produce in California.

▼ Besides being a tomato capital, Sacramento is also a dairy and beef capital. A cattle drive over Tower Bridge kicks off the Farm-to-Fork Festival each year.

▲ The *Delta King* riverboat, permanently docked in Old Sacramento, has been a hotel since the 1980s.

▲ For nearly fifty years the Governor's Mansion sat empty; Ronald Reagan was the last governor to live there before Jerry Brown moved there in 2015.

▶ Tower Bridge is a monument of streamline moderne architecture, standing tall in deep burnished gold since 1935.

▶ Sacramento's dairy history is the secret recipe for the best ice cream in the state. The hard part is choosing where to buy a cone.

CENTRAL CALIFORNIA

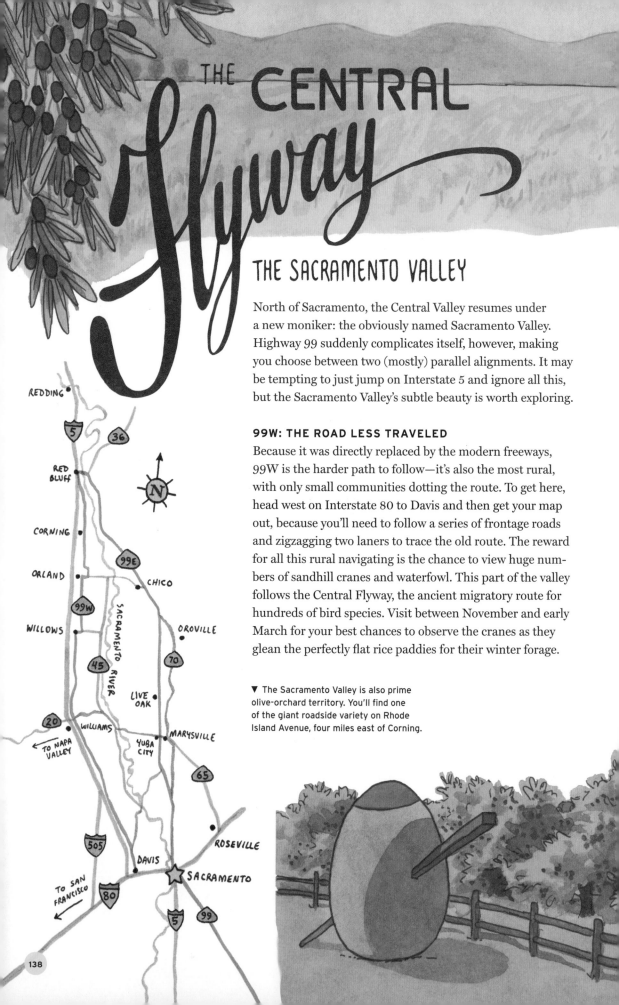

THE CENTRAL *Flyway*

THE SACRAMENTO VALLEY

North of Sacramento, the Central Valley resumes under a new moniker: the obviously named Sacramento Valley. Highway 99 suddenly complicates itself, however, making you choose between two (mostly) parallel alignments. It may be tempting to just jump on Interstate 5 and ignore all this, but the Sacramento Valley's subtle beauty is worth exploring.

99W: THE ROAD LESS TRAVELED

Because it was directly replaced by the modern freeways, 99W is the harder path to follow—it's also the most rural, with only small communities dotting the route. To get here, head west on Interstate 80 to Davis and then get your map out, because you'll need to follow a series of frontage roads and zigzagging two laners to trace the old route. The reward for all this rural navigating is the chance to view huge numbers of sandhill cranes and waterfowl. This part of the valley follows the Central Flyway, the ancient migratory route for hundreds of bird species. Visit between November and early March for your best chances to observe the cranes as they glean the perfectly flat rice paddies for their winter forage.

▼ The Sacramento Valley is also prime olive-orchard territory. You'll find one of the giant roadside variety on Rhode Island Avenue, four miles east of Corning.

99E: THE FAST (SLOW) ROAD

The eastern alignment of Highway 99, accessible from
Interstate 5 immediately north of Sacramento, is a more
heavily traveled road, thanks to the cities of Yuba City and
Chico. The crops here differ from the ones along 99W, on
the other side of the river: there's hardly any rice here, a lot
more walnuts, and even a few tangerines. If you get hungry,
you can grab some fresh produce at one of several roadside
stands along the way.

Also of note is the Chinese American heritage of this
route. Like in Sacramento, the gold rush and railroad boom
of the mid-eighteenth century brought Chinese immigrants
here as well, and various Chinese enclaves popped up along
the Sacramento River and the California Delta. The largest
and best preserved near 99E are Marysville and Oroville. The
beautifully restored Oroville Chinese temple is now a museum
worth the short detour into town. Marysville is home to the
Chinese American Museum of Northern California, as well as
the Bok Kai parade each March. The event, which began in
1882, is the oldest continually held parade in the state.

▲ The Sandhill crane is easy to
identify, with its six-foot wingspan,
its black beak, its distinctive red
crown, and its loud, trilling call.

A REUNION OF ROUTES

The two 99s merge once more at Red Bluff, home to a
well-preserved historic downtown. You'll jump back onto
Interstate 5 here and continue northward. Along the way,
you'll see the valley floor give way to rolling hills and oak
trees—this is the threshold between quintessential California
and the Pacific Northwest.

▼ Several of Marysville's buildings
are reminiscent of the Lingnan style
of Cantonese architecture, reflecting
the culture of the majority of
California's first Chinese immigrants.

ON SHASTA'S DOORSTEP

GREATER REDDING

Heading northward, Redding is the last sizable city until Eugene, Oregon—more than three hundred miles away. It's also the last bastion of the warm, mild climate of the Central Valley. This makes it a good place to spend the night—or at least stretch your legs—before making the long climb to the Siskiyou Summit.

LESS GOLD, MORE GRIT

Like the state capital, Redding lies on the Sacramento River and has its roots in the 1849 gold rush. However, while most of the wealth passed through Sacramento and San Francisco, Redding's earliest incarnation was called Poverty Flat. Copper and mineral mining in the early twentieth century, however, brought real money to the local economy—as did the building of the Shasta Dam a few miles to the north.

THE MIRACLE MILE

With the construction boom of the 1930s and the recreational traffic that followed, Redding suddenly had a lot of visitors. A series of motor lodges popped up along Highway 99 (Market Street), each with an eye-catching Googie design to lure customers. This strip was nicknamed the Miracle Mile and is mostly intact today.

◄ Many of the signs of the Miracle Mile were inspired by the shapes and lettering styles of the famous neon signs of Las Vegas.

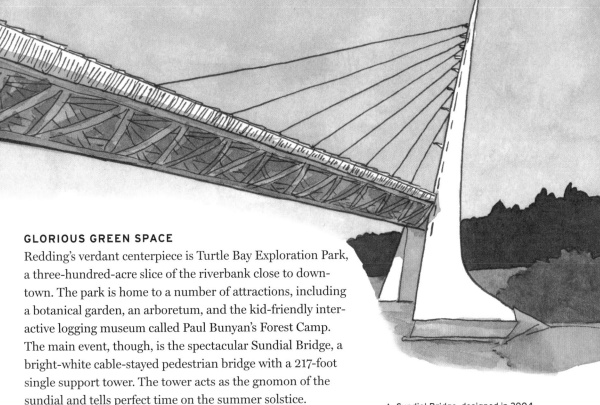

GLORIOUS GREEN SPACE

Redding's verdant centerpiece is Turtle Bay Exploration Park, a three-hundred-acre slice of the riverbank close to downtown. The park is home to a number of attractions, including a botanical garden, an arboretum, and the kid-friendly interactive logging museum called Paul Bunyan's Forest Camp. The main event, though, is the spectacular Sundial Bridge, a bright-white cable-stayed pedestrian bridge with a 217-foot single support tower. The tower acts as the gnomon of the sundial and tells perfect time on the summer solstice.

THE NORCAL LAUNCHPAD

Redding's location makes it the ideal starting point for a host of mountain adventures. Shasta Lake is the closest, with several camping and water-recreation opportunities available. To the east lies Lassen Volcanic National Park, which protects Lassen Peak, the southernmost of the Cascade volcanoes. Westward, a series of rugged mountain roads leads to Whiskeytown National Recreation Area, a favorite of wilderness hikers and high-country campers. Finally, it's a long, *long* drive, but Redding connects to one of the few highways that cross the Coast Range to Eureka and the Redwood Coast (page 70; route map on page 200).

▲ Sundial Bridge, designed in 2004 by Spanish architect Santiago Calatrava, is one of the largest functioning sundials in the world.

▼ Shasta City State Park, six miles west of Redding, encompasses a ghost town that once served as a mining hub until the railroad came to Redding.

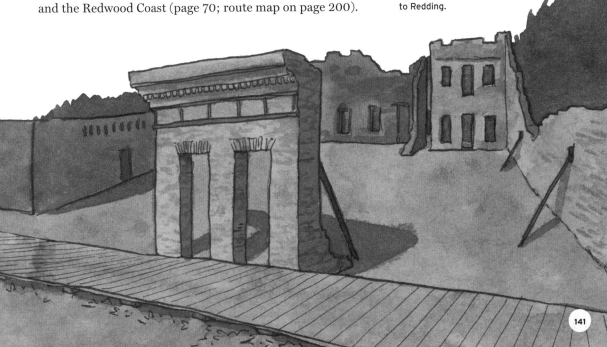

THE RING OF FIRE

Past Redding, Highway 99 climbs rapidly into the mountains, on its way to the Siskiyou Summit and the Oregon border. Because the terrain is so steep through here, it has been all but obliterated by the interstate. A few stretches remain along the way, mostly as the main streets of the towns, but unless you want to stop many times along the way, the easiest course of action is to stick to the interstate all the way to the Oregon line.

VULCAN TERRITORY

Mount Shasta is the first of many volcanoes you'll pass on this trip. You've entered the Ring of Fire, the band of volcanic activity that partly encircles the Pacific Ocean, created by plate tectonics and subduction zones. The white-capped peaks you'll pass are not dormant—each is still very much an active volcano.

MOUNTAIN ADVENTURES

In addition to the obvious recreation spots of Mount Shasta and Shasta Lake, a good mountain destination is Castle Crags State Park near Dunsmuir. You can see the dramatic crags briefly from the highway, but stopping at the park will give you time to enjoy the experience. While you're in Dunsmuir, check out the electric marquee at the California Theatre (page 108). Just before the town of Weed is the dramatic cinder cone of Black Butte. And as you hurtle toward the state line, keep your eyes peeled for the giant roadside dragon made from rusted farm implements in Yreka (pronounced "why-REEK-a").

CANADA

MOUNT BAKER
10,781 FEET

GLACIER PEAK
10,541 FEET

SEATTLE

Washington

OLYMPIA

MOUNT RAINIER
14,410 FEET

MOUNT SAINT HELENS

8,330 FEET

MOUNT ADAMS
12,277 FEET

PORTLAND

MOUNT HOOD
11,240 FEET

SALEM

MOUNT JEFFERSON
10,495 FEET

NORTH SISTER
10,085 FEET

MIDDLE SISTER
10,047 FEET

THREE
SISTERS

SOUTH SISTER
10,358 FEET

MOUNT BACHELOR
9,068 FEET

Oregon

CRATER LAKE
(MOUNT MAZAMA)
8,159 FEET

MOUNT McLOUGHLIN
9,495 FEET

ASHLAND

California

MEDICINE LAKE
VOLCANO
7,913 FEET

MOUNT SHASTA
14,163 FEET

REDDING

LASSEN PEAK
10,456 FEET

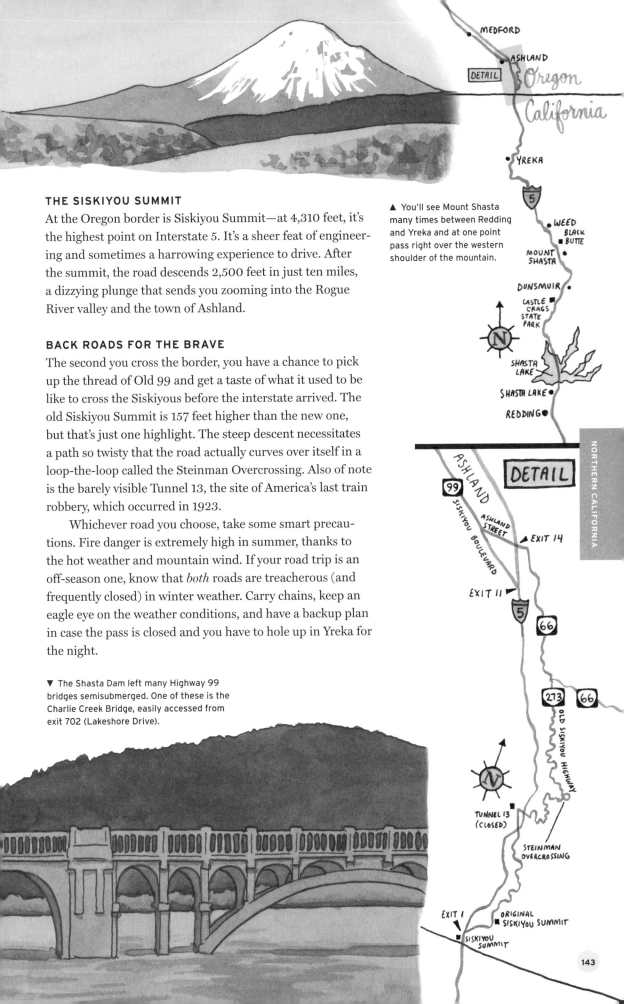

THE SISKIYOU SUMMIT

At the Oregon border is Siskiyou Summit—at 4,310 feet, it's the highest point on Interstate 5. It's a sheer feat of engineering and sometimes a harrowing experience to drive. After the summit, the road descends 2,500 feet in just ten miles, a dizzying plunge that sends you zooming into the Rogue River valley and the town of Ashland.

BACK ROADS FOR THE BRAVE

The second you cross the border, you have a chance to pick up the thread of Old 99 and get a taste of what it used to be like to cross the Siskiyous before the interstate arrived. The old Siskiyou Summit is 157 feet higher than the new one, but that's just one highlight. The steep descent necessitates a path so twisty that the road actually curves over itself in a loop-the-loop called the Steinman Overcrossing. Also of note is the barely visible Tunnel 13, the site of America's last train robbery, which occurred in 1923.

Whichever road you choose, take some smart precautions. Fire danger is extremely high in summer, thanks to the hot weather and mountain wind. If your road trip is an off-season one, know that *both* roads are treacherous (and frequently closed) in winter weather. Carry chains, keep an eagle eye on the weather conditions, and have a backup plan in case the pass is closed and you have to hole up in Yreka for the night.

▼ The Shasta Dam left many Highway 99 bridges semisubmerged. One of these is the Charlie Creek Bridge, easily accessed from exit 702 (Lakeshore Drive).

▲ You'll see Mount Shasta many times between Redding and Yreka and at one point pass right over the western shoulder of the mountain.

NORTHERN CALIFORNIA

143

All the World's a Stage

ASHLAND

It's easy to blow right by Ashland on your descent out of California. But skip this mountain hamlet at your peril: tucked away in a narrow valley, against the wooded wall of the Siskiyous, this place is an Oregon treasure.

DRINK DOWN ALL UNKINDNESS

Ashland first became a tourist destination with the discovery of a bubbling mineral spring in 1907. Dubbed Lithia Springs for the natural lithia water (which here contains lithium oxide), the town quickly grew into a resort town, where hotels and spas hawked the "healthful" benefits of the spring water. The oldest of these is the Ashland Springs Hotel, a hundred-year-old grande dame decorated with natural-history specimens and bird drawings. And there are still public fountains downtown, if you're curious—to be honest, the slightly fizzy water has a strong mineral taste that borders on unpleasant.

TONGUES IN TREES, BOOKS IN BROOKS, SERMONS IN STONES

Ashland's real draw is the Oregon Shakespeare Festival, an annual fixture that began as a summer festival in 1935 and has grown into an eight-month multiproduction extravaganza. Over the years, the OSF has produced all

◀ The Allen Elizabethan Theatre is a replica of the Fortune Theatre, built in London in 1599.

thirty-seven of Shakespeare's plays a combined total of more than three hundred times. What really makes the festival special is the semi-outdoor Allen Elizabethan Theatre. There's something magical about watching Shakespeare performed in Ashland's mountain setting—as if the bard himself were speaking to you through the trees or the rushing Lithia Springs.

Tickets to the mainstage performances can be a hot commodity, but there are also a number of free outdoor performances, plus several satellite venues offering both Shakespeare and non-Shakespeare performances. And for young theater buffs, the local Southern Oregon University offers a Shakespearean studies program.

THE WINTER OF OUR DISCONTENT

There are no Shakespeare performances between November and the end of February, but don't let the discontent get to you. If winter sports are your thing, Mount Ashland delivers both downhill skiing and the Grouse Gap Nordic Trails for cross-country enthusiasts. The downtown outfit Main Street Adventure Tours also offers equipment rentals and snow-shoe tours of the region.

EXIT, PURSUED BY A BEAR

It's hard to leave Ashland at all, but when you're ready to continue northward, the thread of Highway 99 runs all the way along the Rogue Valley, first through the pear orchards and then through a tight mountain passage—where you might just spot a bear or two.

▲ The Butler-Perozzi Fountain in Lithia Park was originally built for the 1916 Panama-Pacific International Exposition in San Francisco.

▼ The picture-postcard view of downtown Ashland, with its iconic hotel and seasonal Shakespeare banners, looks nearly identical to when the festival began in 1935.

"IT'S THE CLIMATE"

THE ROGUE RIVER VALLEY

Southwestern Oregon is home to an unusual pocket of warm weather, thanks to a meteorological phenomenon called the Brookings effect—named for the town on the Oregon coast (page 78). This phenomenon is the reason behind the Oregon banana belt, a region that includes the Rogue River valley from Ashland and Grants Pass all the way to the ocean.

YES, WE HAVE NO BANANAS

This balmy band isn't quite warm enough to grow actual bananas, but it turns out to be the ideal environment for pears. The widest part of the Rogue Valley, around Medford, is world famous for its Comice pears, a variety prized for both its flavor and its hardiness for shipping. Medford's most famous mail-order pear grower is Harry & David, that purveyor of office-party Christmas gifts and fruit-of-the-month clubs. You can still shop for Comice pears at the Harry & David store in Medford—or for the full farm-to-fruit experience, visit Eden Valley Orchards, just west of town.

ON THE RIVERBANKS

Highway 99 continues intact, hugging the Rogue as it wends its way toward Grants Pass. You'll pass a giant Paul Bunyan sign outside of Medford and the Oregon Vortex—an illusion attraction in the spirit of the Santa Cruz Mystery Spot (page 45) or Confusion Hill in the Redwoods (page 75)—in Gold Hill. Farther on, note the handsome Depression-era arch bridges as you cross and recross the river on your way to Grants Pass.

▲ The famous climate sign in Grants Pass was installed in 1920 and was restored in time for its ninetieth anniversary in 2010.

▼ The fragrant pear orchards of the Rogue Valley are also an ideal place for local beekeepers—honey is one of southern Oregon's prized crops.

146

▶ The Caveman Bridge was designed by Conde McCullough, engineer of the famous Oregon coast bridges (page 82) and the Grave Creek covered bridge.

CALLING ALL CONSUMPTIVES

In the summer Grants Pass enjoys hot days and downright cold nights; winters are mild despite the mountain setting. This made people flock to the city to take in the climate and is still a tourist selling point today—hence the restored "It's the Climate" sign that hangs over Highway 99 downtown. The city is also a common staging ground for travelers heading to Crater Lake National Park (page 148).

For southbound interstate travelers, Grants Pass is also the gateway to the Redwood Empire (page 70). US Highway 199 meets Old 99 here and cuts a winding diagonal toward Crescent City, California. The range of coast redwood habitat reaches into Oregon along this route, making the road an excellent scenic byway.

HEAD FOR THE HILLS

They may not look it, but the Siskiyous are some of the most rugged mountains in the Northwest. There are hardly any roads through here (and almost none with pavement). Still, the Rogue River is famous for its white-water rafting opportunities; trips leave from both Grants Pass and Gold Beach, just north of Brookings.

One attraction that might be worth the long drive, however, is Oregon Caves National Monument. Located fifty miles southwest of Grants Pass, these natural marble caverns (dubbed the Marble Halls of Oregon) are open for tours and spelunking adventures.

▼ On the Old 99 alignment of Sixth Street downtown, a lumpy roadside caveman statue celebrates Grants Pass's proximity to Oregon cave country.

OREGON

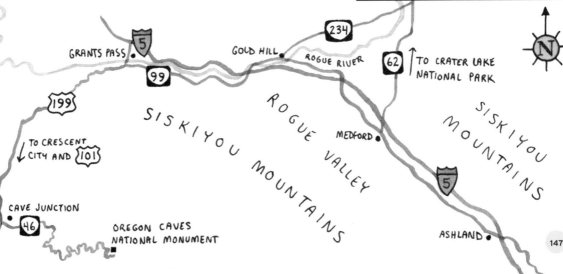

CRATER Lake

SIDE TRIP

NATIONAL PARK

One of America's oldest national parks, Crater Lake is a Pacific Northwest icon. This is the image you'll see on the Oregon state quarter, but no coin will ever do it justice. There's simply no way to convey, either in words or in images, the sheer scale of Crater Lake or the impossible sapphire hues of the water. Early white settlers didn't even try: in 1853, when John Wesley Hillman, the first white man to lay eyes on the lake, stumbled upon the place, he dubbed it the ever-so-creative Deep Blue Lake.

Well, deep and blue it is—we'll give him that. Formed in the caldera of the ancient volcano Mount Mazama, which erupted around 7,700 years ago, the lake is six miles wide and nearly two thousand feet deep—the deepest lake in the United States. There are no rivers or streams feeding the lake, making it entirely rain and snow fed. The water gets its color from its depth and clarity. Though light can penetrate hundreds of feet downward, light on the red end of the spectrum, with its longer wavelength, gets absorbed by the depth, enhancing the effect of light on the blue end of the spectrum.

A PERFECT CIRCLE OF PANORAMAS

From Medford, follow State Route 62 up to the park. Rim Drive is the main park road, open year-round (weather permitting) as far as Rim Village and then only from July to October for the rest of the distance. The road makes a full loop of the caldera rim, offering viewpoints of Wizard Island, the rock formation called Phantom Ship, and the surrounding mountains of the Cascades. Pro tip: early-season mosquitoes thrive on the puddles left from the snowmelt; August is a better time to visit, when everything has dried out a bit.

▼ The park rangers like to say that the strenuous trail down to Cleetwood Cove is "one mile down and ten miles back up."

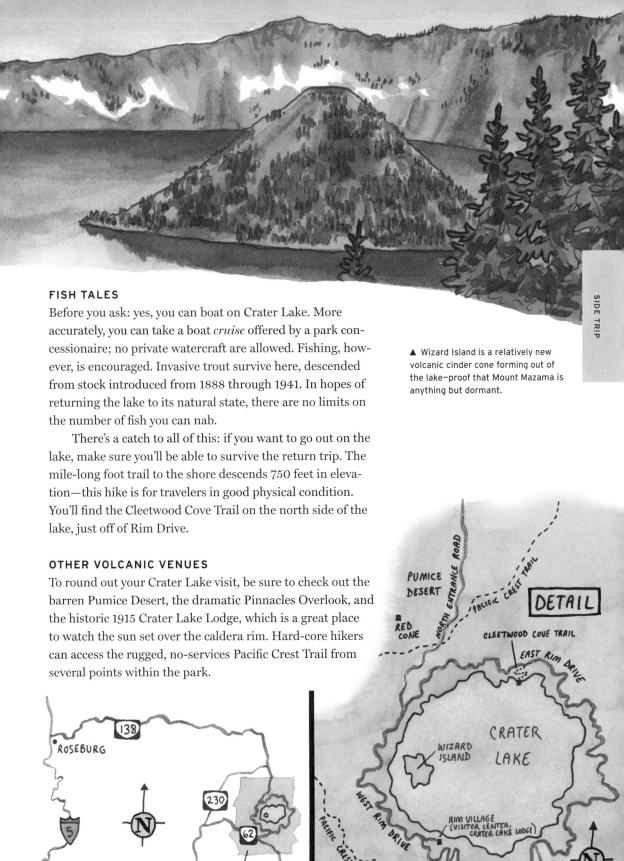

FISH TALES

Before you ask: yes, you can boat on Crater Lake. More accurately, you can take a boat *cruise* offered by a park concessionaire; no private watercraft are allowed. Fishing, however, is encouraged. Invasive trout survive here, descended from stock introduced from 1888 through 1941. In hopes of returning the lake to its natural state, there are no limits on the number of fish you can nab.

There's a catch to all of this: if you want to go out on the lake, make sure you'll be able to survive the return trip. The mile-long foot trail to the shore descends 750 feet in elevation—this hike is for travelers in good physical condition. You'll find the Cleetwood Cove Trail on the north side of the lake, just off of Rim Drive.

OTHER VOLCANIC VENUES

To round out your Crater Lake visit, be sure to check out the barren Pumice Desert, the dramatic Pinnacles Overlook, and the historic 1915 Crater Lake Lodge, which is a great place to watch the sun set over the caldera rim. Hard-core hikers can access the rugged, no-services Pacific Crest Trail from several points within the park.

▲ Wizard Island is a relatively new volcanic cinder cone forming out of the lake—proof that Mount Mazama is anything but dormant.

DETAIL

PUMICE DESERT

RED CONE

NORTH ENTRANCE ROAD

PACIFIC CREST TRAIL

CLEETWOOD COVE TRAIL

EAST RIM DRIVE

WIZARD ISLAND

CRATER LAKE

RIM VILLAGE (VISITOR CENTER, CRATER LAKE LODGE)

WEST RIM DRIVE

PACIFIC CREST TRAIL

PINNACLES OVERLOOK

ROSEBURG

138

5

230

62

62

CRATER LAKE NATIONAL PARK

234

GRANTS PASS

GOLD HILL

MEDFORD

62

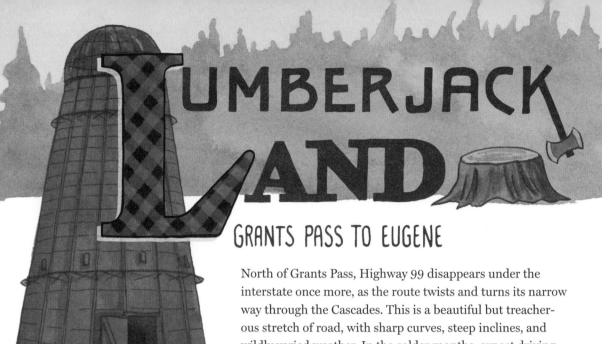

LUMBERJACK LAND

GRANTS PASS TO EUGENE

North of Grants Pass, Highway 99 disappears under the interstate once more, as the route twists and turns its narrow way through the Cascades. This is a beautiful but treacherous stretch of road, with sharp curves, steep inclines, and wildly varied weather. In the colder months, expect driving rain and even snow (goodbye, banana belt); you may need to break out those tire chains again. Even so, parts of this stretch feel like a tribute to California, with patches of chaparral hills and oak trees interrupting the misty evergreen forests and lush blue greens that dominate much of the Pacific Northwest.

HIDDEN TREASURES

You'll have to exit the freeway to see them, but the Grave Creek Bridge and the Wolf Creek Tavern are essential Highway 99 landmarks. The bridge, built in 1920, feels like a small slice of New England, with its shake roof and Gothic-style windows. Twenty miles north of Grants Pass is the historic Wolf Creek Tavern, formerly known as the Wolf Creek Inn. This mountain hideaway is Oregon's oldest continually operating hotel, built in 1883 along the Applegate Trail (a southern spur of the Oregon Trail). The inn is now operated by Oregon State Parks and has a reputation for being haunted.

▲ Wigwam burners, used to destroy scrap wood, once dominated the Northwest logging regions. Only a few remain today; one is visible just northeast of Drain.

▼ Grave Creek Bridge in Sunny Valley is one of many covered spans in Western Oregon but the only one that ever carried Highway 99.

TIMBER TOWN

Roseburg, nicknamed the Timber Capital of the Nation, sits on the Umpqua River. Highway 99 is a major thoroughfare through here, with many vintage neon signs still standing. An odd holiday-season fixture is the world's largest nutcracker. This guy gets hauled out each year for the Umpqua Valley Festival of Lights, held at River Forks Park west of town. Carved out of redwood and cedar, the nutcracker has actual working jaws that crack coconuts.

A DETOUR DOWN THE DRAIN

There's a sizable section of Old 99 that loops through the tiny towns of Yoncalla and Drain. Drain is especially charming, with a covered pedestrian bridge (see below) downtown and a number of restored Victorian houses.

GO OFF ON A TRESTLE TANGENT

If Grave Creek gave you a taste for covered bridges, you'll want to check out this mountain stretch, which is home to many more, with several requiring a bit of a back-road trek to find. Douglas County, covering the southern half of the route, has seven within reach of the interstate. Highlights include the Canyon Creek Bridge, near Pioneer Park in Canyonville. The town of Myrtle Creek is home to two: Horse Creek Bridge and Neal Lane Bridge. Heading northward, Lane County has a whopping nineteen more covered bridges, including seven near the town of Cottage Grove (nicknamed, naturally, the Covered Bridge Capital of Oregon). The best are the windowed Centennial Covered Bridge (at Main Street and River Road downtown) and the Chambers Railroad Bridge (at River Road and Harrison Street), the last covered railroad bridge in the state. The oldest, Mosby Creek Bridge (found along the Row River Trail), is right next to the railroad trestle bridge featured in the 1986 film *Stand by Me*.

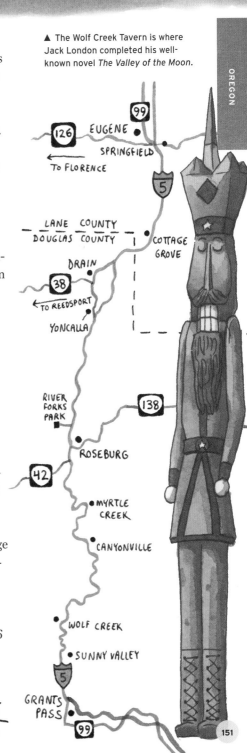

▲ The Wolf Creek Tavern is where Jack London completed his well-known novel *The Valley of the Moon*.

The Cherry on Top

EUGENE AND SALEM

As you enter the Willamette Valley (map on page 154), take a deep breath. You've left the mountains behind you for a good long while. For the rest of Oregon, the terrain is gentle, and a series of cities leads you toward Portland like a trail of bread crumbs.

GREEN EUGENE

The first burg you encounter is the largest before Portland: environmentally conscious Eugene, seat of the University of Oregon (home of the Ducks, the second-most Oregon-y team name on earth). This liberal enclave has built its entire tourism industry around celebrating nature and the arts—sometimes combined.

Some of Eugene's best attractions are outdoors. Start at the Saturday Market, the longest-running open-air artisan craft fair in America. Then walk downtown along the Eugene Ale Trail, and take your pick of many craft breweries. Finally, hike off the calories at Mount Pisgah Arboretum. Located five miles southeast of downtown, this two-hundred-acre park protects one of the savannas of Oregon white oak that blanketed the Willamette Valley before settlers started cultivating the land.

If you're the indoor type, visit the U of O's Jordan Schnitzer Museum of Art to see a top-notch collection of Russian and Asian artwork. For one-stop shopping, try the Fifth Street Public Market (public markets are a thing in the Northwest). It is perched on several levels around a central courtyard and features a wide variety of eateries, coffee shops, retail stores, and small food and wine markets. The market feels a bit more mall-like than Seattle's Pike Place Market (page 176) and is certainly more modern, but it has an open and inviting feel to it.

▲ The *Oregon Pioneer* statue at the top of the capitol is nicknamed Gold Man for the gold leaf that coats the hollow sculpture.

▼ On Salem's northern outskirts is the Oregon Electric Railway Museum, where visitors can ride on a historic double-decker trolley.

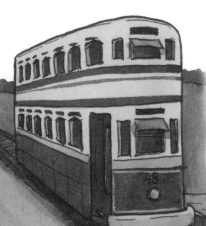

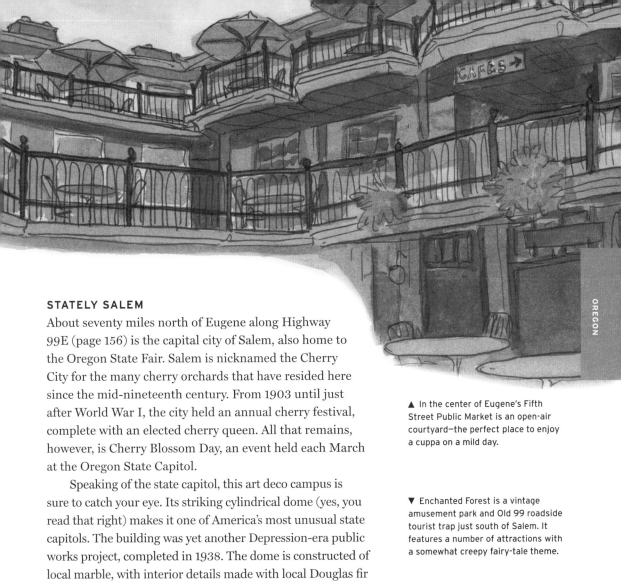

STATELY SALEM

About seventy miles north of Eugene along Highway 99E (page 156) is the capital city of Salem, also home to the Oregon State Fair. Salem is nicknamed the Cherry City for the many cherry orchards that have resided here since the mid-nineteenth century. From 1903 until just after World War I, the city held an annual cherry festival, complete with an elected cherry queen. All that remains, however, is Cherry Blossom Day, an event held each March at the Oregon State Capitol.

Speaking of the state capitol, this art deco campus is sure to catch your eye. Its striking cylindrical dome (yes, you read that right) makes it one of America's most unusual state capitols. The building was yet another Depression-era public works project, completed in 1938. The dome is constructed of local marble, with interior details made with local Douglas fir wood. When you go, make sure to pop into the state library on Court Street. On the second floor are a number of folk-style illustrated vignettes that highlight Oregon's natural resources: timber, wool, hazelnuts, etc.

Before you continue northward, be sure to check out some of Salem's preserved historic enclaves. The downtown historic district, centered around Commercial Street (Old 99E), boasts a number of restored Victorian storefronts, each painted in period colors. Just south of downtown is the Gaiety Hill/Bush's Pasture Park Historic District, home to more than a hundred historic properties, including two nineteenth-century house museums: the Bush House Museum and the historic Deepwood Museum & Gardens. For a more eclectic mix of historic homes, try the Court-Chemeketa Residential Historic District, located just east of the state capitol.

▲ In the center of Eugene's Fifth Street Public Market is an open-air courtyard—the perfect place to enjoy a cuppa on a mild day.

▼ Enchanted Forest is a vintage amusement park and Old 99 roadside tourist trap just south of Salem. It features a number of attractions with a somewhat creepy fairy-tale theme.

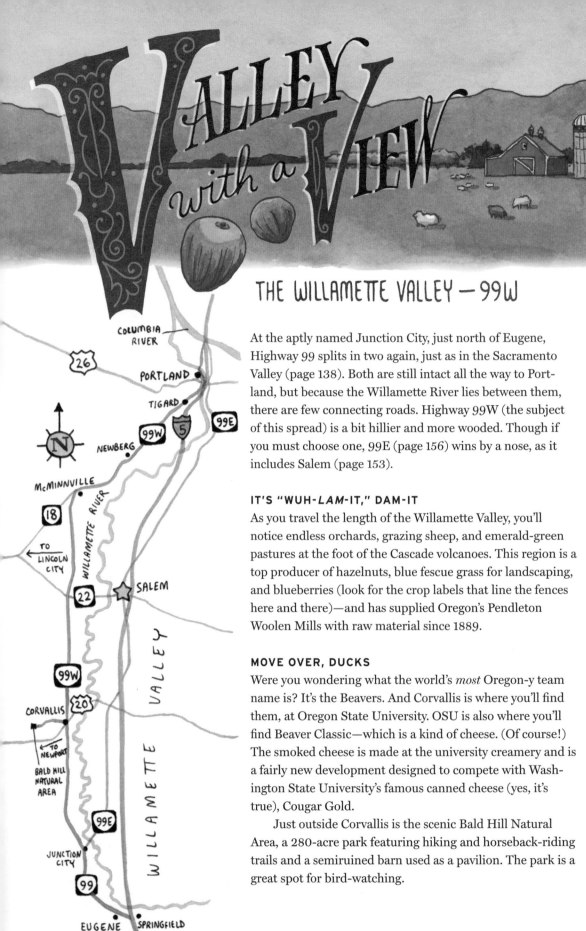

Valley with a View

THE WILLAMETTE VALLEY — 99W

At the aptly named Junction City, just north of Eugene, Highway 99 splits in two again, just as in the Sacramento Valley (page 138). Both are still intact all the way to Portland, but because the Willamette River lies between them, there are few connecting roads. Highway 99W (the subject of this spread) is a bit hillier and more wooded. Though if you must choose one, 99E (page 156) wins by a nose, as it includes Salem (page 153).

IT'S "WUH-*LAM*-IT," DAM-IT

As you travel the length of the Willamette Valley, you'll notice endless orchards, grazing sheep, and emerald-green pastures at the foot of the Cascade volcanoes. This region is a top producer of hazelnuts, blue fescue grass for landscaping, and blueberries (look for the crop labels that line the fences here and there)—and has supplied Oregon's Pendleton Woolen Mills with raw material since 1889.

MOVE OVER, DUCKS

Were you wondering what the world's *most* Oregon-y team name is? It's the Beavers. And Corvallis is where you'll find them, at Oregon State University. OSU is also where you'll find Beaver Classic—which is a kind of cheese. (Of course!) The smoked cheese is made at the university creamery and is a fairly new development designed to compete with Washington State University's famous canned cheese (yes, it's true), Cougar Gold.

Just outside Corvallis is the scenic Bald Hill Natural Area, a 280-acre park featuring hiking and horseback-riding trails and a semiruined barn used as a pavilion. The park is a great spot for bird-watching.

A HEADY BOUQUET

The Willamette Valley wine region is centered around
McMinnville, with several wineries and estates open for
tours and tastings. Also in the region are a handful of
lavender farms; for artists, there's a plein air painting
festival each July called the Oregon Lavender Paint Out.
Here, 99W turns northeastward to make its final approach
toward greater Portland.

▲ Oregon produces 99 percent of the
US hazelnut crop—as well as a whole
lot of grass-fed lamb chops.

THE OUTER BURBS

Tigard (pronounced "TIE-gerd") and the other towns outside of Portland are now a blur of suburban sprawl, unfortunately, with a number of malls obscuring any vintage traces
of Highway 99. The route gets a bit confusing here, too, as
the street grid condenses with more and more thoroughfares. Stay on 99W, which changes its name from Pacific
Highway Southwest to Southwest Barbur Boulevard.

GATEWAY TO *PORTLANDIA*

Barbur Boulevard winds its way into Portland through the
Southwest Hills, before dumping you out on Fourth Avenue
Southwest downtown (map on page 161). For a scenic alternative, turn left onto Terwilliger Boulevard and follow that
into town instead, through George Himes Park. (From here
you'll see great views of Mount Hood and also 99E, visible
far below on the other side of the river.) This route becomes
Sixth Avenue Southwest.

▶ Don't miss the impeccably preserved
Benton County courthouse in Corvallis, a
pyramidal masterpiece built in 1888.

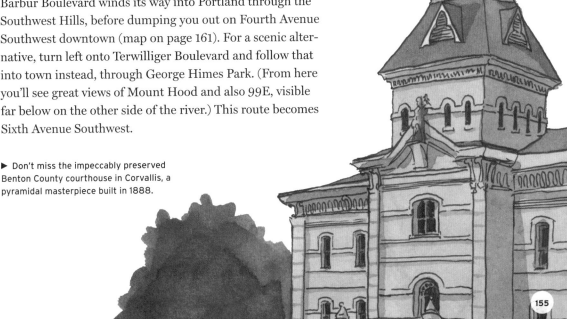

155

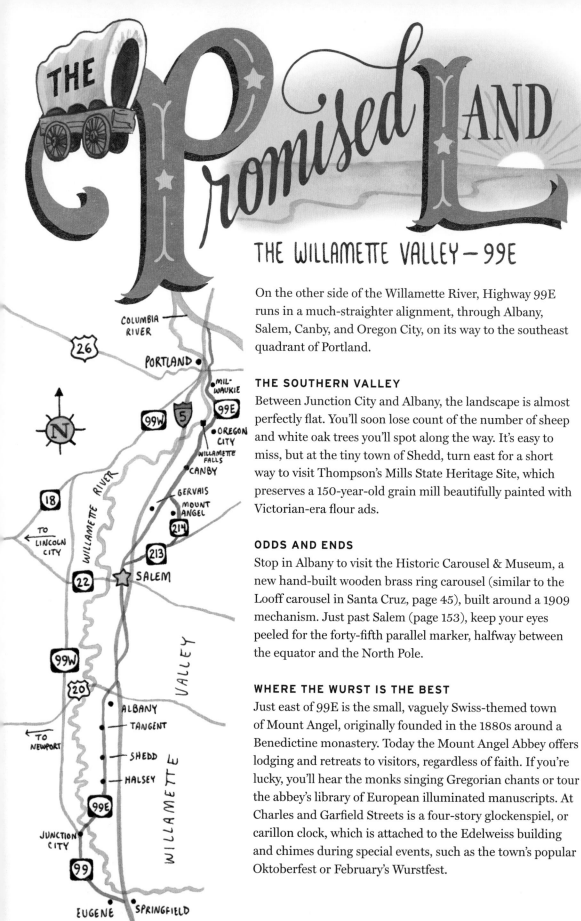

THE WILLAMETTE VALLEY — 99E

On the other side of the Willamette River, Highway 99E runs in a much-straighter alignment, through Albany, Salem, Canby, and Oregon City, on its way to the southeast quadrant of Portland.

THE SOUTHERN VALLEY

Between Junction City and Albany, the landscape is almost perfectly flat. You'll soon lose count of the number of sheep and white oak trees you'll spot along the way. It's easy to miss, but at the tiny town of Shedd, turn east for a short way to visit Thompson's Mills State Heritage Site, which preserves a 150-year-old grain mill beautifully painted with Victorian-era flour ads.

ODDS AND ENDS

Stop in Albany to visit the Historic Carousel & Museum, a new hand-built wooden brass ring carousel (similar to the Looff carousel in Santa Cruz, page 45), built around a 1909 mechanism. Just past Salem (page 153), keep your eyes peeled for the forty-fifth parallel marker, halfway between the equator and the North Pole.

WHERE THE WURST IS THE BEST

Just east of 99E is the small, vaguely Swiss-themed town of Mount Angel, originally founded in the 1880s around a Benedictine monastery. Today the Mount Angel Abbey offers lodging and retreats to visitors, regardless of faith. If you're lucky, you'll hear the monks singing Gregorian chants or tour the abbey's library of European illuminated manuscripts. At Charles and Garfield Streets is a four-story glockenspiel, or carillon clock, which is attached to the Edelweiss building and chimes during special events, such as the town's popular Oktoberfest or February's Wurstfest.

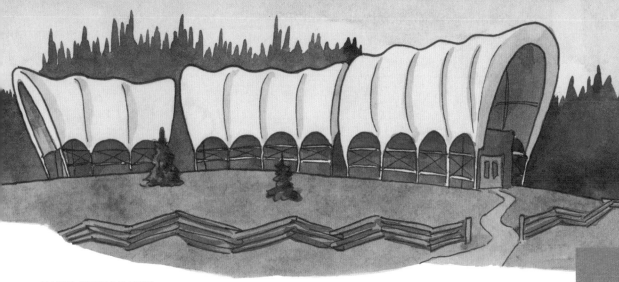

BLUE-RIBBON FUN

If you pass through Canby in August, be sure to stop for the Clackamas County Fair, a weeklong extravaganza of the Willamette Valley's bounty. In late September the fairgrounds hosts the Oregon Flock & Fiber Festival, a perennial favorite of knitters and weavers.

▲ The End of the Oregon Trail Interpretive Center is built in the shape of a huge Conestoga wagon train.

THE END OF THE TRAIL

Oregon City, located at Willamette Falls (illustration on page 111), was the first territorial capital of Oregon. It also marks the symbolic end of the Oregon Trail, a defining element of the American West (not to mention a computer game familiar to anyone who grew up in the 1980s and '90s). Worth a stop is the End of the Oregon Trail Interpretive Center, though it mostly presents the Oregon Trail from the point of view of white settlers and their descendants. For a more complete cultural picture (page 110), you may need to look elsewhere, like one of the traveling lectures by Oregon Black Pioneers, a history group based in Salem. The only Oregon Trail museum that tells the story from the Indigenous point of view is the Tamástslikt Cultural Institute, located two hundred miles east of Portland in Pendleton, Oregon.

CITY LIGHTS

To go on to Portland, continue on 99E, which turns into the busy McLoughlin Boulevard. For a scenic alternative, explore the lovely Portland neighborhood of Sellwood, home to a number of independent shops and cafés.

▶ The Mount Angel glockenspiel opens when it chimes, revealing lederhosen-clad animatronic figures inside the clock movement.

157

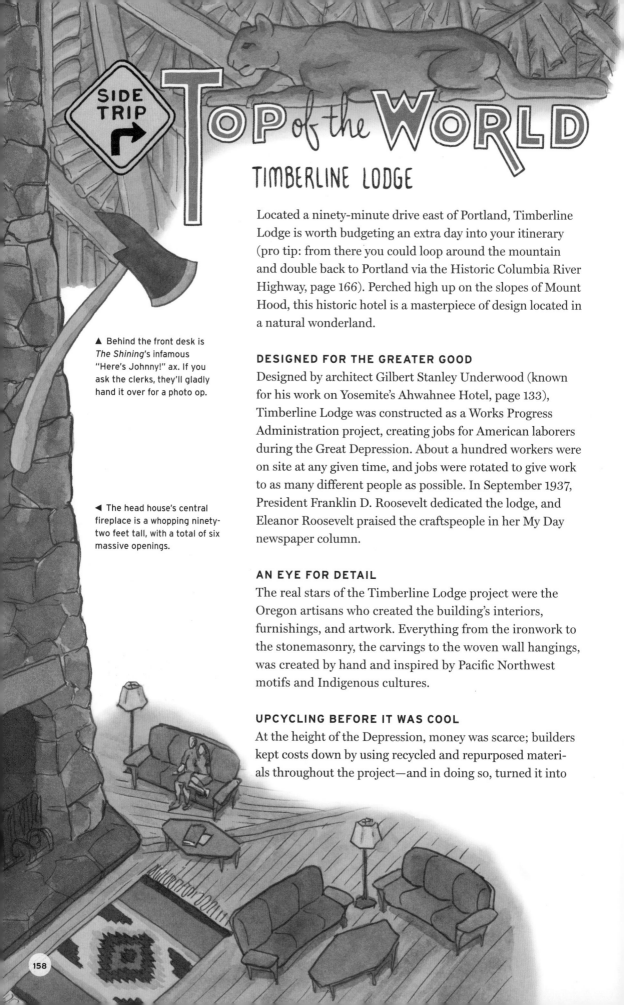

SIDE TRIP

TOP of the WORLD

TIMBERLINE LODGE

Located a ninety-minute drive east of Portland, Timberline Lodge is worth budgeting an extra day into your itinerary (pro tip: from there you could loop around the mountain and double back to Portland via the Historic Columbia River Highway, page 166). Perched high up on the slopes of Mount Hood, this historic hotel is a masterpiece of design located in a natural wonderland.

DESIGNED FOR THE GREATER GOOD

Designed by architect Gilbert Stanley Underwood (known for his work on Yosemite's Ahwahnee Hotel, page 133), Timberline Lodge was constructed as a Works Progress Administration project, creating jobs for American laborers during the Great Depression. About a hundred workers were on site at any given time, and jobs were rotated to give work to as many different people as possible. In September 1937, President Franklin D. Roosevelt dedicated the lodge, and Eleanor Roosevelt praised the craftspeople in her My Day newspaper column.

AN EYE FOR DETAIL

The real stars of the Timberline Lodge project were the Oregon artisans who created the building's interiors, furnishings, and artwork. Everything from the ironwork to the stonemasonry, the carvings to the woven wall hangings, was created by hand and inspired by Pacific Northwest motifs and Indigenous cultures.

UPCYCLING BEFORE IT WAS COOL

At the height of the Depression, money was scarce; builders kept costs down by using recycled and repurposed materials throughout the project—and in doing so, turned it into

▲ Behind the front desk is *The Shining*'s infamous "Here's Johnny!" ax. If you ask the clerks, they'll gladly hand it over for a photo op.

◄ The head house's central fireplace is a whopping ninety-two feet tall, with a total of six massive openings.

158

an engine for innovation. Old utility poles were carved into newel posts, portraying nineteen different local animals and birds. Railroad steel and tire chains transformed into fireplace andirons and screens. Old oxen yokes became light fixtures. Nothing was wasted, and the team learned to think outside the box.

MOVIE MAYHEM

Timberline Lodge reached a new level of fame when director Stanley Kubrick used the exterior of the building as the setting for his 1980 horror film, *The Shining*. (The interiors were filmed on a sound stage modeled after the interior of the Ahwahnee Hotel.) These days the lodge does late-night screenings of the movie—and a winter visit is guaranteed to give you the heebie-jeebies.

RETRO RUSTIC

A stay at Timberline Lodge is a step back in time. Keep in mind that the rooms are small and basic, and the cheaper ones have shared bathrooms. In the winter the window in your room might be completely blocked by snow (even accounting for climate change, Mount Hood receives an average of about a hundred feet of snow each year). If that sounds like a deal breaker, a day trip can be just as rewarding. In the summer the surrounding wildflower meadows make for a colorful hike. And the Cascade Dining Room offers an unforgettable view of the volcanoes of the Pacific crest.

▲ The lodge, with its steep-pitched Cascadian-style roof, is designed to evoke the silhouette of Mount Hood.

▼ The 750-pound bronze weathervane atop the head house is an abstract representation of a snow goose.

▲ The White Stag sign has changed its slogan many times over the years, beginning as a sporting-goods billboard and transforming into a city-owned landmark.

▼ Portland's food carts are often clustered together in pods. Yet in recent years builders have eyed these pods for development, resulting in a tense battle over zoning and gentrification.

Don your plaid flannel shirt, crack open a craft beer, tune up your bike, start growing your beard, and get ready to take up backyard urban farming. Welcome to Portland—the Northwest's counterculture capital. Highway 99 gives you an old-school, in-depth tour as it continues its split along the length of the city. The 99E segment runs up the east side of the river, and 99W follows a series of historic alignments downtown and beyond. The twin roads merge just before the Columbia River bridge, which now carries Interstate 5.

KEEP PORTLAND WEIRD

Thanks to the loving spoofs provided by the television show *Portlandia*, the world knows that the bumper stickers don't lie. Individuality is an art form here; peccadilloes and personal quirks are strongly encouraged. If you want to blend in in Portland, learn to stand out.

TWO PLUS TWO EQUALS FIVE

Here's a strange thing: Portland is a city of five quadrants (see map, right). That's not a typo, and it's no accident. Rather, call it a gift of the Willamette and Columbia Rivers, which flow together just beyond the northern enclave of St. Johns. Burnside Street is the north-south division line, with the rivers and the interstate doing the rest of the work. Each quadrant feels like a distinct entity with an individual flavor all its own.

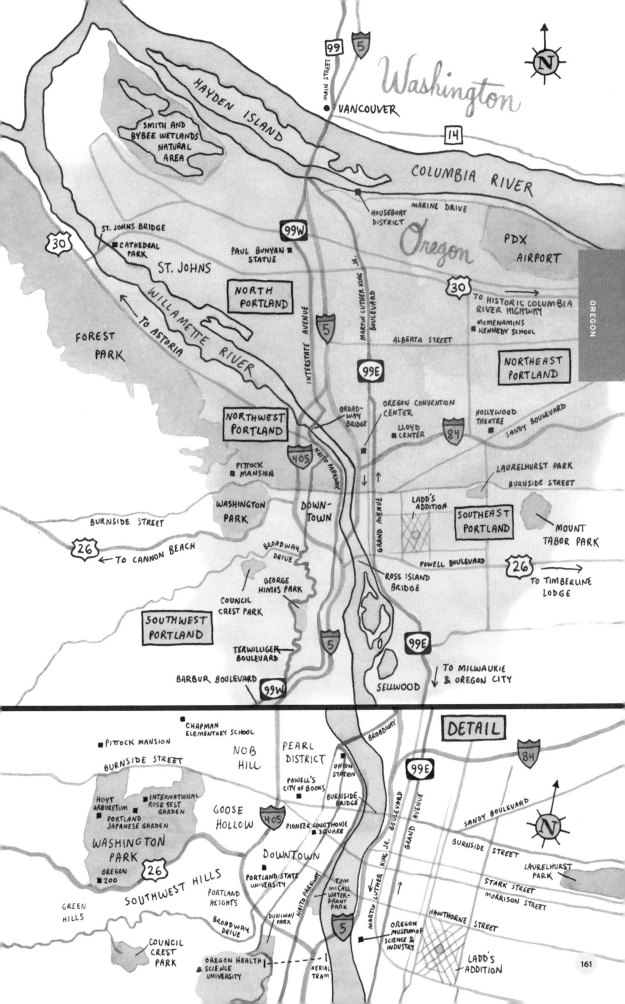

N

HAYDEN ISLAND

Washington

99 5

Main Street

VANCOUVER

14

COLUMBIA RIVER

SMITH AND BYBEE WETLANDS NATURAL AREA

MARINE DRIVE

HOUSEBOAT DISTRICT

Oregon

PDX AIRPORT

OREGON

ST. JOHNS BRIDGE

30

CATHEDRAL PARK

99W

PAUL BUNYAN STATUE

ST. JOHNS

NORTH PORTLAND

30

TO HISTORIC COLUMBIA RIVER HIGHWAY

McMENAMINS KENNEDY SCHOOL

FOREST PARK

To Astoria

WILLAMETTE RIVER

INTERSTATE AVENUE

5

MARTIN LUTHER KING JR. BOULEVARD

ALBERTA STREET

99E

NORTHEAST PORTLAND

OREGON CONVENTION CENTER

HOLLYWOOD THEATRE

SANDY BOULEVARD

NORTHWEST PORTLAND

BROADWAY BRIDGE

LLOYD CENTER

84

405

NAITO PARKWAY

PITTOCK MANSION

LAURELHURST PARK

BURNSIDE STREET

WASHINGTON PARK

DOWNTOWN

GRAND AVENUE

LADD'S ADDITION

SOUTHEAST PORTLAND

MOUNT TABOR PARK

BURNSIDE STREET

26

TO CANNON BEACH

BROADWAY DRIVE

GEORGE HIMES PARK

COUNCIL CREST PARK

POWELL BOULEVARD

ROSS ISLAND BRIDGE

26

TO TIMBERLINE LODGE

SOUTHWEST PORTLAND

5

99E

TERWILLIGER BOULEVARD

TO MILWAUKIE & OREGON CITY

BARBUR BOULEVARD

99W

SELLWOOD

PITTOCK MANSION

CHAPMAN ELEMENTARY SCHOOL

NOB HILL

PEARL DISTRICT

Broadway

DETAIL

84

BURNSIDE STREET

UNION STATION

99E

POWELL'S CITY OF BOOKS

HOYT ARBORETUM

INTERNATIONAL ROSE TEST GARDEN

GOOSE HOLLOW

BURNSIDE BRIDGE

SANDY BOULEVARD

N

PORTLAND JAPANESE GARDEN

405

PIONEER COURTHOUSE SQUARE

MARTIN LUTHER KING JR. BOULEVARD

GRAND AVENUE

BURNSIDE STREET

WASHINGTON PARK

DOWNTOWN

LAURELHURST PARK

OREGON ZOO

26

STARK STREET

GREEN HILLS

SOUTHWEST HILLS

PORTLAND STATE UNIVERSITY

MORRISON STREET

PORTLAND HEIGHTS

TOM McCALL WATERFRONT PARK

HAWTHORNE STREET

DUNIWAY PARK

NAITO PARKWAY

BROADWAY DRIVE

COUNCIL CREST PARK

5

OREGON MUSEUM OF SCIENCE & INDUSTRY

LADD'S ADDITION

OREGON HEALTH & SCIENCE UNIVERSITY

AERIAL TRAM

SOUTHWEST: TOWERS AND TREES

This massive quadrant encompasses both downtown and the region known as the Southwest Hills. The city center lies within the Willamette floodplain, so it is perfectly flat and extremely walkable. Start at Portland's Living Room: Pioneer Courthouse Square, home to a number of seasonal events. Hit up the Oregon Historical Society for state and regional lore, or view an exhibit at the Portland Art Museum across the street. The long, skinny South Park Blocks are home to the city's largest farmers' market, while along the riverfront, the Portland Saturday Market boasts a number of artisan vendors and food trucks but no produce.

The historic neighborhood of Goose Hollow marks the transition to Portland Heights and the Southwest Hills. "Mountains" might be a more apt description, as this part of town sits up to a thousand feet above downtown. Council Crest Park is the highest point in the city, offering 360-degree views of Mount Hood, downtown, and, when it decides to cooperate with the weather, Mount Saint Helens. Closer in, Washington Park commands an enormous presence, with a hundred miles of hiking trails and the many tree and plant species of the Hoyt Arboretum. The park is also home to the Oregon Zoo, the Portland Children's Museum, a number of memorials, and the World Forestry Center. The two jewels of the park are the International Rose Test Garden, home to over five hundred flower varieties, and the Portland Japanese Garden, with its teahouse and raked sand beds.

▲ With their steep hills and many pedestrian trails, the Southwest Hills are great for a wooded hike—complete with countless vista points for peekaboo panoramas.

▼ Powell's City of Books organizes its 3,500 sections into nine color-coded rooms, creating a multistory book labyrinth that is a tourist attraction in its own right.

NORTHWEST: ALPHABET CITY

Across Burnside Street lie the Pearl District, Old Town, and Portland's tiny Chinatown. The Pearl is densely packed with shops, restaurants, and bars. Grab a pastry at the Pearl Bakery, a pint at Deschutes Brewery, or a fancy Peruvian meal at Andina. The quadrant's anchor point is Powell's City of Books—occupying a full city block, it's the world's largest independent bookstore. To help you navigate the area, the streets are alphabetical from *B* (Burnside) to *Y* (York). Fun fact: Flanders Street was the inspiration for Ned Flanders in *The Simpsons*.

Naito Parkway, along the riverfront, will lead you up and out to a large industrial area. Above is a vast wall of trees: this is Forest Park, one of the largest urban forests in America. Just seven miles in length, the park encompasses eighty miles of woodland trails.

NORTH: OLD-SCHOOL AND INCREASINGLY COOL

Mixed use from the beginning, North Portland is experiencing rapid residential and commercial growth. Still, a number of old roadside icons survive beside the new light-rail line that runs along Interstate Avenue (99W)—especially the Palms Motel, the Alibi (page 99), and the thirty-foot Paul Bunyan statue. Tucked away to the west is the enclave of St. Johns. Originally its own town, this up-and-coming neighborhood is centered around the beautiful St. Johns Bridge, a spired copper affair that is the last river crossing until the bridge over the Columbia to Longview, Washington.

▲ If you're tired from all that hill hiking, consider catching a ride on the aerial tram, which offers views of Mount Hood on clear days.

▼ Cathedral Park lies underneath St. Johns Bridge, the pillars of which resemble the arches of a Gothic cathedral.

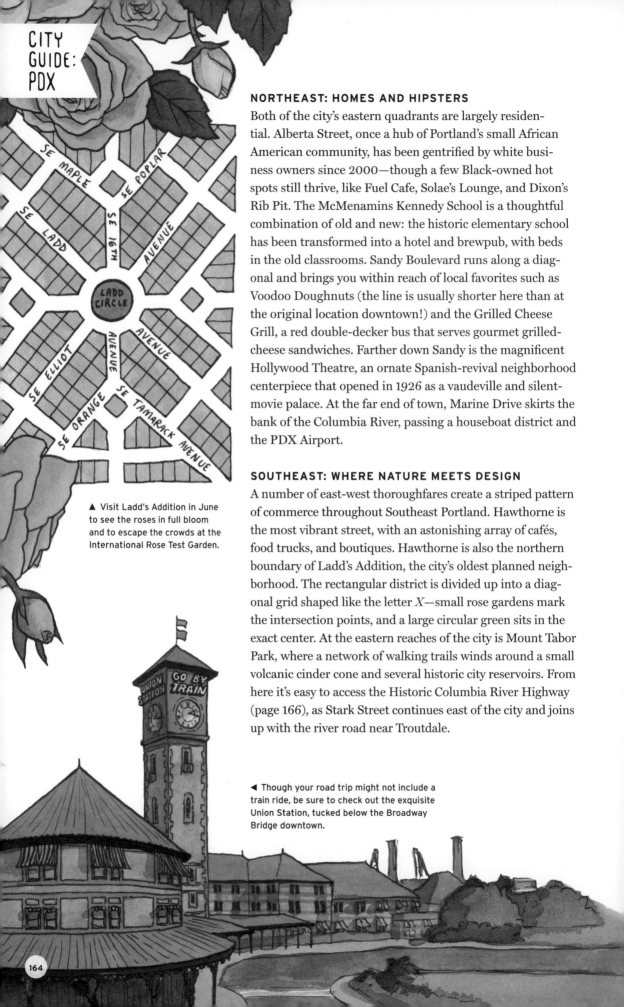

NORTHEAST: HOMES AND HIPSTERS

Both of the city's eastern quadrants are largely residential. Alberta Street, once a hub of Portland's small African American community, has been gentrified by white business owners since 2000—though a few Black-owned hot spots still thrive, like Fuel Cafe, Solae's Lounge, and Dixon's Rib Pit. The McMenamins Kennedy School is a thoughtful combination of old and new: the historic elementary school has been transformed into a hotel and brewpub, with beds in the old classrooms. Sandy Boulevard runs along a diagonal and brings you within reach of local favorites such as Voodoo Doughnuts (the line is usually shorter here than at the original location downtown!) and the Grilled Cheese Grill, a red double-decker bus that serves gourmet grilled-cheese sandwiches. Farther down Sandy is the magnificent Hollywood Theatre, an ornate Spanish-revival neighborhood centerpiece that opened in 1926 as a vaudeville and silent-movie palace. At the far end of town, Marine Drive skirts the bank of the Columbia River, passing a houseboat district and the PDX Airport.

SOUTHEAST: WHERE NATURE MEETS DESIGN

A number of east-west thoroughfares create a striped pattern of commerce throughout Southeast Portland. Hawthorne is the most vibrant street, with an astonishing array of cafés, food trucks, and boutiques. Hawthorne is also the northern boundary of Ladd's Addition, the city's oldest planned neighborhood. The rectangular district is divided up into a diagonal grid shaped like the letter *X*—small rose gardens mark the intersection points, and a large circular green sits in the exact center. At the eastern reaches of the city is Mount Tabor Park, where a network of walking trails winds around a small volcanic cinder cone and several historic city reservoirs. From here it's easy to access the Historic Columbia River Highway (page 166), as Stark Street continues east of the city and joins up with the river road near Troutdale.

▲ Visit Ladd's Addition in June to see the roses in full bloom and to escape the crowds at the International Rose Test Garden.

◄ Though your road trip might not include a train ride, be sure to check out the exquisite Union Station, tucked below the Broadway Bridge downtown.

PORTLAND ICONS

▶ On September evenings spectators flock to Chapman Elementary School to watch up to ten thousand Vaux's swifts return to their roost inside the school chimney.

▼ The Paul Bunyan statue is both an Oregon icon and a Highway 99 legend. Naturally, Portland's original hipster is decked out in a beard and flannel shirt.

◀ Portland's many food trucks offer everything from a quick bite to a gourmet meal—you can find them, either alone or in pods, in every quadrant.

OREGON

▼ Portland enjoys many nicknames, including Bridgetown, Stumptown, and the Rose City.

▲ The Pittock Mansion, perched on forty-six acres above downtown, is now a historic museum and park run by the City of Portland.

▼ With fourteen unique spans (like the Fremont Bridge, below), Portland has the most diverse array of bridges in the country.

▶ Rodents of unusual size *do* exist here: the beaver-size nutria, introduced from South America, is an unwelcome addition to the urban fauna.

◀ The Pioneer Courthouse, built in 1869, is the oldest federal building west of the Mississippi.

▶ Between the landmark store Powell's City of Books and the Portland Book Festival, Portland has become a hub for literature and writers.

Gorge-ous

SIDE TRIP ↱

THE HISTORIC COLUMBIA RIVER HIGHWAY

Before you cross the mighty Columbia into Washington, consider taking a short side jaunt to explore the river itself. Just as it carried Lewis and Clark to the Pacific Ocean (page 88), the Columbia River swept the first auto tourists into a new era of exploration.

TAKE ME TO THE RIVER

Just east of Portland, the Columbia cuts its way through a deep mountain gorge as it crosses the Pacific crest and enters the leeward side of the Cascades. Interstate 84 follows the river on the Oregon side; if you go far enough east, you can watch the lush forests peter out and the semidesert climate take over. While the interstate runs upstream along the riverbank, the Historic Columbia River Highway twists and turns its way to Multnomah Falls, high above the modern freeway on the cliff side.

DEATH-DEFYING DESIGN

Rather than a simple thoroughfare, the Columbia River Highway was specifically designed as the nation's first scenic byway. Designer and promoter Sam Hill knew what wonders the Gorge held and anticipated that with help, America's new class of motorists and road trippers would view the journey itself as the destination. Between 1913 and 1916, engineers and laborers created the route out of impossible grades, cuts, and bridges along the stone cliffs of the Gorge. Some of the project's stonemasons went on to work on Timberline Lodge, and the highway became the model for national park routes like Glacier's Going-to-the-Sun Road.

◀ The Benson Footbridge, built in 1914, was designed both to complement the landscape and to give pedestrians a simultaneous view of both tiers of Multnomah Falls.

TAKE THE LONG VIEW

The Columbia River Highway's most famous landmark is the
Vista House, perched on the volcanic promontory of Crown
Point. Completed in 1918, the octagonal building is a combination of roadside rest stop and monument to the pioneers
of the Oregon Trail.

FALL HEAD OVER HEELS

Two major waterfalls punctuate the Columbia River Gorge
experience. First up is Bridal Veil Falls, reached by a short
ADA-accessible trail. Farther on is Multnomah Falls, one
of Oregon's top tourist destinations. This six-hundred-foot
waterfall plunges down in two tiers, with a stone bridge hov-
ering above the transition point. As the falls sit on the north
face of a cliff, they are nearly always in shadow. Visit around
the summer solstice, however, and just before sunset you'll
see the last rays of light illuminate the cascade.

THE RETURN TRIP

Most visitors opt to return to Portland via the interstate,
but if you're not quite ready to let go of the Gorge, you can
continue on to the town of Hood River (thirty miles east
of Multnomah Falls), where the next bridge can carry you
across to the Washington side. There, scenic State Route 14
can carry you back to Highway 99.

▲ The Vista House is built from
sandstone, with interior details of
pink marble, white limestone, and
green glass.

EVERGREEN Dreams

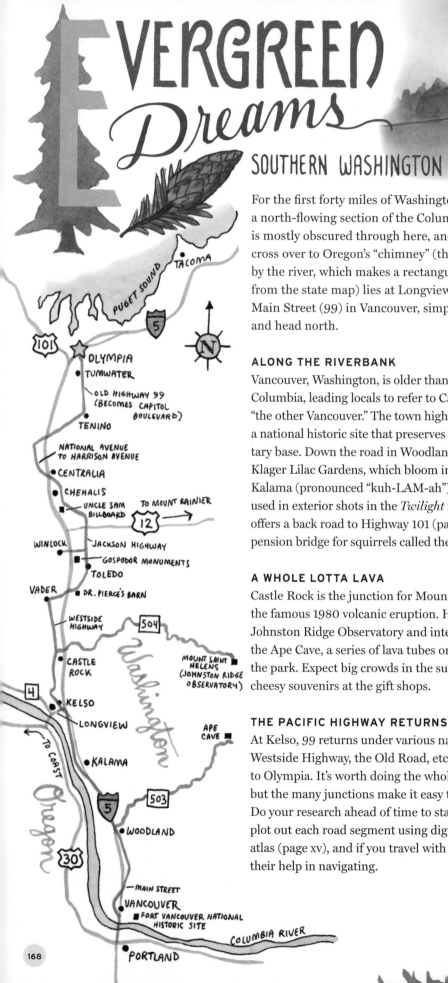

SOUTHERN WASHINGTON

For the first forty miles of Washington, the interstate hugs a north-flowing section of the Columbia River. Highway 99 is mostly obscured through here, and the next bridge to cross over to Oregon's "chimney" (the stub of land defined by the river, which makes a rectangular shape stick out from the state map) lies at Longview. After checking out Main Street (99) in Vancouver, simply jump on the freeway and head north.

ALONG THE RIVERBANK

Vancouver, Washington, is older than the one in British Columbia, leading locals to refer to Canada's (page 196) as "the other Vancouver." The town highlight is Fort Vancouver, a national historic site that preserves a Victorian-era military base. Down the road in Woodland, check out the Hulda Klager Lilac Gardens, which bloom in late April or early May. Kalama (pronounced "kuh-LAM-ah") boasts the high school used in exterior shots in the *Twilight* movies, while Longview offers a back road to Highway 101 (page 90) and a mini suspension bridge for squirrels called the Nutty Narrows.

A WHOLE LOTTA LAVA

Castle Rock is the junction for Mount Saint Helens, site of the famous 1980 volcanic eruption. Highlights include the Johnston Ridge Observatory and interpretive center and the Ape Cave, a series of lava tubes on the southern end of the park. Expect big crowds in the summer and delightfully cheesy souvenirs at the gift shops.

THE PACIFIC HIGHWAY RETURNS

At Kelso, 99 returns under various names (Jackson Highway, Westside Highway, the Old Road, etc.) and runs all the way to Olympia. It's worth doing the whole turn-by-turn route, but the many junctions make it easy to get turned around. Do your research ahead of time to stay on the correct path: plot out each road segment using digital maps or your paper atlas (page xv), and if you travel with a companion, enlist their help in navigating.

Dr. PIERCE'S

▲ A Victorian-era barn with a hand-painted snake-oil advertisement still stands near Toledo.

ROADSIDE ODDBALLS

Near Toledo, check out the Gospodor Monuments, a strange attraction between the Jackson Highway and the interstate. The trio of eighty-foot columns were designed by an octogenarian millionaire to pay tribute to Mother Teresa, the Holocaust, and the American Indian. In the town of Winlock, a regional egg-and-poultry capital, is the self-proclaimed world's largest egg statue. In 1931 representatives from Long Beach brought in their world's largest frying pan (page 91) for a festival and used it to fry an omelet using more than seven thousand fresh eggs!

▲ Mount Saint Helens, dramatically altered since its 1980 eruption, is visible from many spots along the old Highway 99.

TWIN C-TOWNS

Next up are the sister cities of Chehalis (pronounced "shuh-HAY-liss") and Centralia ("cen-TRAY-lia"). Near Centralia, visible from Rush Road, is the infamous Uncle Sam billboard. Built by Alfred Hamilton after the government used eminent domain on his land in the 1960s, this homemade sign belts out ever-changing libertarian screeds. Alfred's equally cantankerous descendants continue his legacy, alternately amusing and infuriating interstate travelers. Centralia is the quainter city, with a number of good antique shops and a vintage Chinese restaurant with a neon butterfly sign out front (page ix).

▼ Sadly, "world's largest" eggs (even larger than the one in Winlock) can be found in Wilson, Kansas, and Mentone, Indiana.

COUNTDOWN TO THE CAPITAL

The last town before Olympia is historic Tumwater, site of the first permanent white settlement in Washington and the 1896 former Olympia Brewery building. Highway 99 crosses over Tumwater Falls on a totem-pole-adorned bridge and arrives in Olympia via Capitol Way.

WASHINGTON EGG & CO-OPERATIVE POULTRY ASSOCIATION

WINLOCK WORLD'S Largest EGG

CAPITOL *Idea*

OLYMPIA

(page 90)

At Olympia, Highway 99 completes the thread between all three West Coast capitals. Capitol Way (which carries 99) intersects with the original Highway 101 at Fourth Avenue; from here you can head west to the Olympic Peninsula (page 90) or turn right on Fourth to continue along the original 99 route.

Olympia lies at the southern end of Puget Sound, that large saltwater inlet that defines the Seattle area. From here on out you'll be shadowing the Salish Sea as Highway 99 heads closer and closer to the shore. Olympia is home to a small waterfront and commercial port, as well as the large shoreline reserve of Priest Point Park. Slightly farther afield are the Black Hills, the northeastern arm of the Coast Range, and the southern end of the Olympic Mountains. Don't miss the Mima Mounds Natural Area Preserve, located just southwest of town. Nobody knows how these mysterious, circular earthen mounds got here, but the trail that winds over and around them is a joy to hike and explore.

▲ Theories about the origins of the Mima Mounds range from pocket gophers and strong winds to ancient civilizations and earthquakes—none have yet been ruled out.

▼ With its cherry and maple trees, the state capitol campus bursts with color in spring and fall.

TOWER AND DOME

Olympia has had two state capitols over the years. The first, after it lost its tall central tower in a 1928 fire, was relegated to the Thurston County courthouse. The current capitol, completed that same year out of stone, has also seen its fair share of natural disasters (mostly earthquakes). Its stone dome still stands, though, as the tallest masonry dome in the nation. The capitol rotunda is open to the public, and Deschutes Parkway offers a scenic drive around Capitol Lake and views of the dome.

THIS LITTLE PIGGY WENT TO MARKET

At the far end of downtown is the Olympia Farmers Market, one of the best in the Northwest. The market stands near the spot where Indigenous peoples traded food and goods before white settlers arrived; today's market began in 1930. Now housed in an open-air pavilion, the market offers local produce and cranberries, seafood and meats, and handmade crafts. Don't miss the giant bins that house every conceivable variety of pears and apples—Washington *is* the Apple State, after all.

THAT IS SO PUNK ROCK

Thanks in part to the Evergreen State College, Olympia is the birthplace of the Riot Grrrl movement of feminist punk and rock musicians. Proud daughters of Olympia include Carrie Brownstein (*Portlandia* actress whose band Sleater-Kinney is named for a road that parallels Old 99) and Kathleen Hanna (of Bikini Kill, Le Tigre, and the Julie Ruin), and the record labels Kill Rock Stars and K Records. The punk-rock vibe still permeates the culture here, as Olympia's thriving community of artists and musicians belies the city's small size of around fifty thousand people.

▲ The Olympia Farmers Market is a proving ground for new apple varieties and hybrids, making it the perfect spot to score an exotic fruit snack.

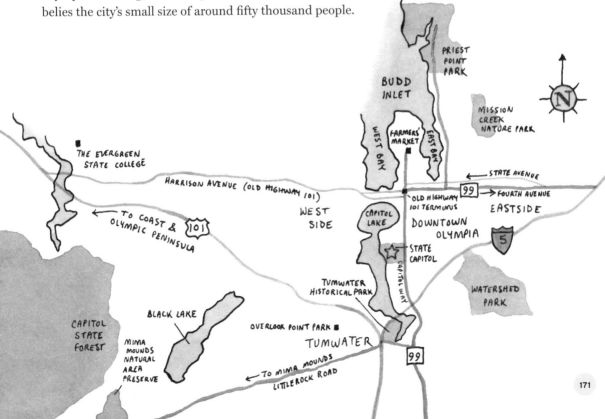

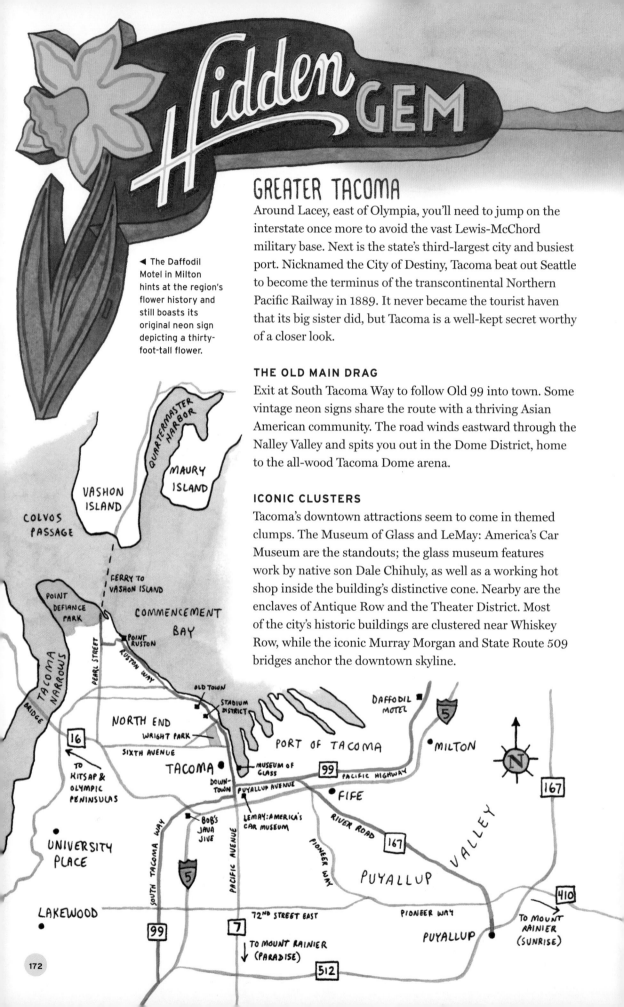

Hidden GEM

GREATER TACOMA

Around Lacey, east of Olympia, you'll need to jump on the interstate once more to avoid the vast Lewis-McChord military base. Next is the state's third-largest city and busiest port. Nicknamed the City of Destiny, Tacoma beat out Seattle to become the terminus of the transcontinental Northern Pacific Railway in 1889. It never became the tourist haven that its big sister did, but Tacoma is a well-kept secret worthy of a closer look.

THE OLD MAIN DRAG

Exit at South Tacoma Way to follow Old 99 into town. Some vintage neon signs share the route with a thriving Asian American community. The road winds eastward through the Nalley Valley and spits you out in the Dome District, home to the all-wood Tacoma Dome arena.

ICONIC CLUSTERS

Tacoma's downtown attractions seem to come in themed clumps. The Museum of Glass and LeMay: America's Car Museum are the standouts; the glass museum features work by native son Dale Chihuly, as well as a working hot shop inside the building's distinctive cone. Nearby are the enclaves of Antique Row and the Theater District. Most of the city's historic buildings are clustered near Whiskey Row, while the iconic Murray Morgan and State Route 509 bridges anchor the downtown skyline.

◄ The Daffodil Motel in Milton hints at the region's flower history and still boasts its original neon sign depicting a thirty-foot-tall flower.

SMALL TOWNS INSIDE A BIG CITY

The mostly residential North End comprises a number of mini village centers, such as Old Town and the walkable Proctor District. The Stadium District is home to the high school that featured as a movie set in *10 Things I Hate About You*; just uphill is the horror house from *The Hand That Rocks the Cradle*. Wright Park features a lush lawn, arboretum, and Victorian-era crystal greenhouse conservatory. At Point Ruston, the hundred-year-old Asarco copper smelter has been transformed from an environmental disaster into a thriving waterfront community.

THE MOTHER LODE OF PARKS

At the northern tip of the peninsula is Point Defiance, the second-largest city park in the nation. Home to a zoo, a large flower garden, a pebbly beach, and a five-mile forest drive, Point Defiance is a destination by itself. Don't miss the newly restored Japanese-style pagoda or the Fort Nisqually Living History Museum. You can catch a ferry here to Vashon Island or take the nearby Tacoma Narrows Bridge for a shortcut to the Kitsap (page 101) and Olympic (page 90) Peninsulas.

CROPS, HOPS, AND DAFFODIL QUEENS

East of Tacoma, Highway 99 continues through a fertile valley once known for its daffodil and hop farms. Nearby Puyallup (pronounced "pew-ALL-up") is home to the Washington State Fair and the annual Daffodil Parade.

▲ The entire Tacoma waterfront is public property. The Ruston Way walking trail offers spectacular views of Mount Rainier, Vashon Island, and Commencement Bay.

▲ Bob's Java Jive, located in the Nalley Valley on South Tacoma Way, opened as a coffee shop but now operates as a beloved dive bar.

▼ Unique buildings downtown, including the historic Union Station (now the federal courthouse) and the Museum of Glass, are part of Tacoma's unusual skyline.

NATIONAL PARK

Ever wanted to see an active volcano up close? Look no farther than America's fifth-ever national park, which protects Washington's highest peak and some of the most pristine alpine landscapes in the Northwest.

A WIDDERSHINS LOOP

There are several roads that lead here, but each makes for a long drive. Plan at least a long day for your side trip; an overnight is even better, especially if you plan to do the whole counterclockwise park loop. Experienced hikers might opt to do a different circuit on foot: the ninety-three-mile Wonderland Trail makes a wilderness loop of the mountain and links to the Pacific Crest Trail.

MOVING ON UP

Starting at the western entrance at Ashford, the park road is generally open year-round (weather permitting) as far as Paradise. The first stop on the way up is Kautz Creek, site of a 1947 lahar flow, in which a landslide of muddy volcanic ash raced down the mountain in a matter of seconds. Next up is Longmire, home of a historic museum constructed in the classic early-twentieth-century rustic park style. Continuing up the road, keep an eye out for Christine Falls adjacent to the roadside, and pull over at the Ricksecker Point scenic lookout.

▲ Depending on the season, the Paradise meadows are home to wild lupines, paintbrush, lilies, bear grass, saxifrage, buttercups, trillium, and many other plants.

▼ The reward for getting to Sunrise at dawn is seeing the alpenglow, a fleeting moment where the mountain appears pink.

PARADISE ON EARTH

Subalpine wildflower meadows are the big attraction at Paradise. July is generally a good time to see them, but as the bloom depends on the winter snowpack, visit the park website for up-to-date information. Many hikes lead up and over the meadows from here. Upon your return you can grab a snack or a souvenir at the visitor center or stay at the Paradise Inn, built in 1916. In the winter only the visitor center remains open, but the meadows, buried under up to twenty feet of snow, become the ideal location for sledding or a snowball fight.

EAST OF EDEN

Past the Paradise summit, the road is open only in the summer—and some years the winter rains wash out the road completely. If you're lucky enough to continue, this is the way to Ohanapecosh, a grove of old-growth fir and cedar trees. From there the road turns northward; keep an eye out for the turn to Chinook Pass. It's worth taking this short detour to Tipsoo Lake, where a brief hike will show you the mountain reflected in the glassy water.

SUNRISE AT THE END OF THE DAY

The last stop on your park loop is Sunrise Point—at 6,400 feet, it's the highest point in the park to which you can drive. A small parking lot at the top of the hairpin switchbacks provides a jaw-dropping view of the peak. On clear days you can also see Mount Adams in a notch to the left of Rainier. There's a lodge up here, but it no longer offers overnight accommodations, so if you'd like to see Sunrise Point at actual sunrise, you'll need to either drive in the dark (yikes) or snag a campsite in one of the campgrounds on this side of the park.

▲ The sixty pendant lamps in the Paradise Inn lobby are individually hand painted, each with a different species of wildflower found at the Paradise meadows.

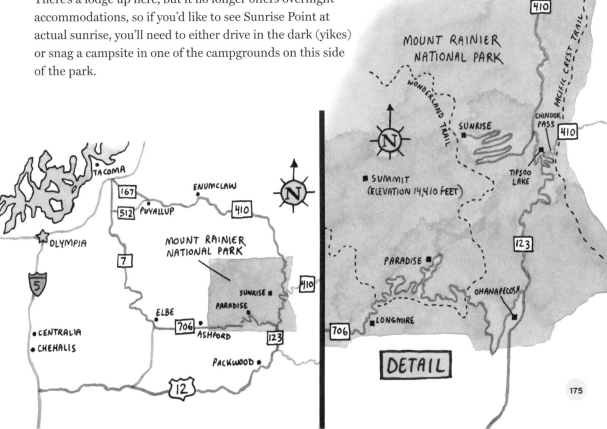

Seattle

▲ Many of the businesses along the Alaskan Way waterfront occupy historic wharf buildings, each constructed on wooden piers jutting out over the water.

▼ Oxbow Park holds a Highway 99 relic: the giant cowboy hat and boots that were once part of the 1950s-era Premium Tex gas station.

The Puget Sound region's largest city is a technology hub with a beating heart. Constantly reinventing itself since its settlement in the 1850s, Seattle is a city of boom and bust, birth and rebirth. Along Highway 99 you can see this drama play out anew, as old buildings get knocked down in favor of new skyscrapers and gleaming condos.

WELCOME TO THE EMERALD CITY

Seattle works hard and takes play just as seriously. On weekdays the working waterfront and tech campuses are busy hives of industry, while on weekends the coffee shops and festivals are teeming with laid-back families and hipsters. On sunny days, never taken for granted here, the entire city turns out to experience Seattle's outdoor treasures. As you explore, get ready for a workout: parking is precious, and the hills are steep. The best course of action is to park your car for the day and start hoofing it. And don't be afraid to get a little wet: Seattleites have a chip on their shoulder about the rain (come on, it's not that bad!), so if you want to blend in with the locals, put your umbrella away.

WHERE HISTORY MEETS THE FUTURE

For a sense of Seattle's past, start in Pioneer Square, a throwback from the city's early days as a supply hub for the 1890s Klondike gold rush. Downtown are the seafood stands and produce stalls of Pike Place Market, one of America's oldest and most beloved public markets. The University of Washington still holds hints of its roots as the campus of the 1909 Alaska-Yukon-Pacific Exposition. For an in-depth look at all this history and more, visit the Museum of History & Industry (MOHAI) at Lake Union Park.

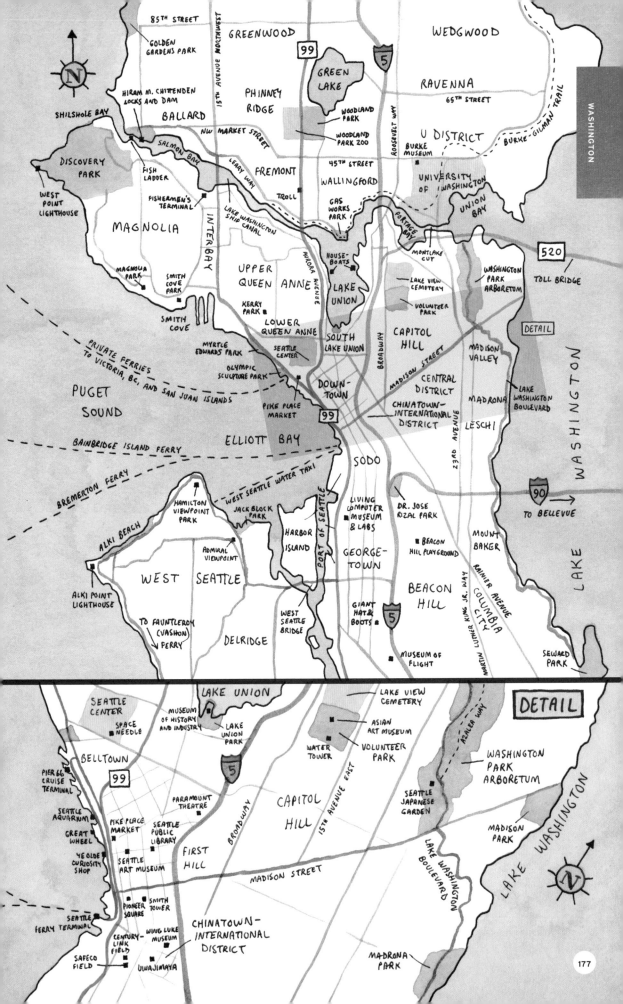

85TH STREET
GREENWOOD
WEDGWOOD
GOLDEN GARDENS PARK
99
RAVENNA
GREEN LAKE
65TH STREET
PHINNEY RIDGE
HIRAM M. CHITTENDEN LOCKS AND DAM
BALLARD
WOODLAND PARK
U DISTRICT
BURKE-GILMAN TRAIL
SHILSHOLE BAY
NW MARKET STREET
WOODLAND PARK ZOO
BURKE MUSEUM
DISCOVERY PARK
SALMON BAY
FISH LADDER
FREMONT
45TH STREET
UNIVERSITY OF WASHINGTON
WEST POINT LIGHTHOUSE
FISHERMEN'S TERMINAL
LEARY WAY
WALLINGFORD
TROLL
GAS WORKS PARK
UNION BAY
PORTAGE BAY
LAKE WASHINGTON SHIP CANAL
MAGNOLIA
520
HOUSE-BOATS
MONTLAKE CUT
TOLL BRIDGE
AURORA AVENUE
LAKE VIEW CEMETERY
WASHINGTON PARK ARBORETUM
MAGNOLIA PARK
UPPER QUEEN ANNE
LAKE UNION
VOLUNTEER PARK
SMITH COVE PARK
KERRY PARK
DETAIL
SMITH COVE
LOWER QUEEN ANNE
SOUTH LAKE UNION
CAPITOL HILL
MADISON VALLEY
PRIVATE FERRIES TO VICTORIA, BC, AND SAN JUAN ISLANDS
MYRTLE EDWARDS PARK
SEATTLE CENTER
BROADWAY
MADISON STREET
CENTRAL DISTRICT
MADRONA
LAKE WASHINGTON BOULEVARD
PUGET SOUND
OLYMPIC SCULPTURE PARK
DOWN-TOWN
CHINATOWN-INTERNATIONAL DISTRICT
LESCHI
PIKE PLACE MARKET
99
23RD AVENUE
BAINBRIDGE ISLAND FERRY
ELLIOTT BAY
SODO
BREMERTON FERRY
WEST SEATTLE WATER TAXI
HAMILTON VIEWPOINT PARK
JACK BLOCK PARK
LIVING COMPUTER MUSEUM & LABS
DR. JOSE RIZAL PARK
90
TO BELLEVUE
ALKI BEACH
HARBOR ISLAND
MOUNT BAKER
ADMIRAL VIEWPOINT
PORT OF SEATTLE
GEORGE-TOWN
BEACON HILL PLAYGROUND
WEST SEATTLE
BEACON HILL
RAINIER AVENUE
COLUMBIA CITY
ALKI POINT LIGHTHOUSE
WEST SEATTLE BRIDGE
GIANT HAT & BOOTS
5
MARTIN LUTHER KING JR. WAY
SEWARD PARK
TO FAUNTLEROY (VASHON) FERRY
DELRIDGE
MUSEUM OF FLIGHT
LAKE WASHINGTON

DETAIL

SEATTLE CENTER
LAKE UNION
LAKE VIEW CEMETERY
MUSEUM OF HISTORY AND INDUSTRY
SPACE NEEDLE
LAKE UNION PARK
ASIAN ART MUSEUM
AZALEA WAY
BELLTOWN
5
WATER TOWER
VOLUNTEER PARK
WASHINGTON PARK ARBORETUM
PIER 66 CRUISE TERMINAL
99
PARAMOUNT THEATRE
BROADWAY
15TH AVENUE EAST
SEATTLE AQUARIUM
PIKE PLACE MARKET
SEATTLE PUBLIC LIBRARY
CAPITOL HILL
SEATTLE JAPANESE GARDEN
GREAT WHEEL
MADISON PARK
YE OLDE CURIOSITY SHOP
SEATTLE ART MUSEUM
FIRST HILL
LAKE WASHINGTON BOULEVARD
MADISON STREET
PIONEER SQUARE
SMITH TOWER
SEATTLE FERRY TERMINAL
CHINATOWN-INTERNATIONAL DISTRICT
LAKE WASHINGTON
CENTURY-LINK FIELD
WING LUKE MUSEUM
SAFECO FIELD
UWAJIMAYA
MADRONA PARK

▼ Operating continuously since 1907, the labyrinthine Pike Place Market is home to fresh fish and produce stands, plus a number of retail shops and restaurants.

Seattle's futuristic streak begins at the Space Needle, built for the 1962 Seattle World's Fair. Nearby is the Museum of Pop Culture, designed in an even more futuristic style by Frank Gehry. The Living Computer Museum gives a hands-on look at the influence of Microsoft and other Seattle tech companies, while the Museum of Flight details Seattle's history as an aerospace hub. And you can witness a living experiment in tech and commerce at the South Lake Union Amazon campus, where backpack-wearing employees buzz around the glass-domed Amazon Spheres. (Don't forget to grab your free banana at the Community Banana Stand!)

MAKE A SPLASH

The weather isn't the only thing here that's wet; Seattle is defined by its waterways. Visit Fishermen's Terminal and the Hiram M. Chittenden Locks to see the salmon boats in action. The giant orange container cranes at the Port of Seattle are visible from the downtown waterfront. A series of drawbridges add their own unique rhythm to the flow of traffic, and an endless succession of public ferries crosses Elliott Bay, bringing cars and foot traffic to the Kitsap and Olympic Peninsulas. The Seattle Aquarium provides a glimpse of the marine life of Puget Sound, and various whale-watching trips leave from Alaskan Way. Magnolia's Discovery Park, Ballard's Golden Gardens, and West Seattle's Alki Beach offer saltwater access, while Lake Union offers boat rentals and floatplane flights. Finish up with a beautiful eight-mile waterfront drive along Lake Washington Boulevard.

PUBLIC MARKET

THE OUTDOORSY TYPE

Seattle is the perfect place to get outside—and you can stock up on gear (or try the climbing wall) at the REI flagship store. For an easy waterfront stroll, visit the Olympic Sculpture Park, run by the Seattle Art Museum. The Washington Park Arboretum, designed by the Olmsted brothers (who designed New York City's Central Park), is home to more than two hundred acres of Northwest trees and plants—don't miss the Azalea Way walking path in the spring. The Burke-Gilman Trail connects Lake Washington to the sound, and the Pike Street Hill Climb links Alaskan Way to Capitol Hill. If you can bear a few more steps, climb the Volunteer Park water tower (another Olmsted masterpiece) for a 360-degree view from one of the highest points in the city.

CULTURAL CAPITAL

Despite being one of the whitest major cities in America, Seattle has been shaped by many other cultures. You can sample Indigenous Seattle at the University of Washington's Burke Museum (read more about Salish culture on page 98) or the Coast Salish galleries at the Seattle Art Museum. The Chinatown-International District, once a Japanese American enclave, underwent massive change during World War II, when Japanese nationals were forced to leave the city. Today the neighborhood is a vibrant pan-Asian melting pot home to Seattle's Chinese, Japanese, and Vietnamese communities. The excellent Wing Luke Museum, named for a Chinese American city and state politician, is the only pan-Asian-Pacific community museum in America. If all these museums make you peckish, grab a snack at the sprawling Uwajimaya supermarket and food court or a fine meal at Maneki, an institution of Seattle sushi since 1904.

▲ Steampunk and sci-fi fans love the setting and views at Gas Works Park, a preserved, historic gas plant located on a small peninsula on the north shore of Lake Union.

▼ The International District is the site of a number of pan-Asian American celebrations, including a Lunar New Year festival, a summer night market, and Dragon Fest.

▲ Though the film *Sleepless in Seattle* made them famous in 1993, the city's houseboat districts have been a fixture since the 1920s.

To continue your cultural tour, head back downtown to the Central Library, an all-glass modern masterpiece by Dutch architect Rem Koolhaas. If live performances are more your thing, Benaroya Hall hosts the Seattle Opera and the Seattle Men's Chorus holiday concert. Seasonal crowd-pleasers include Folklife Festival on Memorial Day, the Bumbershoot music festival on Labor Day, and the Seattle International Film Festival in late spring.

NORTHWEST FLAVORS

Seattle cuisine tends to emphasize whatever is fresh and local: expect dishes celebrating local favorites like wild huckleberries, grilled oysters, and fresh salmon. From raw ingredients to sit-down restaurants, it's hard to go wrong here. New eateries seem to pop up daily, while perennial favorites include the Dahlia Lounge, the Athenian (seafood), Paseo (Cuban sandwiches!), the Salumi deli, Molly Moon's ice cream, Dick's Drive-In, Alki Spud (fish-and-chips), and Beecher's Handmade Cheese.

Of course, no visit would be complete without a stop at a coffee shop. Seattle brought coffee culture to America, and indie establishments like Zeitgeist and Victrola keep the tradition strong. Top Pot offers fresh-baked doughnuts to go with your latte or drip coffee. If you're just passing through, there are a million drive-through espresso huts, and since everyone asks, the original Starbucks can be found next to Pike Place Market. But for best results, choose a mom-and-pop java joint, curl up in a corner, and linger awhile.

◄ The Smith Tower was the West Coast's tallest building until the Space Needle arrived. Sip a cocktail at the top-floor bar, and take in the view.

SEATTLE ICONS

▶ The *Seattle Post-Intelligencer* is now an online-only newspaper, but this spinning neon globe still lights up the waterfront.

▲ The sound is too cold to do much swimming—good thing Washington State Ferries offers easy access to cities on the other side.

▼ Seattleites drink more joe than any other Americans and wouldn't trade their eight hundred coffee shops for all the tea in China.

◀ The salmon-tossing fishmongers delight Pike Place Market crowds with their fishy showmanship. (Look for their orange rubber overalls.)

◀ Home to a Lenin statue and a twenty-foot troll, the Fremont neighborhood is proud of its quirks—proclaiming itself the center of the universe.

NORTH POLE
LENIN STATUE
XANADU
RAPUNZEL
TROLL
TIMBUKTU
INTERURBAN
CENTER OF THE UNIVERSE

▼ Visit the Museum of Pop Culture to acquaint yourself with the region's rich music history, from Hendrix to Heart and Nirvana to Neko Case.

▶ The Space Needle, Seattle's most iconic landmark, is home to a revolving restaurant that offers an ever-changing bird's-eye view of the city and sound.

◀ Despite not being an original part of Indigenous culture here (page 98), Seattle's many totem poles are now an integral part of the cityscape.

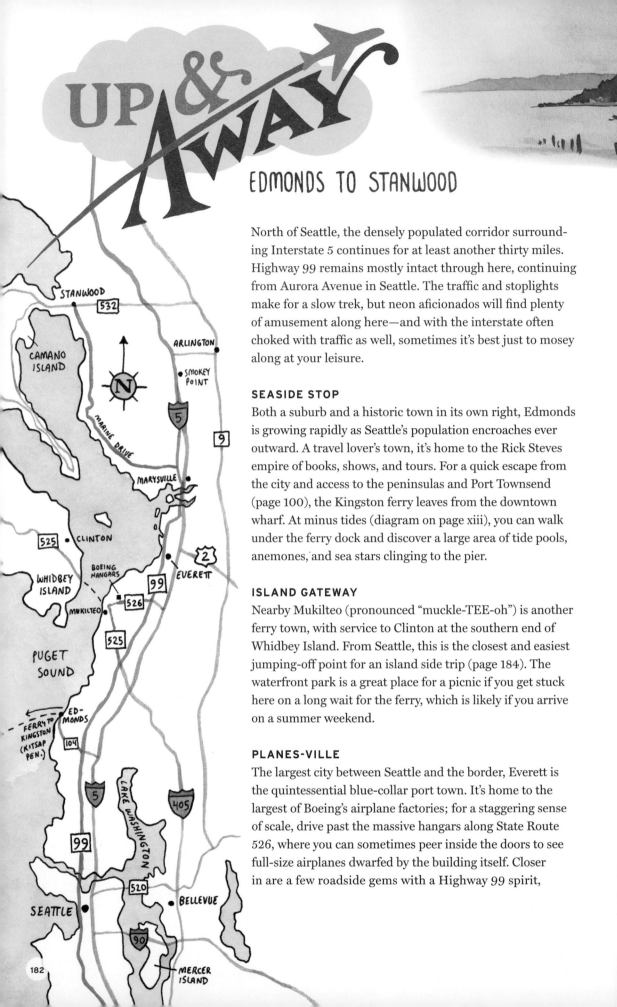

UP & AWAY

EDMONDS TO STANWOOD

North of Seattle, the densely populated corridor surrounding Interstate 5 continues for at least another thirty miles. Highway 99 remains mostly intact through here, continuing from Aurora Avenue in Seattle. The traffic and stoplights make for a slow trek, but neon aficionados will find plenty of amusement along here—and with the interstate often choked with traffic as well, sometimes it's best just to mosey along at your leisure.

SEASIDE STOP

Both a suburb and a historic town in its own right, Edmonds is growing rapidly as Seattle's population encroaches ever outward. A travel lover's town, it's home to the Rick Steves empire of books, shows, and tours. For a quick escape from the city and access to the peninsulas and Port Townsend (page 100), the Kingston ferry leaves from the downtown wharf. At minus tides (diagram on page xiii), you can walk under the ferry dock and discover a large area of tide pools, anemones, and sea stars clinging to the pier.

ISLAND GATEWAY

Nearby Mukilteo (pronounced "muckle-TEE-oh") is another ferry town, with service to Clinton at the southern end of Whidbey Island. From Seattle, this is the closest and easiest jumping-off point for an island side trip (page 184). The waterfront park is a great place for a picnic if you get stuck here on a long wait for the ferry, which is likely if you arrive on a summer weekend.

PLANES-VILLE

The largest city between Seattle and the border, Everett is the quintessential blue-collar port town. It's home to the largest of Boeing's airplane factories; for a staggering sense of scale, drive past the massive hangars along State Route 526, where you can sometimes peer inside the doors to see full-size airplanes dwarfed by the building itself. Closer in are a few roadside gems with a Highway 99 spirit,

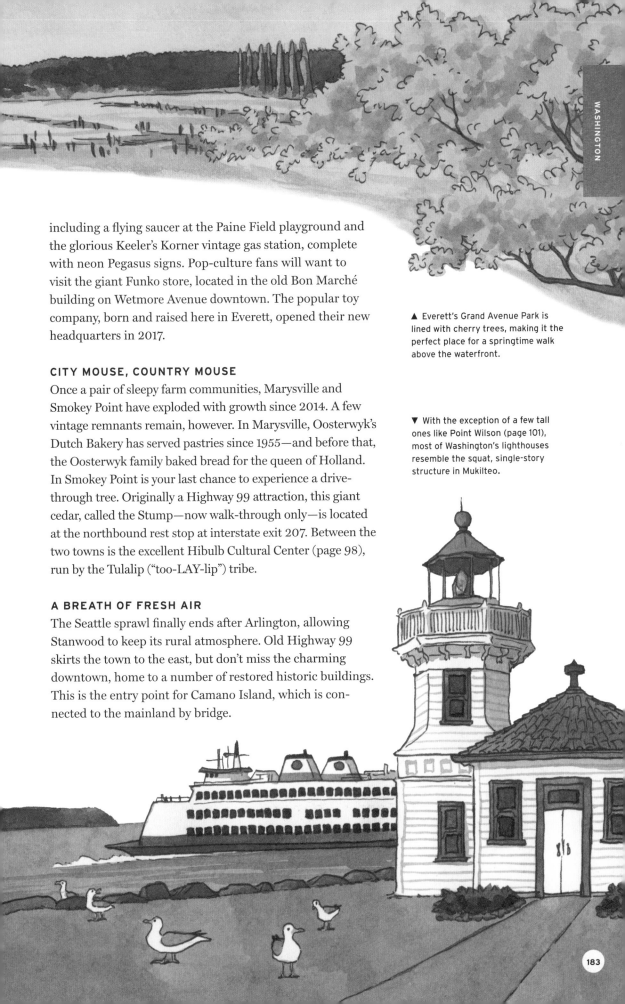

including a flying saucer at the Paine Field playground and the glorious Keeler's Korner vintage gas station, complete with neon Pegasus signs. Pop-culture fans will want to visit the giant Funko store, located in the old Bon Marché building on Wetmore Avenue downtown. The popular toy company, born and raised here in Everett, opened their new headquarters in 2017.

▲ Everett's Grand Avenue Park is lined with cherry trees, making it the perfect place for a springtime walk above the waterfront.

CITY MOUSE, COUNTRY MOUSE

Once a pair of sleepy farm communities, Marysville and Smokey Point have exploded with growth since 2014. A few vintage remnants remain, however. In Marysville, Oosterwyk's Dutch Bakery has served pastries since 1955—and before that, the Oosterwyk family baked bread for the queen of Holland. In Smokey Point is your last chance to experience a drive-through tree. Originally a Highway 99 attraction, this giant cedar, called the Stump—now walk-through only—is located at the northbound rest stop at interstate exit 207. Between the two towns is the excellent Hibulb Cultural Center (page 98), run by the Tulalip ("too-LAY-lip") tribe.

▼ With the exception of a few tall ones like Point Wilson (page 101), most of Washington's lighthouses resemble the squat, single-story structure in Mukilteo.

A BREATH OF FRESH AIR

The Seattle sprawl finally ends after Arlington, allowing Stanwood to keep its rural atmosphere. Old Highway 99 skirts the town to the east, but don't miss the charming downtown, home to a number of restored historic buildings. This is the entry point for Camano Island, which is connected to the mainland by bridge.

SIDE TRIP

Island-Hopping

▼ Deception Pass Bridge features a narrow pedestrian walkway. If you can brave the dizzying heights, low railing, and choking crowds, stunning views are the reward.

The jewels in Washington's crown are its many islands. From towering old-growth forests to sweeping open meadows and historic towns to picturesque lighthouses, the Salish Sea is peppered with island havens. Several lie within easy reach of Highway 99—a few by bridge, and others by Washington State Ferries, which offers both pedestrian and auto crossings.

Whidbey and Camano

CAMANO ISLAND

Accessible by bridge from Stanwood, crescent-shaped Camano (pronounced "ca-MAY-no") is small, rural, and easy to explore in a day. Start at Iverson Spit Preserve for bird-watching, or check out the old cedar cabins at Cama Beach Historical State Park. Art lovers will enjoy the island's vibrant artist community, including many studios and rural galleries, usually open on weekends in the summer or by appointment at other times.

WHIDBEY ISLAND

Washington's largest island is packed with history and natural beauty. At the southern end, the quaint town of Langley is home to the Whidbey Island Fair and a number of boutique shops, restaurants, and inns. Langley is also the site of the world's cutest pest-control problem: the town is overrun with feral European rabbits, descended from pet bunnies that escaped the fair.

▶ Coupeville is located on Penn Cove, world famous for its mussels. Visit in March for the annual MusselFest, or simply grab a bowl at a local bistro.

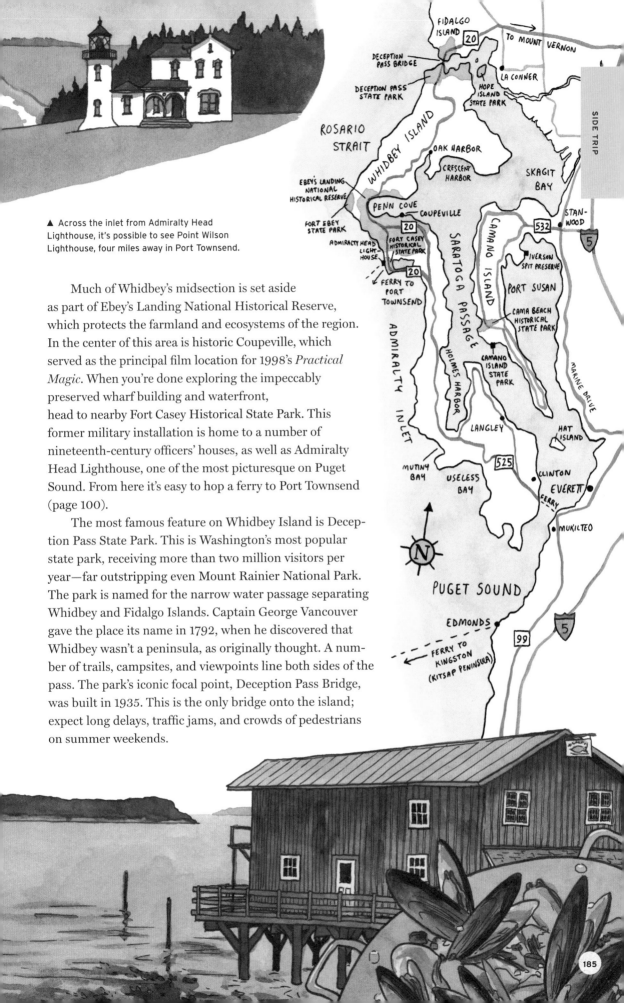

Map labels:

FIDALGO ISLAND · 20 · TO MOUNT VERNON · DECEPTION PASS BRIDGE · LA CONNER · DECEPTION PASS STATE PARK · HOPE ISLAND STATE PARK · ROSARIO STRAIT · WHIDBEY ISLAND · OAK HARBOR · CRESCENT HARBOR · SKAGIT BAY · EBEY'S LANDING NATIONAL HISTORICAL RESERVE · PENN COVE · COUPEVILLE · STAN-WOOD · FORT EBEY STATE PARK · 20 · 532 · 5 · ADMIRALTY HEAD LIGHT-HOUSE · FORT CASEY HISTORICAL STATE PARK · SARATOGA PASSAGE · CAMANO ISLAND · IVERSON SPIT PRESERVE · PORT SUSAN · 20 · FERRY TO PORT TOWNSEND · CAMA BEACH HISTORICAL STATE PARK · ADMIRALTY INLET · HOLMES HARBOR · CAMANO ISLAND STATE PARK · MARINE DRIVE · LANGLEY · HAT ISLAND · MUTINY BAY · USELESS BAY · 525 · CLINTON · EVERETT · FERRY · MUKILTEO · PUGET SOUND · N · EDMONDS · 99 · 5 · FERRY TO KINGSTON (KITSAP PENINSULA)

▲ Across the inlet from Admiralty Head Lighthouse, it's possible to see Point Wilson Lighthouse, four miles away in Port Townsend.

Much of Whidbey's midsection is set aside as part of Ebey's Landing National Historical Reserve, which protects the farmland and ecosystems of the region. In the center of this area is historic Coupeville, which served as the principal film location for 1998's *Practical Magic*. When you're done exploring the impeccably preserved wharf building and waterfront, head to nearby Fort Casey Historical State Park. This former military installation is home to a number of nineteenth-century officers' houses, as well as Admiralty Head Lighthouse, one of the most picturesque on Puget Sound. From here it's easy to hop a ferry to Port Townsend (page 100).

The most famous feature on Whidbey Island is Deception Pass State Park. This is Washington's most popular state park, receiving more than two million visitors per year—far outstripping even Mount Rainier National Park. The park is named for the narrow water passage separating Whidbey and Fidalgo Islands. Captain George Vancouver gave the place its name in 1792, when he discovered that Whidbey wasn't a peninsula, as originally thought. A number of trails, campsites, and viewpoints line both sides of the pass. The park's iconic focal point, Deception Pass Bridge, was built in 1935. This is the only bridge onto the island; expect long delays, traffic jams, and crowds of pedestrians on summer weekends.

The San Juans

An archipelago consisting of over 400 islands (128 of which are named), the San Juans are among Washington's most visited destinations. Deep, cold channels provide habitat for the islands' most famous stars: the critically endangered Southern Resident orcas (the distinct J, K, and L pods). The luckiest visitors might just spot them from the Anacortes (pronounced "anna-COR-tiss") ferry, which goes to the four largest islands.

SAN JUAN ISLAND: ISLAND IN THE SUN

The most populous island is home to the bustling town of Friday Harbor, a small airport, and the San Juan County Fairgrounds. Part of the island lies within the Olympic rain shadow (page 100), making it a haven of bucolic farmland, including the Pelindaba Lavender Farm. At the north end of the island, Roche Harbor is home to the historic Hotel de Haro and its lush flower garden. A ring of parks runs along the shoreline of the island, including Lime Kiln Point State Park (where it's possible to view orcas from a shoreline overlook) and San Juan Island National Historical Park, encompassing the American and English military camps. Here, a Canadian boundary dispute (the San Juans were omitted when the forty-ninth parallel border was drawn in 1846) erupted into the 1859 Pig War, an armed standoff between the two sides triggered by a trespassing pig.

LOPEZ: THE FRIENDLY ISLE

Lopez Island has rolling terrain ideal for cycling—and bike-conscious motorists famous for waving hello as they pass you by (hence the nickname). Grab a scoop of locally made ice cream in Lopez Village, then head to Spencer Spit State Park for a beachfront stroll. Or you can check out the views at Iceberg Point, accessible by public hiking trail—despite a series of confusing Private Property and No Parking signs in the vicinity.

▲ While you're island-hopping, keep a sharp eye out for orcas, Washington's state marine mammal. They occasionally perform a behavior called spy-hopping to get a look at the horizon.

▼ Near Cattle Point on San Juan Island, the madronas and conifers end abruptly, leaving a treeless plain with panoramic views of water and mountains.

ORCAS: THE MISTY MOUNTAIN

The largest island in the archipelago stands in stark contrast to San Juan Island. Orcas Island is home to mountainous terrain, old-growth forests, and many more rainy days per year. Visit Moran State Park and take the winding road up Mount Constitution: a short trail leads to a watchtower, the highest point in the San Juans at 2,400 feet. Afterward, head down to the village of Eastsound, perched on a beautiful bit of shoreline at the head of a fjord. A favorite overnight spot for nature lovers is Doe Bay Resort, which offers rustic accommodations and spaces for artists' and writers' retreats.

SHAW: A WELL-KEPT SECRET

The smallest island serviced by the ferry, Shaw is overlooked by tourists, and all the better for it. A community of Benedictine nuns runs a working farm at the visitor-friendly Our Lady of the Rock Monastery. Shaw County Park and Blind Island State Park offer some great hiking. And you can wait for your return ferry with a sandwich and a cuppa joe at Shaw General Store.

BEYOND THE FERRY

If you have access to your own boat or a charter service, there are many other spots worthy of a visit. Several small islands offer public marine campgrounds, including Sucia Island Marine State Park, Strawberry Island Park, and James Island Marine State Park. Both Stuart Island, near Roche Harbor, and Patos Island, the northernmost in the archipelago, have historic lighthouses.

▶ The Orcas Hotel is perched directly above the ferry terminal, making it the ideal place to stay if you have an early-morning boat to catch.

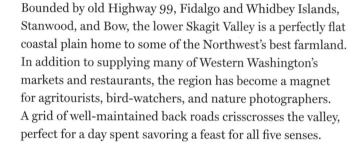

Seasonal SPLENDOR
THE LOWER SKAGIT VALLEY

▲ It's easy to tell the migrating bird species apart. Snow geese have distinctive black wing tips, while the swans' noisiness lives up to their jazzy name.

▼ The Skagit Valley's historic barns are popular with photographers. Around fifty are listed on Washington's Heritage Barn Register.

Bounded by old Highway 99, Fidalgo and Whidbey Islands, Stanwood, and Bow, the lower Skagit Valley is a perfectly flat coastal plain home to some of the Northwest's best farmland. In addition to supplying many of Western Washington's markets and restaurants, the region has become a magnet for agritourists, bird-watchers, and nature photographers. A grid of well-maintained back roads crisscrosses the valley, perfect for a day spent savoring a feast for all five senses.

WINTER: BIRD-WATCHING SEASON

Though the trees are bare and the weather usually wet and chilly, winter might just be the best time to visit the Skagit Valley. This is because from November to March, the region hosts tens of thousands of snow geese and trumpeter swans, which migrate down from the Arctic and spend the winter here. If you're lucky, you'll witness the dramatic display of an entire flock taking off or landing, blotting out the landscape with a sea of white wings. February is the best time to goose watch, as hunting season ends in January. Many of the birds congregate on Fir Island, where local farmers participate in a Barley for Birds program, planting subsidized winter grain to help the birds fatten up for the long flight back north in the spring. In addition to the Arctic visitors, keep an eye out for bald eagles and other raptors, as well as a host of waterfowl gleaning tidbits from the stubbly fields.

SPRING: AN EXPLOSION OF COLOR

In April, once the hordes of geese depart, new hordes of tourists arrive to see the Skagit Valley's famous Tulip Festival, thanks to the Dutch bulb farmers who arrived in the 1950s. Due to crop rotation, the location of the rainbow tulip fields changes from year to year, so plan to go exploring along the various country roads. Visiting on a weekday or very early in the morning will help you outsmart the crowds; be prepared to pay for parking and admission to some of the fields. The bulb farms also grow daffodils, which bloom in March, and irises, appearing in late spring.

SUMMER: GREEN FIELDS, BLUE SKIES

Come summer, the farms are in full swing and the weather is at its sunniest. Many creameries, wineries, and cideries are open to the public, and farm stands like Snow Goose Produce offer fresh fruit and veggies. Pop by historic La Conner for a bit of antiquing, or visit the Berry Dairy Days festival in Burlington.

AUTUMN: THE BOUNTIFUL HARVEST

Fall is an exciting time here, especially for folks traveling with children. The Skagit Valley Giant Pumpkin Festival is the seasonal centerpiece, held in Mount Vernon. End your day at a farm-to-table restaurant in La Conner or Anacortes, and taste the very best of the local harvest.

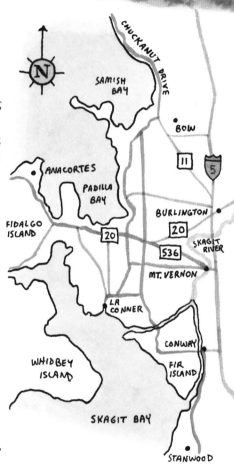

189

NORTHERN BASTION

GREATER BELLINGHAM

Continuing northward, Washington has one more city up its sleeve and one more dramatic highway to drive. Interstate travelers speed by on the much-newer inland route, but old Highway 99 brings travelers into Bellingham by way of a twenty-mile cliff-side coastal adventure.

RIDE THE CLIFFS

At the north end of the Skagit Valley, Farm-to-Market Road ends at State Route 11. A left turn here will put you onto Chuckanut Drive Scenic Byway, the original Highway 99 alignment. The road climbs quickly, clinging to the only mountain arm of the Cascades that touches the Salish Sea. Stop at Larrabee State Park to hike or fish, or just to look at the million-dollar views. Far below the road, you'll see the oyster beds that line Samish Bay. You can shuck 'em yourself at the Taylor Shellfish Farms store or enjoy a sit-down shellfish meal at Chuckanut Manor, a high-end roadhouse that has served local seafood for over fifty years. Timing your drive for late afternoon or early evening will give you an unforgettable sunset vista of the San Juan Islands (page 186).

NO NEED FOR A TIME MACHINE

Chuckanut Drive dumps you out in the Fairhaven Historic District. The Victorian buildings here hint at both the early prosperity and the rough-and-tumble history of Bellingham. Today the mostly residential neighborhood boasts a number of shops, restaurants, and hotels, as well as Village Books, a three-story indie bookstore. Nearby is the Bellingham Cruise Terminal (check out the view from the Dome Room!), the southern terminus of the Alaska Marine Highway. This state-run ferry system offers connections all the way to the Aleutian Islands.

▲ Bellingham Bay and the islands add a picturesque backdrop to the Victorian buildings of Fairhaven.

◄ Bellingham's old city hall is now the Whatcom Museum, devoted to Northwest art and history.

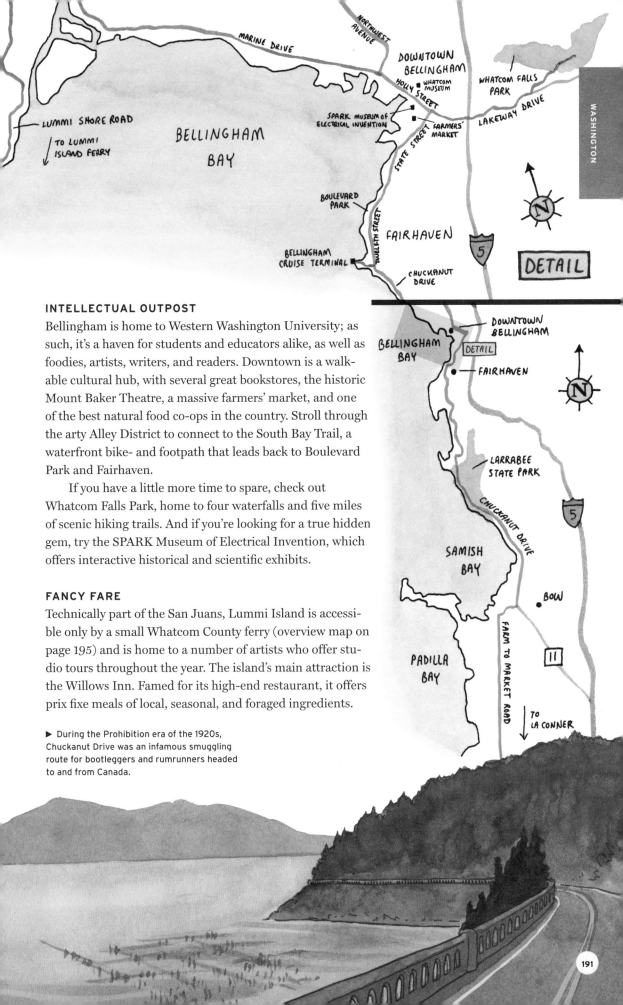

Map labels (top detail):

MARINE DRIVE

NORTHWEST AVENUE

DOWNTOWN BELLINGHAM

HOLLY STREET

WHATCOM MUSEUM

WHATCOM FALLS PARK

LAKEWAY DRIVE

SPARK MUSEUM OF ELECTRICAL INVENTION

FARMERS' MARKET

STATE STREET

LUMMI SHORE ROAD

TO LUMMI ISLAND FERRY

BELLINGHAM BAY

BOULEVARD PARK

TWELFTH STREET

FAIRHAVEN

5

WASHINGTON

N

DETAIL

BELLINGHAM CRUISE TERMINAL

CHUCKANUT DRIVE

INTELLECTUAL OUTPOST

Bellingham is home to Western Washington University; as such, it's a haven for students and educators alike, as well as foodies, artists, writers, and readers. Downtown is a walkable cultural hub, with several great bookstores, the historic Mount Baker Theatre, a massive farmers' market, and one of the best natural food co-ops in the country. Stroll through the arty Alley District to connect to the South Bay Trail, a waterfront bike- and footpath that leads back to Boulevard Park and Fairhaven.

If you have a little more time to spare, check out Whatcom Falls Park, home to four waterfalls and five miles of scenic hiking trails. And if you're looking for a true hidden gem, try the SPARK Museum of Electrical Invention, which offers interactive historical and scientific exhibits.

FANCY FARE

Technically part of the San Juans, Lummi Island is accessible only by a small Whatcom County ferry (overview map on page 195) and is home to a number of artists who offer studio tours throughout the year. The island's main attraction is the Willows Inn. Famed for its high-end restaurant, it offers prix fixe meals of local, seasonal, and foraged ingredients.

▶ During the Prohibition era of the 1920s, Chuckanut Drive was an infamous smuggling route for bootleggers and rumrunners headed to and from Canada.

Map labels (lower detail):

DOWNTOWN BELLINGHAM

BELLINGHAM BAY

DETAIL

FAIRHAVEN

N

LARRABEE STATE PARK

CHUCKANUT DRIVE

SAMISH BAY

5

BOW

FARM TO MARKET ROAD

11

PADILLA BAY

TO LA CONNER

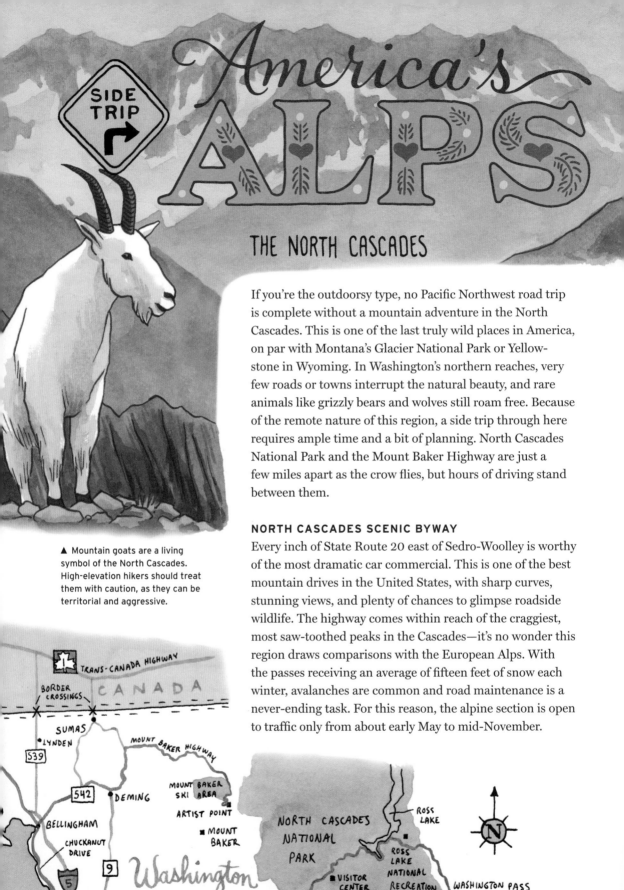

America's ALPS

SIDE TRIP ↱

THE NORTH CASCADES

If you're the outdoorsy type, no Pacific Northwest road trip is complete without a mountain adventure in the North Cascades. This is one of the last truly wild places in America, on par with Montana's Glacier National Park or Yellowstone in Wyoming. In Washington's northern reaches, very few roads or towns interrupt the natural beauty, and rare animals like grizzly bears and wolves still roam free. Because of the remote nature of this region, a side trip through here requires ample time and a bit of planning. North Cascades National Park and the Mount Baker Highway are just a few miles apart as the crow flies, but hours of driving stand between them.

NORTH CASCADES SCENIC BYWAY

Every inch of State Route 20 east of Sedro-Woolley is worthy of the most dramatic car commercial. This is one of the best mountain drives in the United States, with sharp curves, stunning views, and plenty of chances to glimpse roadside wildlife. The highway comes within reach of the craggiest, most saw-toothed peaks in the Cascades—it's no wonder this region draws comparisons with the European Alps. With the passes receiving an average of fifteen feet of snow each winter, avalanches are common and road maintenance is a never-ending task. For this reason, the alpine section is open to traffic only from about early May to mid-November.

▲ Mountain goats are a living symbol of the North Cascades. High-elevation hikers should treat them with caution, as they can be territorial and aggressive.

TRANS-CANADA HIGHWAY

BORDER CROSSINGS

CANADA

SUMAS
LYNDEN
539

MOUNT BAKER HIGHWAY

542   DEMING

MOUNT BAKER SKI AREA

ARTIST POINT

BELLINGHAM

CHUCKANUT DRIVE

MOUNT BAKER

NORTH CASCADES NATIONAL PARK

ROSS LAKE

ROSS LAKE NATIONAL RECREATION AREA

N

9   Washington

5

VISITOR CENTER

WASHINGTON PASS

20

NORTH CASCADES HIGHWAY

SEDRO-WOOLLEY

LAKE CHELAN NATIONAL RECREATION AREA

WINTHROP

MOUNT VERNON

SR 20 provides access to several National Park Service properties, including North Cascades National Park, Ross Lake National Recreation Area, and Lake Chelan National Recreation Area. Each of these is a wilderness park; while the highway crosses through each park, most access is available only through permitted backcountry hiking and camping. Information and backcountry permits are available at park service visitor centers located in Sedro-Woolley and Marblemount. East of the parks, the North Cascades Highway reaches its climax at Washington Pass and its finale in the historic Wild West hamlet of Winthrop, about 130 miles east of Sedro-Woolley.

▲ The Washington Pass Overlook affords dizzying views of the road below. Just west of the pass, a short hiking trail leads to the overlook.

THE MOUNT BAKER HIGHWAY

Bellingham provides easy access to the Mount Baker Highway (State Route 542) and Mount Baker Ski Area. The road is open mostly year-round as far as the ski area, where the lanes split into a one-way loop around Picture Lake and offer a carousel of views of Mounts Baker and Shuksan. The last three miles, however, are open only from July through October each year. It's well worth planning your trip around this period—those last three miles are a doozy. The road climbs quickly, via a series of steep, razor-sharp hairpins, up to its terminus at Artist Point, more than 5,200 feet above sea level. From there you can take a walk along the Artist Point hiking trail—see if that doesn't inspire you to pull out a sketchbook.

▼ Visit Artist Point in late September or early October to see the heather and huckleberry meadows turn a bright autumn red.

193

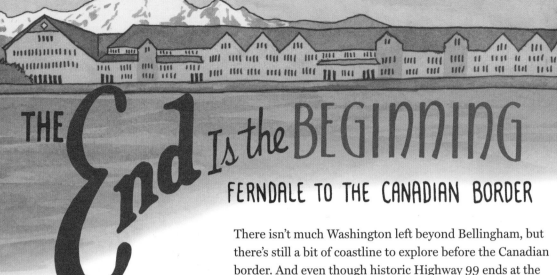

THE End Is the BEGINNING
FERNDALE TO THE CANADIAN BORDER

There isn't much Washington left beyond Bellingham, but there's still a bit of coastline to explore before the Canadian border. And even though historic Highway 99 ends at the forty-ninth parallel, British Columbia continues the thread with BC Highway 99 (page 196), which connects, via a series of provincial roads, all the way to the ALCAN (Alaska–Canada) Highway.

▲ The Semiahmoo Resort sits adjacent to a golf course designed by famed PGA golfer Arnold Palmer.

▼ Many of the beachfront houses, cottages, and condos in Birch Bay are available as vacation rentals—these can be an affordable alternative to resorts like Semiahmoo.

THE LAST STRETCH OF COASTLINE

Past Bellingham, the Old 99 route gets swallowed by Interstate 5 again. It's tempting to blow past the next town, Ferndale, but Hovander Homestead Park and, especially, Pioneer Park are worth a stop for their preserved buildings and kid-friendly interpretive programs.

Leaving Ferndale on Portal Way, turn west on State Route 548 and head for Birch Bay. Here, a quiet beach community hugs a pristine half-moon cove. Get yourself a clamming license and dig at Birch Bay State Park, or continue up the waterfront to Semiahmoo (pronounced "sem-ee-AAH-moo") Park, located on a mile-and-a-half-long sandspit. What used to be an Alaskan cannery is now the swanky Semiahmoo Resort, offering rooms and meals with views of the Peace Arch, Drayton Harbor, and the Canadian city of White Rock. The resort is also accessible by the MV *Plover*, a free summer "foot ferry" (what Washingtonians call a passenger-only boat) operating out of Blaine.

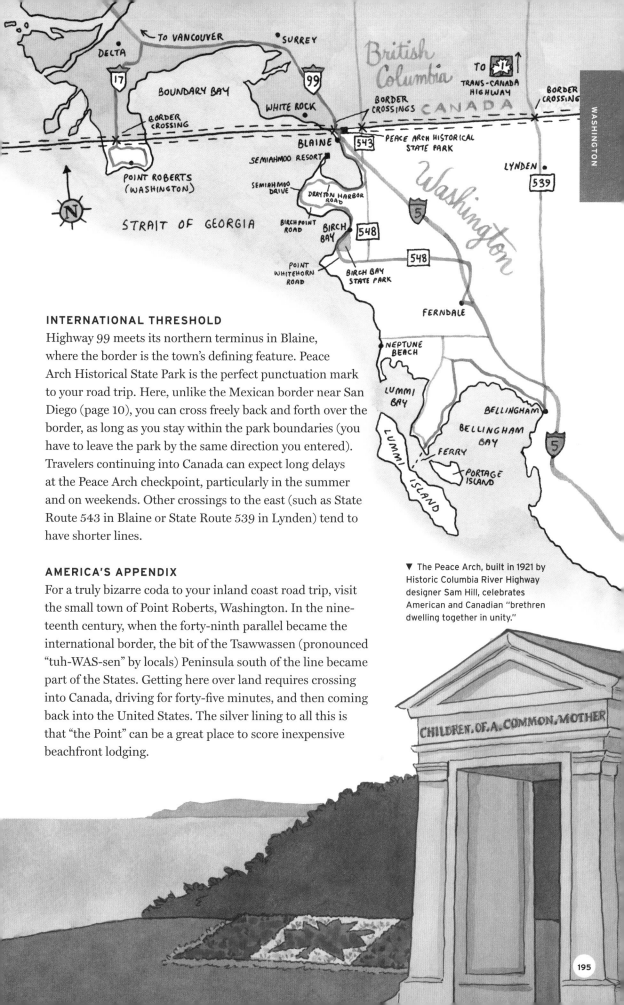

INTERNATIONAL THRESHOLD

Highway 99 meets its northern terminus in Blaine, where the border is the town's defining feature. Peace Arch Historical State Park is the perfect punctuation mark to your road trip. Here, unlike the Mexican border near San Diego (page 10), you can cross freely back and forth over the border, as long as you stay within the park boundaries (you have to leave the park by the same direction you entered). Travelers continuing into Canada can expect long delays at the Peace Arch checkpoint, particularly in the summer and on weekends. Other crossings to the east (such as State Route 543 in Blaine or State Route 539 in Lynden) tend to have shorter lines.

AMERICA'S APPENDIX

For a truly bizarre coda to your inland coast road trip, visit the small town of Point Roberts, Washington. In the nineteenth century, when the forty-ninth parallel became the international border, the bit of the Tsawwassen (pronounced "tuh-WAS-sen" by locals) Peninsula south of the line became part of the States. Getting here over land requires crossing into Canada, driving for forty-five minutes, and then coming back into the United States. The silver lining to all this is that "the Point" can be a great place to score inexpensive beachfront lodging.

▼ The Peace Arch, built in 1921 by Historic Columbia River Highway designer Sam Hill, celebrates American and Canadian "brethren dwelling together in unity."

SIDE TRIP

VANCOUVER

BRITISH COLUMBIA

If you brought the right identification with you, end your road trip in Vancouver, the multicultural Canadian city perched where the Salish Sea meets the North Shore Mountains. Continuing the thread of your trip, BC Highway 99 leads right through the center of town.

AROUND TOWN

Vancouver is a relatively young city, with a tendency toward constant renewal. Gleaming, ultramodern high-rises dominate the city center, but the area's easy walkability keeps everything on a human scale. Start with a visit to the excellent Granville Island Public Market, easily reached on foot via the tiny False Creek ferryboats. Back downtown, the West End is home to a vibrant LGBTQ community, while Gastown is one of the city's few preserved historic districts. Must-see spots there include the whimsical steam clock and Maple Tree Square, the oldest intersection in Vancouver. Several public beaches stretch westward from Kitsilano toward the University of British Columbia, a sprawling campus encompassing huge swaths of parkland. Don't miss the acclaimed Museum of Anthropology at UBC, home to half a million artifacts and ethnographic objects. The heart of the museum is the First Nations collection, featuring both historic and contemporary artwork.

PARK-ARAMA

Vancouver boasts many world-class parks, including massive Stanley Park: home to a thousand acres of wooded green space, a collection of Indigenous totem poles, a lighthouse, and Lions Gate Bridge. For a scenic stroll, try the Seawall, a fourteen-mile pedestrian and bike path that runs along most of Vancouver's waterfront, from Stanley Park all the way to UBC. If you're looking for something even more dramatic, visit North Vancouver's Capilano Suspension Bridge, a dizzying five-hundred-foot span hanging above a deep, wooded gorge.

▲ As you stroll along the Stanley Park Seawall, keep an eye out for one of the park's many black squirrels, introduced here in the 1910s.

▼ In addition to the famous suspension bridge, Capilano River Regional Park has added a heart-stopping suspended path called the Cliffwalk.

▶ From Horseshoe Bay it's easy to hop on the BC ferry system for service to Victoria (page 104).

FOODIES REJOICE

With exciting options in every neighborhood, Vancouver is a cuisine capital of both Canada and the West Coast. A number of downtown restaurants (like Blue Water Cafe and YEW) support the Ocean Wise program for sustainable seafood. The Vancouver street-food scene rivals that of Portland (page 160)—local favorites include Tacofino and Japadog. If you're looking to try the Canadian delicacy of poutine (fries with cheese curds and gravy), look no farther than the downtown hole-in-the-wall Belgian Fries. In Canada's largest Chinatown, old-school dim sum parlors coexist with contemporary Asian-fusion restaurants. The city is also home to some of the best Japanese fare this side of the Pacific, including the tapas-style gastropub Guu Izakaya. And if you just can't choose, try the massive food and cooking festival called EAT!, held every autumn.

THE GRAND FINALE

If you have the time, the perfect end to a West Coast road trip is a journey up to Whistler, along the stretch of BC 99 known as the Sea to Sky Highway. Starting in Horseshoe Bay, the route hugs the dramatic fjord of Howe Sound, then makes a winding alpine climb up to the Whistler ski resort. The drive frequently makes the list of best scenic roads in the world, and the experience will end your trip on an unforgettable high note.

▶ The Dr. Sun Yat-Sen Classical Chinese Garden was the first formal, traditional scholar's garden built outside of China.

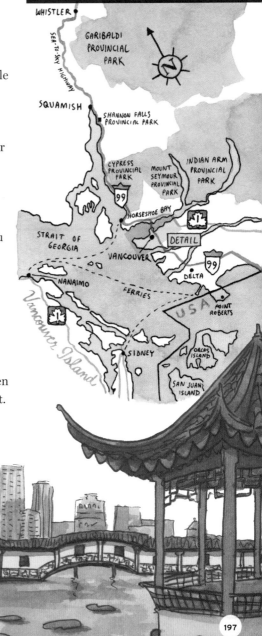

AFTER-WORD · The ROAD AHEAD

▼ Thanks to road planners who wanted to make Yosemite accessible to all, the historic park road brings you within spitting distance of wonders like El Capitan.

This book has been a labor of love—which is exactly how I view every road trip I've ever taken. To see the West Coast by car takes more time, extra planning, and a host of skills one might never employ on an airplane or cruise. Yet I believe the "work" required is part of what makes road trips so rewarding and so memorable.

COME UP WITH A THEME

This book treats each route like one giant, all-encompassing trip—yet having an entire region at your feet can feel a bit overwhelming. With so much to see and do, and only so many hours in a day, you'll have to pick and choose your stops along the way. One logical way to do this is to arrange your trip around some sort of central theme. You might embark on a scavenger hunt for roadside attractions, or visit all twenty-one California missions (page 5), or hit every public lighthouse from border to border. Giving your trip a theme creates a manageable framework for your journey—as well as a built-in bit of fun if you're traveling with kids.

When all else fails, treat your trip like it's merely the first of many to come. If you don't get to everything, don't worry. Each road trip tends to inspire others, as you squirrel away ideas and recommendations for future trips. And for me, part of the fun is simply planning that next road trip, mile by mile.

DON'T SWEAT IT

Above all, remember to let yourself have a good time. Leave room for serendipity among all your plans—you never know what surprises you might find along the way. And that includes mishaps and stumbles: car trouble, closed roads, canceled plans, and sickness have all been known to happen on the road. Yet in the end they become just another memory and part of the story.

As they say, your mileage may vary. Yet whatever your trip looks like, whatever unexpected things crop up in your path, you'll come away with irreplaceable memories and an exciting tale to tell.

WILDLIFE *Checklist*

The West Coast is a wildlife wonderland, and you're sure to spot at least some animals. Look for these creatures of land, sea, and air:

BEARS AND RACCOONS

Grizzly bears are all but extinct on the American West Coast. More likely to steal your camping snacks are black bears and their wily relatives, raccoons.

WILD DOGS

Wolves inhabit only the most wild and remote places on the West Coast, but coyotes and foxes are fairly common sights.

GOATS AND SHEEP

Look hard, and you might see desert bighorn sheep near Palm Springs—or mountain goats in the North Cascades.

CETACEANS

Sharp-eyed travelers might spot orcas (killer whales), dolphins, porpoises, and gray or humpback whales from the shore or a ferry.

PINNIPEDS

Harbor seals are common, while elephant seals are rare. Golden-colored Steller sea lions really look like lions, while California sea lions look (and bark!) more like dogs.

OTTERS

River otters are generally too elusive to spot, but you might just glimpse a sea otter in the wild at any point along the coast.

DIURNAL RAPTORS

Bald eagles can be found near shorelines, but the osprey (the mascot of the Seattle Seahawks) is a holy grail of bird-watching.

OWLS

Owl species abound on the West Coast, including the snowy owl and the endangered northern spotted owl.

RUNNER BIRDS

Roadrunners frequent the California desert, and quail and wild turkeys can be found up and down the coast.

Connecting ROUTES

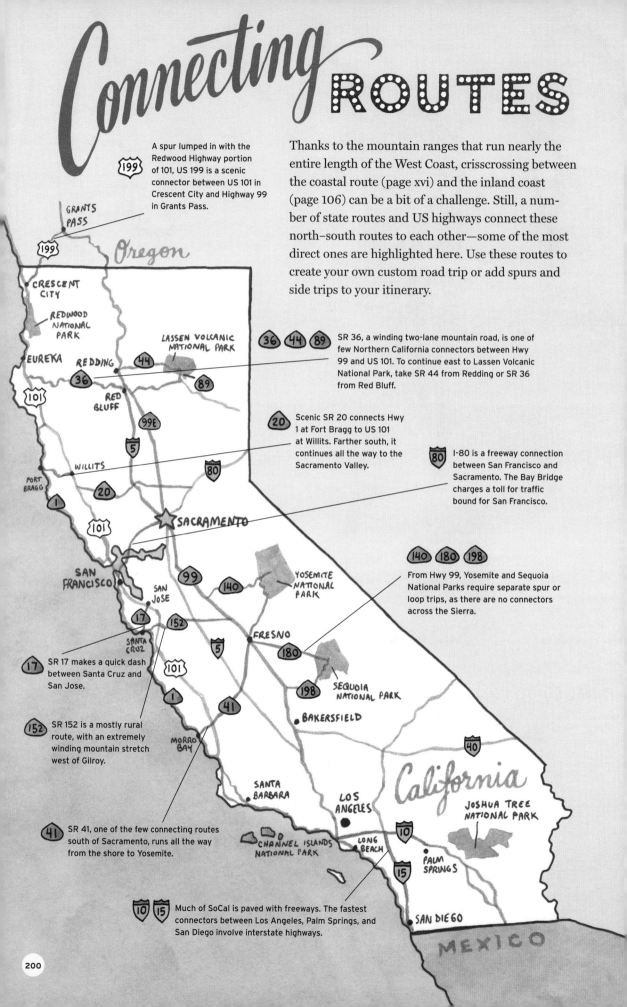

Thanks to the mountain ranges that run nearly the entire length of the West Coast, crisscrossing between the coastal route (page xvi) and the inland coast (page 106) can be a bit of a challenge. Still, a number of state routes and US highways connect these north–south routes to each other—some of the most direct ones are highlighted here. Use these routes to create your own custom road trip or add spurs and side trips to your itinerary.

A spur lumped in with the Redwood Highway portion of 101, US 199 is a scenic connector between US 101 in Crescent City and Highway 99 in Grants Pass.

SR 36, a winding two-lane mountain road, is one of few Northern California connectors between Hwy 99 and US 101. To continue east to Lassen Volcanic National Park, take SR 44 from Redding or SR 36 from Red Bluff.

Scenic SR 20 connects Hwy 1 at Fort Bragg to US 101 at Willits. Farther south, it continues all the way to the Sacramento Valley.

I-80 is a freeway connection between San Francisco and Sacramento. The Bay Bridge charges a toll for traffic bound for San Francisco.

From Hwy 99, Yosemite and Sequoia National Parks require separate spur or loop trips, as there are no connectors across the Sierra.

SR 17 makes a quick dash between Santa Cruz and San Jose.

SR 152 is a mostly rural route, with an extremely winding mountain stretch west of Gilroy.

SR 41, one of the few connecting routes south of Sacramento, runs all the way from the shore to Yosemite.

Much of SoCal is paved with freeways. The fastest connectors between Los Angeles, Palm Springs, and San Diego involve interstate highways.

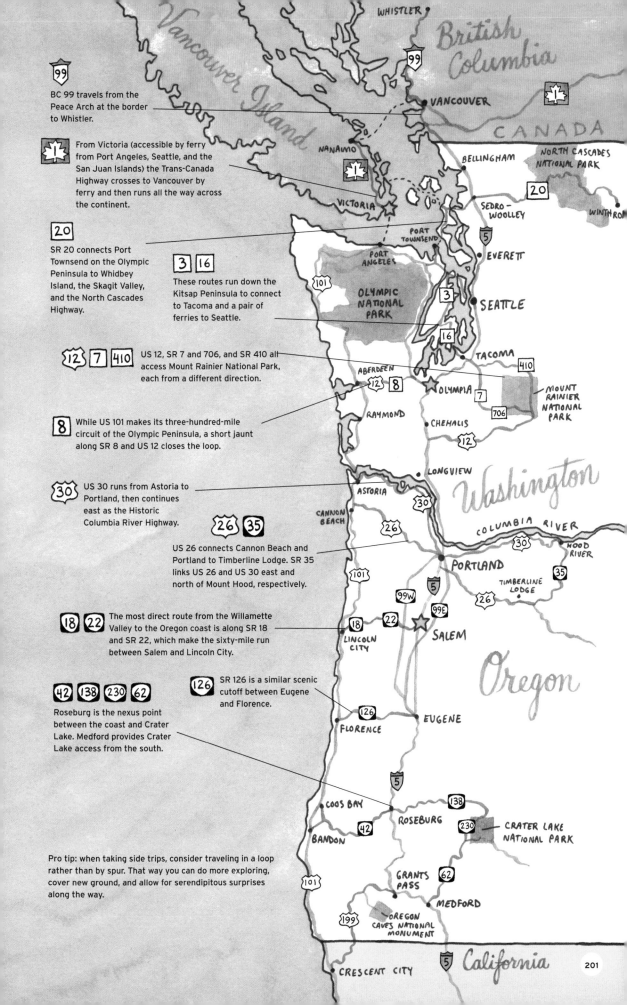

99 BC 99 travels from the Peace Arch at the border to Whistler.

1 From Victoria (accessible by ferry from Port Angeles, Seattle, and the San Juan Islands) the Trans-Canada Highway crosses to Vancouver by ferry and then runs all the way across the continent.

20 SR 20 connects Port Townsend on the Olympic Peninsula to Whidbey Island, the Skagit Valley, and the North Cascades Highway.

3 **16** These routes run down the Kitsap Peninsula to connect to Tacoma and a pair of ferries to Seattle.

12 **7** **410** US 12, SR 7 and 706, and SR 410 all access Mount Rainier National Park, each from a different direction.

8 While US 101 makes its three-hundred-mile circuit of the Olympic Peninsula, a short jaunt along SR 8 and US 12 closes the loop.

30 US 30 runs from Astoria to Portland, then continues east as the Historic Columbia River Highway.

26 **35** US 26 connects Cannon Beach and Portland to Timberline Lodge. SR 35 links US 26 and US 30 east and north of Mount Hood, respectively.

18 **22** The most direct route from the Willamette Valley to the Oregon coast is along SR 18 and SR 22, which make the sixty-mile run between Salem and Lincoln City.

42 **138** **230** **62** Roseburg is the nexus point between the coast and Crater Lake. Medford provides Crater Lake access from the south.

126 SR 126 is a similar scenic cutoff between Eugene and Florence.

Pro tip: when taking side trips, consider traveling in a loop rather than by spur. That way you can do more exploring, cover new ground, and allow for serendipitous surprises along the way.

INDEX of Places

INDEX of Parks and Attractions

RESOURCES

Navigational Aids

MAPS AND ATLASES
AAA (maps are free for members): AAA.com
Better World Club: BetterWorldClub.com
 /travel/maps.cfm
DeLorme Atlas & Gazetteer (recommended):
 Info.Delorme.com
Rand McNally Road Atlas: RandMcnally.com
 /product/road-atlas

TURN-BY-TURN INFORMATION
Google Maps: Maps.Google.com
That Ribbon of Highway (a series of books
 about Highway 99) by Jill Livingston:
 LivingGoldPress.com/ribbonofhighway.htm
US 99 Guides—Historic Highway 99: GBCNet
 .com/ushighways/US99
US 99 Guides—US Highway 101: GBCNet.com
 /ushighways/US101

Travel Information

California Department of Transportation:
 DoT.ca.gov
**National Oceanic and Atmospheric Administration
 (tide info):** NOAA.gov
Oregon Department of Transportation:
 Oregon.gov/odot
Washington Department of Transportation:
 WSDoT.wa.gov
Washington State Ferries: WSDoT.wa.gov/ferries

Outdoor Agencies

California State Parks: Parks.ca.gov
National Park Service: NPS.gov
Oregon State Parks: OregonStateParks.org
Pacific Crest Trail: FS.usda.gov/pct/
Washington State Parks: Parks.wa.gov
US Forest Service: FS.fed.us

Passes and Permits

California annual state park passes:
 Parks.ca.gov/?page_id=1049
National Park Service annual passes:
 NPS.gov/planyourvisit/passes.htm
Oregon annual state park passes:
 OregonStateParks.org/index.cfm?do=visit
 .dsp_dayuse
State fishing and shellfish permits:
 CA: Wildlife.ca.gov/licensing
 OR: DFW.state.or.us/resources/fishing
 WA: WDFW.wa.gov/fishing/shellfish
Washington annual state park pass:
 DiscoverPass.wa.gov
Wilderness camping permits: Visit individual
 national park websites or in person at NPS
 ranger stations for information

Dig Deeper

WEBSITES AND FILMS
AtlasObscura.com
DrawntheRoadAgain.com
RoadArch.com
RoadsideAmerica.com
The National Parks: America's Best Idea by
 Ken Burns (documentary)

BOOKS
Are We There Yet? by Susan Sessions Rugh
A Woman's Guide to the Wild by Ruby
 McConnell
Infinite City: A San Francisco Atlas by Rebecca
 Solnit
Portland Hill Walks by Laura O. Foster
Selected Writings by John Muir
*Sundown Towns: A Hidden Dimension of
 American Racism* by James W. Loewen
The Big Roads by Earl Smith
The Hour of Land by Terry Tempest Williams
The Orange and the Dream of California by
 David Boulé
Travels with Charley by John Steinbeck

THANK YOU

First of all, this book would not exist had I not picked up and moved to Washington a decade ago. To my adopted hometown of Tacoma, and the wonderful folks with whom I share it: thank you for all your support.

I am so grateful to my editor, Hannah Elnan, who trusts my crazy ideas and laughs at my terrible jokes. Thanks also to Anna Goldstein and the team at Sasquatch Books for their guidance and help in bringing this book to life.

To my best travel companion on the road and in life, my husband, Donald Sidman: thank you for your love, your encouragement, and your patience. And to my awesome book- and road-trip-loving brother Adrian: thank you for always championing my work . . . and for your ability to converse entirely in movie references with me.

Big thanks and much love to the Spring family, for welcoming me into their lives, up and down the West Coast: Jessica, Tupper, Margaret, John and Susan, Tina and Diddy. Also, Brown: good boy.

Many friends and fellow travelers hosted me on my coastal journeys, introduced me to hidden gems and local wonders, or lent me their ears (and eyes) as I worked on this book. To Sarah Christianson and Jesse Mullan, Mary Holste and Erik Hanberg, Ellie Mathews and Carl Youngmann, Tony Reese and Christopher Leslie, Ann and Peter Darling, Jeff Markwardt, Laurie Cinotto, Nicole Allin, Allison Baer, Suzanne Moore, Marsha Samuel, Gabi Campanario, and Candace Rardon: thank you all.

Finally, I owe a huge debt of gratitude to my dear friends Mary-Alice Pomputius and Walter Smith (and Chloe, of course), who gave me the best gift of all: a place to write and draw, in their perfect hideaway on San Juan Island.

Images and Text

The illustrations in this book are inspired by my travel sketchbooks, but I've redrawn each one anew in my studio, in order to tell a seamless story and fit the format of these pages. Each scene was drawn by hand and painted with watercolor. All the chapter headings and maps are hand lettered. The main text is set in Miller Text Roman and the captions in Interstate—simply because I can't resist a little typographic irony.